an **a–z** of
social
work
skills

Sara Miller McCune founded SAGE Publishing in 1965 to support the dissemination of usable knowledge and educate a global community. SAGE publishes more than 1000 journals and over 800 new books each year, spanning a wide range of subject areas. Our growing selection of library products includes archives, data, case studies and video. SAGE remains majority owned by our founder and after her lifetime will become owned by a charitable trust that secures the company's continued independence.

Los Angeles | London | New Delhi | Singapore | Washington DC | Melbourne

an **a-z** of
social
work
skills

michaela rogers
dan allen

Los Angeles | London | New Delhi
Singapore | Washington DC | Melbourne

Los Angeles | London | New Delhi
Singapore | Washington DC | Melbourne

SAGE Publications Ltd
1 Oliver's Yard
55 City Road
London EC1Y 1SP

SAGE Publications Inc.
2455 Teller Road
Thousand Oaks, California 91320

SAGE Publications India Pvt Ltd
B 1/I 1 Mohan Cooperative Industrial Area
Mathura Road
New Delhi 110 044

SAGE Publications Asia-Pacific Pte Ltd
3 Church Street
#10-04 Samsung Hub
Singapore 049483

© Michaela Rogers and Dan Allen 2021

Editor: Kate Keers
Assistant editor: Catriona McMullen
Production editor: Martin Fox
Marketing manager: Camille Richmond
Design: Wendy Scott
Typeset by: C&M Digitals (P) Ltd, Chennai, India

Library of Congress Control Number:
2021930235

British Library Cataloguing in
Publication data

A catalogue record for this book is available from the British Library

ISBN 978-1-5264-9282-1
ISBN 978-1-5264-9281-4 (pbk)

Contents

About the authors

Dr Michaela Rogers is Senior Lecturer in Social Work and Director of Learning and Teaching in the Department of Sociological Studies at the University of Sheffield. She is a qualified social worker registered with Social Work England, the profession's regulatory body. Michaela has practice experience in child and families social work along with a career in the equalities and women's sector. Her research primarily focuses on interpersonal and gender-based violence and abuse; gender, trans and gender diversity; hidden and marginalised communities; and multiple social exclusion, using a range of qualitative and narrative methods.

Dr Dan Allen is the Deputy Head of the Social Care and Social Work Department at Manchester Metropolitan University. He works extensively trying to democratise child protection practice with Gypsy, Roma and Traveller families. Dr Allen is particularly interested in examining power relations and the impact of governmentality, subjectivities and ethics on the professional conduct of social workers. Developing a perspective that combines 'neoliberal governmentality' with 'socio-political' influence and 'critical' and 'radical' theory, Dr Allen continually seeks to examine the questions of why, how and so what in the context of dominant discourses affecting regimes of social work practice at individual, cultural and societal levels. Dr Allen is a qualified social worker registered with the professional regulatory body, Social Work England.

About this book

This book offers a compendium of social work skills and represents our commitment to the promotion of skilled social work practice as fundamental to all social work contexts. It seems apposite to begin by clarifying what we mean when we talk of 'skill'. Merriam-Webster dictionary (2020) offers a comprehensive definition of skill as:

1   the ability to use one's knowledge effectively and readily in execution or performance
2   dexterity or coordination especially in the execution of learned physical tasks
3   a learned power of doing something competently: a developed aptitude or ability.
     (Merriam-Webster dictionary, 2020: online)

You might intuitively think that points 1 and 3 clearly reflect the type of skill that we write about in this book. You might also think that the point about dexterity or coordination is not necessarily applicable. But, as we will explore in the pages that follow, you will often be required to use your body in the way that you communicate and in the way that you make use of all your senses. Social work is not simply about what you see or hear; it can also include being alert to what you touch (the feeling and weight of a malnourished child), say (using accessible language and no jargon) and/or taste (even if that is the taste of your own adrenaline).

In social work discourse, skills are defined as interventions through which learning is put into practice (Trevithick et al., 2004) and as specific practitioner behaviours in the helping process (Shulman, 2008). In social work discourse we also talk about 'skills' or 'being skilled' in recognition of the vast array of techniques, methods and tools that are needed in practice.

As you will see when you move through this book, the skills, tools and methods that we describe are not the only critical aspects of social work practice; they do not exist on their own. Being the best social worker that you can be demands that you blend these things with knowledge and personal qualities that are fundamentally underpinned by a strong commitment to a value base and ethical code that is also reflected in social work practice frameworks (including the values of social justice, human rights, equality and anti-discrimination). That said, the connection that exists between social work practice and the blend of skills, knowledge, values and personal qualities is not always considered. In a review of social work literature on the theme of skill, for example, Karpetis (2018) notes how the theoretical underpinning of social work skills is often neglected, so too is the process through which skill is operationalised in social work practice contexts. In recognition of this gap, we are pleased, therefore, to present this A–Z book as it speaks to these combinations, processes and the relationship between them.

For reasons that will hopefully become clear to you, we do not believe that it is enough to be a skilled communicator. Throughout your entire learning journey, you need certain knowledge to know what to do with the information that you gather from another person during an exchange of communication. You need to be clear about the purpose of your communication and be transparent so that the other person understands why you are meeting and exchanging information with them. Similarly, being value-driven in your approach to building relationships requires you to be skilled in managing communication along with the dilemmas and/or conflicts that may arise from your legal duties and responsibility as a social worker. This book integrates a good deal of essential knowledge and explores the values associated with social work practice in the attention we have given to the broad areas of skills identified in the earlier paragraph.

At the time of writing this introduction, we are in the midst of the global pandemic (COVID-19) and intermittent lockdowns in the UK. Critical discussions around the Black Lives Matter (BLM) movement have re-emerged following the tragic death of George Floyd in the US in 2020. These are just two examples of social phenomena that affect social work and the practice contexts that we describe. For example, during a lockdown period most people (who could) suddenly began to work from home, but social workers, like many others in the field of health and social care, have continued to work, and adapt their skills in very different contexts. Court cases and safeguarding work is being conducted using video conferencing software and social workers are now communicating with young people using social media that is familiar to today's younger generation (but not to all social workers). As social workers throughout the world continue to protect and enhance the lives of those who are most vulnerable, their adaptability and willingness to work present a range of skills that go far and above those essential components that are presented here.

The death of George Floyd has rightly led to renewed and vigorous discussions centring on the issues raised by BLM; discussions which have reached new levels. In our everyday worlds (in university and social work settings), we are having reflective discussions about the ways in which social work education should reflect the issues of inequality, discrimination and marginalisation still affecting many Black and minority ethnic people in all our communities. This discussion inevitably intertwines with issues of skilled practice and some of the skills associated with fairer approaches to social work are introduced in subsequent sections. The task for all of us is to build on our knowledge to provide a reflective and flexible approach to social work that everyone can be proud of.

We recognise that the practice of social work covers many different fields including children and families social work, adult social care, mental health and palliative social work. Simultaneously, social work crosses boundaries and enables us to work with people from all types of social locations and backgrounds. We work with people from diverse communities and ethnicities, and from across the life course (from babies to people nearing the end of their life), and with diverse identities in relation to gender identity, sexual orientation, age, health and physical ability. Whilst we work with people from different socio-economic backgrounds, the majority of social work is undertaken with people who experience poverty and for whom there are more structural barriers to accessing resources and building capital. Recognising this point is important as we need to understand the complexity of poverty, social inequalities and exclusion in contemporary social work contexts and how this affects the relationships that we build and the roles that we take (Featherstone et al., 2018). For us, this complexity highlights the important combination of skills, knowledge and values that should enable you to undertake social work in a way that is inclusive, relational, socially informed and anti-oppressive.

You might be getting the picture about skills, tools and methods and a flavour of this book, but we wish to emphasise that being skilled in all aspects of everyday practice is critical. Being reflective before, during and after each exchange with another is incredibly important as you must develop the ability to turn a mirror onto yourself and your practice (Rogers & Allen, 2019). Knowing the areas in which you are skilled, those areas in which you need to work on, and being able to learn from your own practice is key to ensuring that you will be the best practitioner that you can be. Moreover, as a qualified and registered social worker, it is imperative that you continue to meet the needs of your regulatory body, by drawing on your knowledge, values and skills to address the social care needs of individuals and their families, work in collaboration with others, communicate with others and respond quickly to potentially harmful or dangerous situations.

At qualification, you will be required to meet the minimum standards of the social work profession and continue to demonstrate areas of skills and knowledge throughout your entire career journey. We hope that this book can provide the foundation for that journey and a springboard that ignites a commitment to your ongoing professional development.

Structure and features of the book

The chapters (entries) in this A–Z are succinct, getting straight to the heart of the skill under discussion. We call each entry a chapter even though it does not follow a traditional chapter structure (with an introduction and conclusion) due to its length (much longer than a traditional A–Z entry but shorter than a traditional book chapter). Each chapter introduces the main principles of the skill under discussion. If there is a relevant theoretical underpinning, we have sought to include this.

The range of skills presented in each chapter will be mapped to different categories that exist to support various communities of practice. For example, each skill chapter will be labelled with a **Main Associated Theory**. These will include: cognitive-behavioural theory; crisis intervention theory; ecological theory; empowerment theory; humanistic theory; narrative theory; psychosocial theory; strengths-based theory; systems theory; and task-centred theory (see the box below for a brief explanation of each). In addition, each skill will be labelled with an associated **Skill Category** that will include: anti-oppressive practice; assessment; communication; critical thinking and analysis; interventions; reflection and reflexivity; and relational practice. The purpose of this labelling for each chapter is to enrich your knowledge about social work skills, but also to help you to understand how you might use the tools and methods being described to translate your developing knowledge of social work theory into practice.

Theory explained

Cognitive-Behavioural Theory draws upon techniques from behaviourism, social learning theory and cognitive theory. It assumes that a person's thoughts, feelings and attitudes influence behaviour. Applied to social work, this theory provides the basis for change. It is used to recognise that if a person's thoughts and feelings are changed, their behaviour will also change.

Crisis Intervention Theory asserts that social work is most effective if it focuses on brief interventions and deals with immediate issues rather than longer term problems. It is a theory that is based on psychology and cognitive-behavioural models of practice and assumes that serious events have an impact on the way people think about themselves and their emotional reactions. The central premise of the theory is that a crisis can be a significant motivator and enabler of change.

Ecological Theory suggests that people's lives are interdependent with various levels of influence including on a personal, family, community or societal basis. It recognises that as people move through their unique life course, they may encounter challenges that they find difficult to cope with and that affect their wellbeing or growth. Applied to social work, this theory provides the basis for supporting interdependent relationships and the development of coping mechanisms that might exist in the environment, in social networks, or within the individual person.

Empowerment Theory focuses on understanding solutions rather than on problems. Applied to social work, it avoids diagnostic labelling separating the person from the problem and it promotes social action and change with approaches to enablement and advocacy.

Humanistic Theory establishes the principles of empathy, congruence and unconditional positive regard as necessary in the helping relationship. Applied to social work practice, it requires social workers to take a non-directive approach, based on the faithful belief that everyone has the capacity to develop and grow.

Narrative Theory argues that the stories that people tell define their understanding of themselves and their lives. For this reason, it encourages social workers to facilitate opportunities for people to describe their life in their own words. Applied to social work, a narrative approach supports the person to feel in control of their story and draw their attention to the possibility of a different story for the future.

Psychosocial Theory draws on psychological and social theories and it has evolved considerably from its Freudian and ego psychological underpinnings. Applied to social work, it is based on the idea that the lives of people are determined by their engagement and interpretation of the world. By understating how people perceive the world, the psychosocial theory attempts to understand the full impact of significant life events.

Strengths-Based Theory highlights the importance of the collaborative process that is required between the social worker and the person they are working to support. Applied to social work, the focus on strengths and resources enables social workers to build relationships that can facilitate opportunities for collaborative activities that draw on an individual's aspirations and assets.

Systems Theory explains that people are not isolated. Instead, they operate as part of wider networks or systems that may be informal (friends and family) or formal (education, health, housing, employment). The theory assumes that difficulties may arise if there is an element with the system that is not working as it should. Applied to social work, this theory provides the basis for social work action, which seeks to identify the cause of any difficulties that a person is experiencing by examining both informal and formal networks.

Task-Centred Theory determines a time-limited approach to social work. It argues that social work practice is more likely to be successful if it focuses on actionable solutions to specific problems. For this reason, task-centred theory requires social workers to facilitate interventions that are brief, direct and easily measurable. The aim of this theory is to identify problems, outline goals, create and execute a specific plan and evaluate the results.

Further reading

Payne, M. (2021) *An A–Z of Social Work Theory*. London: Sage.

Whilst we have tried to be holistic and comprehensive, the compilation of skills contained in this book is by no means exhaustive and we appreciate that there will be skills that we do not cover but we hope that we have included the absolute core of skills and some extra ones too. By associating skills that can be grouped under the themes of anti-oppressive practice, communication, critical thinking and analysis, interventions, reflection and reflexivity, and relational practice, we do not consider the role of social work theory in equal depth. For example, we do not have a specific chapter on strengths-based practice, but we consider skills that might enable it. By filling the gap that has been identified by Karpetis (2018), we wanted to provide an introduction to key skills that could be read alongside a text book on social work theory, not instead of one.

In making decisions about what to include (and exclude), we have tried to be holistic but as we have kept chapters succinct and to the point, where possible, we also link and signpost you to other chapters that associate with and/or are related to the chapter that you have just read. In some cases, it is essential that you read the complementary or linked chapters. For example, if you read the chapter on **interviewing**, we would expect you to read the chapters on **active listening** and **questioning**.

Throughout the book, we have used a number of different features including:

- *Danger Zone* – this is a section that introduces some of the dangers of the skills that are introduced
- *Skills in Action* – this provides a short case study to illuminate the skill in practice
- *Stop–Reflect* – this feature encourages you to participate in a reflective activity to help you to understand the value of the skill in that chapter
- *Top Tips* – a list of tips for good practice
- *Theory Explained* – an explanation of relevant theory related to or underpinning the skill (as shown above).

Each chapter ends with a small number of items in 'Further Reading' which signpost you to some key or specialist texts that will enable you to read in greater depth around the skill in discussion.

Conclusion

This introduction has set out the rationale for this book in that we have illustrated the importance of skill and skills in social work practice. As you read the various chapters, try to associate the skills that we describe to the relevant social work standards and consider how the requirement for excellent practice can be equated to skilled practice that is formally recognised and required. We hope that you find this book to be of value and use.

A

Active listening is a fundamental skill that underpins all elements of social work practice. It comprises the building blocks of interpersonal communication and it acts as an essential component of the coaching, counselling, interview, person-centred process. Used to gather detailed information, active listening provides an essential communication method that can enable you to begin to clarify and verify your interpretation of what others are telling you and provide a potential springboard for change.

If you minimise the importance of active listening, and the need to understand the views, wishes and perspectives of the people you are working to support, you might miss an important opportunity to enable and encourage them to tell their story in their own way and in their own time. However, if you seek to use active listening skills carefully, you can begin to refine your commitment to demonstrate **empathy**, understanding and genuine positive regard. Indeed, the need to listen, clarify and verify information that another person is communicating to you is crucially important, especially in the strengths-based approach to the **assessment**, planning, intervention and review cycle.

Active listening forms an essential component of your human agency. In other words, it can enable you to begin to transfer your professional power to situate the person you are working to support at the centre of the conversation. Whilst listening, you should try to be patient, accepting of short periods of silence, and ready to ask questions that enable the person who is communicating to describe the detail of their situation, their thoughts and feelings, so long as they consent to do so.

Of course, we all seek to listen to others, but in doing so, do we know whether the person who is communicating always thinks and feels that they are being listened to? Consider the Stop–Reflect activity below and think about the skill of listening from the perspective of the person who is communicating.

Stop–reflect

Listening and active listening

Imagine that you are observing a conversation between two people. One person, the listener, is looking through social media on a mobile phone. The other person, the speaker, is trying to share important information about their day. Whilst the listener is looking at the phone, they might respond to the speaker, to indicate that they are listening, by

(Continued)

uttering words like 'yeah' and 'right'. However, although they might think that they are demonstrating sufficient attention to show that they are hearing what is being said, do you think the speaker will think or feel that they are being listened to?

What do you think the person looking at their phone might do to demonstrate to the person speaking that they are listening?

Active listening is the core skill that can help you to apply many theories associated with social work practice. By paying close attention to the person who is communicating in an active way, you can show that you are listening by using both verbal and **non-verbal communication** methods. You might, for example, demonstrate that you are listening by tuning into the other person, focusing your entire attention on them, perhaps smiling, sitting in comfortable proximity to them or maintaining comfortable eye contact. You might also seek to be attentive and sensitive to the speaker's thoughts and feelings and for this reason you would do well to avoid fidgeting, looking at your phone or watch, doodling on a notebook, playing with your hair, slouching in a chair or anything else that gives an impression that you are not interested. In summary, the fundamental skill of active listening is to focus all of your energy and genuine interest onto the speaker.

Once tuned in to the person who is communicating, verbal signs of active listening can include repeating, paraphrasing or summarising what the person has said. By doing this you can begin to demonstrate other skills, such as empathy, shown via your commitment to understand and accept the perspectives of others with detail and accuracy. To gain further clarity, you might also ask deliberate questions designed to help you understand the speaker's views and wishes in more detail. This additional information could also help you to verify your interpretation of what is being communicated.

Consider the example in the box below and consider how you might respond to the things that people tell you in your own life.

Skills in action

Ignoring and contradicting, or repeating, paraphrasing and summarising?

Ian is visiting a young person, Kim, who is living with a foster family. Kim has recently joined a local football team and is required to attend a team training session that evening. When Ian asks Kim how the football practise is going, Kim exclaims, 'I don't want to go there anymore, I hate it! It's rubbish!' Ian, in a rush to get to his next appointment quickly responds, 'Yeah you do. You're great at football. I know loads of kids who say they don't want to go to football training, but when they get on the pitch, they love it. Now, stop being miserable and go and get your boots on'.

Do you think that Ian demonstrated the skills associated with active listening? The answer is plain, he did not. Ian contradicted Kim and he minimised her view, opinion and perspective when he compared her situation to the situation of others. So, what do you think Ian might have done instead?

Through the careful application of active listening techniques, Ian could have responded to the statement 'I don't want to go there anymore' much more professionally and sensitively. Instead of contradicting Kim and being condescending, telling her that she was being miserable, he could have asked her to talk about their views and wishes in more detail.

One question Ian could have asked, to demonstrate active listening, and following a summary of Kim's perspective is:

'You don't want to go to football, you hate it and it's rubbish? You seemed to be really looking forward to football the last time we spoke. Tell me what has changed to make you feel like you don't want to go anymore?'

Other responses might include:

'What is it about going to football that you don't like?' or 'Is there anything that you would prefer to do instead of going to football?' or 'Is there anything that needs to change so that you don't hate it quite so much?'

In no circumstance, regardless of the skill being used, should Ian compare Kim's situation to the experiences of others. To do so obscures her individual experience and circumstance.

By applying active listening skills alongside those other skills listed in this book, Ian might have been able to develop an understanding of why Kim's view of football has changed. What is more important, he could have asked her to tell him what she thinks needs to happen in the future, paving the way to more person-centred practice.

The single biggest threat to active listening skills emerge from the pressures that you might be experiencing in your personal and professional life. If you feel that you are working under pressure, that you are rushed, stressed, under skilled, or if you feel that the speaker is unimportant or does not deserve your attention, then you will be less likely to take time to listen actively. It is also worth noting that some of the people who you work to support might not respond well to active listening techniques either, particularly if they perceive your attempts to listen actively as patronising or condescending.

In light of these limitations, active listening can be a difficult skill to perfect. Yet, with time, practice and patience, your ability to listen actively should become embedded within the personal and professional praxis of everything that you do.

Main associated theory

Humanistic Theory – but all actually apply

Skill category

All

See also: anti-oppressive practice, counselling skills, motivational interviewing, person-centred communication, person-centred planning, solution-focused practice, use of self and reflexivity.

Further reading

Dexter, J., Dexter, G. & Irving, J. (2011) *An Introduction to Coaching*. London: Sage.

Nugent, W.R. & Halvorson, H. (1995) Testing the effects of active listening. *Research on Social Work Practice*, 5(2): 152–175.

Advocacy is a term used to describe the way in which you might promote the views and perspectives of the people you are working to support.

You can begin to demonstrate the skills associated with advocacy when you seek to represent the views, wishes, thoughts and feelings of others to influence the decision-making processes, challenge unjust or unresponsive systems or identify a person's view or concern. In all cases, you should use the principles of advocacy to ensure that the rights of the people you are working to support are enhanced and their entitlement to independence is enabled.

Consistent with a wider commitment to emancipation and **anti-oppressive practice**, you would also do well to ensure that the intent and outcome of advocacy promotes the power of others by helping them to feel more confident, more assertive and more able. However, as shown by Rogers and Allen (2019), you might require a number of other different skills, including the skills of persuasion, influence and professional authority and a detailed knowledge of social work systems, before you can demonstrate effective approaches to advocacy.

As you set out to become an advocate, you will require good **assessment** and communication skills. You need to be able to work in partnership with others to identify and analyse key problems, understanding, as far as practicable and possible, what life is like through the eyes of the person you are working to support and how they might like their life to be different.

You will also need to be able to apply the principles of **person-centred planning** and the ability to identify strengths, resources and opportunity for **collaboration**. Applying the key tenets of **task-centred practice**, for instance, might enable you to seek opportunities for problem resolution, using a variety of other techniques that might include, for example, **motivational interviewing** and **active listening**.

Once an assessment has been conducted, and the plan for action has been agreed, you must feel confident to present your case to others and be ready to defend and substantiate your recommendations. In preparing your argument, you should continue to work in partnership with the individual, family or community to support, develop and review an accurate and up-to-date knowledge of risk, eligibility thresholds, local and national policy, case law and recent examples of evidence-based practice.

Finally, throughout each stage of the advocacy process the views, wishes and feelings of the individual, family or community must remain central and at the forefront of the planning, implementation and review process.

The centrality of the individual, family or community who you are working to support becomes particularly important as the principles of advocacy are often used to support or enable change. For many people, this change may be needed to enhance their sense of power, confidence and empowerment. For this reason, when using advocacy skills, we would recommend that you use supervision, or other formal case work discussions, to reflect on the ways in which advocacy might be used to promote the mental health and wellbeing of the people who you are working to support.

Whilst advocacy has been used to enable projects of social change (consider the social model of disability, for instance), social injustice is seen to endure in a wide range of circumstances. If you are committed to the principles of advocacy, it is important that you are realistic about your scope of influence. Be honest and support others to understand that the proposed plans for change may not be realised or possible. It is also important that you do not use advocacy to compromise your own professionalism. Consider the Danger Zone in the box and the potential tension caused by advocacy in practice.

Danger zone

The importance of independent advocates

A conflict of interest can occur in a situation when the use of advocacy could compromise your professional position. For example, consider a social worker who has devised the content of a care package for a person living with an acquired brain injury. The detail of this plan would be based on assessed need and legal entitlement. A conflict of interest could emerge if the same social worker sought to work with the individual or family to then publicy challenge the content of the care package and advocate for system-wide change in community care services. In this case, the social worker would be responsible

(Continued)

for assessing, planning, implementing and reviewing the care package of commissioning services based upon the relevant eligibility criteria. They might compromise their professional status if they seek to publicly challenge the status quo of community care services at the same time. In this circumstance, the appointment of an independent advocate would be much more appropriate.

Although the statutory nature of some social work transactions may weaken the opportunities for advocacy, always try to consider alternative ways to use your professional skills to influence and promote the views and perspectives of the people you are working to support. In many cases, this alternative way of working is in your ability to refer individuals, families and communities to independent advocacy agencies.

Independent advocacy agencies can advance the principles of democratic and transdisciplinary social work. They can help you to ensure that the voices of individuals, families and communities are promoted, advance the principles of enablement and independence and reduce the personal, professional and political pressures associated with a conflict of interest. The key challenge to independent advocacy in practice is constructed by the concern that there are frequently not enough service providers to meet demand.

Main associated theory

Empowerment Theory

Skill category

Anti-oppressive practice, interventions

See also: challenging skills, communicating (with adults and children)

Further reading

Brandon, D. & Brandon, T. (2001) *Advocacy in Social Work*. Birmingham: Venture Press

Dalrymple, J. & Boylan, J. (2013) *Effective Advocacy in Social Work*. London: Sage.

Wilks, T. (2012) *Advocacy and Social Work Practice*. Maidenhead: Open University Press.

Anti-discriminatory practice
The word 'discrimination' has legal status in law, particularly in relation to a key characteristic. As a social worker, you will routinely apply equality laws and duties, but in doing so, you will also be required to consider the potential impact of discrimination.

Discrimination can be defined as the ability to categorise, recognise and understand the difference. For example, the difference between hot and cold water. When we discriminate, we differentiate between two things in a positive, negative or neutral way. Applied to social work practice, the word discrimination is used to describe the way that differences between people are categorised, recognised and understood. It also extends to describe how this difference is used to justify the inclusion or exclusion of others (Thompson, 2018).

Not only does discrimination have clear implications for contemporary society, it can also have a significant impact on your ability to practise safely, effectively and honestly in line with your professional values and standards.

Understanding what discrimination is, and how it can exist to destabilise lawful social work practice, is a first step towards demonstrating anti-discriminatory skills in practice. The next step is to transfer this learning into action. At all times, you should be prepared to recognise discrimination, in all of its manifestations, and be able to reduce, challenge and eliminate discrimination within your sphere of influence or control. The second step is arguably the hardest one to achieve. Whilst the concepts needed to inform and underpin anti-discriminatory practice have been pursued in a diverse range of applications (Cocker & Hafford-Letchfield, 2014), the skills needed to recognise and challenge discrimination have not been considered in equal depth.

In a book chapter entitled 'Are discriminatory attitudes natural', Allen (2017) shows how discrimination is socially constructed and culturally determined. He argues that whilst some discriminatory views represent long established, historical stereotypes based on perceived biological or physical differences (such as racism, sexism, disablism and ageism) others are more situational (such as Islamophobia and transphobia). Constructed, communicated and reinforced by right-wing governments, social media and mass media, Allen (2017) provides examples of how discriminatory views can contaminate the social work process, compromise the integrity of the social worker and destabilise the equality laws and duties that underpin intervention. However, he concludes that the skills associated with anti-discriminatory practice can be hard to define because discriminatory attitudes often exist in the shadows of personal practice.

Discriminatory attitudes can be subtle and divisive. They can also be used to blame, label and denigrate others. Whilst you might employ the primary assumptions of critical and **radical social work** theories (Turbett, 2014) to challenge discrimination and structural inequality, it is important to recognise that this ambition may not be realistic for you, particularly at the early stages of your career (see the Theory Explained box below for a more detailed explanation).

Of course, we encourage you to challenge institutional discrimination and structural inequality in all of its manifestations, but at the outset of your career you may become frustrated by a perception of the limited impact that you have. We advise you, therefore, to use **reflective**

practice techniques to recognise and challenge any potential discriminatory views that may exist within the shadows of your own personal and professional practice.

Theory explained

Critical and radical social work

Turbett (2014) shows how critical and radical social work theories have been growing in social work since the 1970s. They have roots in emancipatory social movements concerning human rights and the oppression of specific social groups on the basis of key personal characteristics. A key principle of critical and radical social work theories is the focus on unequal social structures that blame the experience of poverty, unemployment, ill health (including mental health) and marginalisation on the actions, or inactions, of the individual. Applied to contemporary practice, critical and radical social work theories encourage social workers to focus more on the external and societal causes of the problems faced by the people they are working to support. Accordingly, the theories require social workers to be engaged in a battle to tackle and change these societal causes, rather than accept the notion that problems should be solved on an individual level.

When considering discrimination, Rogers and Allen (2019) explain that social work is a sense-making activity. They suggest that social work requires individuals to apply their senses to 'make sense' of the situations they encounter, to arrive at safe and effective assessments. However, discrimination can become a factor of influence on your assessment if you do not consider how your own approaches to practice might be determined by prejudicial value judgements and non-reflected personal options.

When visiting an individual, family or community, for example, you might develop positive or negative perceptions about the people, the situations and the challenges that are being faced. These feelings might lead you to categorise, recognise and understand the nature of risk differently.

Anti-discriminatory practice, therefore, requires you to understand the value of your perception, and the need to recognise what knowledge, values, attitudes and beliefs about other people and their complex situation you might bring to the working relationship. Remember discrimination, the act of allowing prejudicial value judgements and non-reflected personal opinions to impact on the assessment process, is problematic because it can lead to unethical decision-making and unethical practice.

At all times, the skills associated with anti-discriminatory practice require you to make specific efforts to identity and isolate discriminatory views, discuss them in supervision and reflect on the potential way that your personal perceptions may influence professional judgements and undermine the legitimacy of any assessment.

Main associated theory

Humanistic Theory – but all actually apply

Skill category

All

See also: critical thinking and analysis, cross-cultural practice, person-centred planning, working with protected characteristics

---

Further reading

Cocker, C. & Hafford-Letchfield, T. (2014) *Rethinking Anti-discriminatory and Anti-oppressive Theories for Social Work Practice*. Basingstoke: Palgrave Macmillan.
Okitikpi, T. & Aymer, C. (2010) *Key Concepts in Anti-discriminatory Social Work*. London: SAGE.
Thompson, N. (2018) *Promoting Equality: Working with Diversity and Difference* (4th edn). London: Palgrave.

Anti-oppressive practice is not the same as anti-discriminatory practice.

Like anti-discriminatory practice, anti-oppressive practice is a central guiding principle of social work. It underpins social work values, standards and codes of practice across the globe (Lyons, 2012). Given the centrality of the skills associated with anti-oppressive practice, we realise that some social workers can sometimes struggle to explain how they demonstrate this approach within the reality of their own assessments and casework.

Before we can think about anti-oppressive practice skill, we need to recognise that oppression is associated with the inherent tensions that can characterise the function of social work and the role of statutory social work in particular. Let us explain further.

In the main, social work is a state sponsored activity. The state, or government, employs social workers, determines the content of the social work training curriculum, and it implements the social policies that define those situations that require social work intervention. In general, the situations that social workers seek to engage often exhibit complex features and intersectional elements of poverty, disadvantage, harm, risk and exclusion (these features and elements can be labelled as examples of structural inequality – that is inequality caused by social and political systems). For many of the individuals who social workers seek to support, the presence of structural inequality (poverty, disadvantage, harm, risk and social exclusion) can become a defining characteristic (Cocker & Hafford-Letchfield, 2014). As agents of the state then (so called because the majority are employed by the government), social workers seek to address and minimise structural inequality (poverty, disadvantage, harm, risk and social exclusion) but they are themselves part of the same social and political system that has caused those challenges. If the function of social work is not sufficiently reflective and reflexive, it could represent a further layer of structural inequality that used a professional identity to label people as vulnerable when they experience poverty, disadvantage, harm, risk and social exclusion.

Let us consider, for instance, the impact that poverty, disadvantage and exclusion have on the lives of the people you are working to support. Research shows us that some families are struggling to feed themselves as a reliance on food banks across the globe increases (Prayogo et al., 2018; Strier & Binyamin, 2014). We also recognise that the frequency and severity of mental health difficulties among school-aged children and adults is increasing, and that the welfare of some children and adults is being jeopardised by the poverty, disadvantage and social exclusion that they experience (Ataguba & Ataguba, 2020). We are also told that poverty, disadvantage and exclusion have a direct impact on infant mortality rates and the life expectance of entire communities (Yan, Chen & Gill, 2020). If a social worker is unable to understand these hardships, and then blames people for the situations that they were in, they may be opening the door to oppressive practice.

Let us consider a further example. If a person living with poverty, disadvantage and social exclusion experiences frequent relapses in a diagnosed mental health difficulty, society might question their resilience to the world in which they live (Yan, Chen & Gill, 2020). Whilst people living with a diagnosed mental health difficulty may be given an increased dose of chemical treatment to assist in their recovery, the challenges and impact associated with poverty, disadvantage and exclusion might not always be addressed. Yes, there are many biological and physiological reasons why people experience mental health difficulties, but we also know that some mental health difficulties can be socially determined too. If a person experiences prejudice, hate, unemployment, debt, limited opportunity, reduced quality of life, disadvantage and social exclusion, it is hard to see how medication can address the cause of these factors at a social level. Therefore, a social worker may not rely solely on medical treatment to aid recovery. Neither would they blame individuals for the situation that they are in. Instead they would work to assess the impact of poverty, disadvantage and exclusion, at all times recognising structural inequality as an oppressive force.

Facilitating opportunities for people to build resilience is an important function of social work, but this work must be contextualised within anti-oppressive assessments that can explain how the impact of poverty, disadvantage, exclusion and other structural inequalities might be exacerbating examples of harm and risk. If the lives and challenges of the people you are working to support are being impacted by prejudice, hate, unemployment, debt, limited opportunity, reduced quality of life, disadvantage and social exclusion, the skills associated with anti-oppressive practice demand that you give equal energy to the act of challenging and minimising the impact of these unequal social structures too.

A pragmatic challenge to anti-oppressive practice can be identified by the care versus control debate, and the power of a social worker to intervene in the lives of others where harm and risk are reported. If we consider human rights legislation and associated policy, including a right to private family life, we might begin to see how some of the more controlling powers that social work has (as a function of the state) can be seen by some as an oppressive action. Indeed, the act of removing a child from a birth parent, or admitting an individual who experiences a mental health difficulty to hospital, highlights the central premise of anti-oppressive practice as a complex ethical dilemma. Yet, if we consider human rights legislation and associated policy through a public protection lens, we come to recognise that every individual has a right to live a life without fear, marginalisation and abuse. To remove a child from an environment that is not safe, or to provide emergency health care to a person who is extremely poorly is not controlling, it is caring. The key is to ensure that whatever action is taken, all appropriate procedures are followed, the right to natural justice is made accessible and the decisions being made are transparent, honest and defensible.

The development of anti-oppressive practice then becomes evident in the way in which we manage and respond to risk. Consider how you might do this using the activity in the following Stop–Reflect box.

Stop–reflect

Care versus control

Anti-oppressive practice reminds us that the removal of a child from a dangerous home situation, the formal admission of an individual to hospital under relevant mental health legislation and the implementation of structured care plans for vulnerable adults living within the community or a formal residential setting are not oppressive or controlling actions when legally justified to provide safety and prevent harm. In each case, the decisions that you take should be supported by law, safeguarding policy and the multi-agency team (including the individual or family who you are working with). However, some families might not agree with the actions taken to provide this type of safety and some might feel that social work is a controlling intrusion into their private family life.

1   Reflecting on skills listed in this book, what do you think you can do or say to help individuals or families understand the reasons why you are involved in their lives?
2   How might you support individuals or families to make a complaint if they feel that social work practice is oppressive or unfair?

Main associated theory

Humanistic Theory – but all actually apply

Skill category

All

See also: advocacy, appreciative inquiry, cross-cultural practice, ethical practice, risk assessment, valuing diversity, working with protected characteristics

Further reading

Cocker, C. & Hafford-Letchfield, T. (2014) *Rethinking Anti-discriminatory and Anti-oppressive Theories for Social Work Practice*. Basingstoke: Palgrave Macmillan.

Strier, R. & Binyamin, S. (2014) Introducing anti-oppressive social work practices in public services: Rhetoric to practice. *British Journal of Social Work*, 44(8): 2095–2112.

Appreciative inquiry We have shown in various chapters presented in

this book that the focus of social work is on solving problems or reducing or diminishing risk. However, we must also recognise that if we allocate resources to solve problems or reduce risk, we must be confident that our **assessment** accurately reflects the lives of the people who we are working to support.

The chapter on **evidence-informed practice** begins to explain how you could verify an assessment by incorporating the views and wishes of the people you are working to support alongside the best available research evidence and your application of social work theory and methods. However, what this chapter does not explain, is that where there is conflict, prejudice, structural ambivalence, limited research and no clear evidence of the 'right way' to act, your ability to draw on evidence-informed approaches to practice can be limited. Where informed practice decisions are limited, or the purpose of action is unclear, it is unlikely that the resources that you allocate to the task, including your own time, will be fully effective.

The foundations of appreciative inquiry (Ai) were created by Cooperrider and Srivastva (1987) and have strong links to the theory of strengths-based practice. It provides the basis from which you can seek to formulate a plan of action based upon the experiences and aspiration of the people you are working to support.

According to Bellinger and Elliott (2011), Ai can be useful, particularly in the absence of clear evidence of the 'right way' to act, because it incorporates strengths-based perspectives and **solution-focused practice**. In contrast to evidence-informed practice, appreciative inquiry relies upon your ability to develop mutually respectful relationships with others.

Consistent with a non-directive or participatory approach to the assessment, the Ai model also assumes that the people you are working to support should, wherever possible, take a lead role in the assessment process. Moving away from a problem-solving risk reduction orientation to social work, the model is designed to enable you to facilitate opportunities to focus on change by recognising success, achievement and understanding what was already working (before you were involved).

As shown in the example in the Skills in Action box below, the Ai model can be accomplished when you can change the way that you use your power and human agency during the assessment and review process.

Skills in action

The four D model of the appreciative inquiry

Ruckman, a student social worker, is working to support Jon, a 19-year-old man living with Downs Syndrome. Ruckman has been asked to support Jon to plan, facilitate and support his move from a children's home to a supported living arrangement.

After meeting with Jon to discuss the move, Ruckman becomes aware that Jon, his parents and his carers are very worried about the impact that the change will have on him. Since being told that he would be moving house by his key worker, Jon has begun to put on weight. He now refuses to leave home to attend college or take exercise.

Based upon his understanding of Ai, Ruckman acknowledges the anxieties being described. However, with the agreement and support of his manager, Ruckman asks Jon, his parents and the carers to consider how a continued focus on their worries and anxieties might be magnifying the problem rather than result in its reduction. Ruckman then introduces Jon, his parents and the carers to the 'four-D model' designed by Hammond (1982) and asks them if he could use this model as a basis of a conversation.

1   Discovery: First Ruckman encourages Jon, his parents and carers to consider what it is about the children's home that Jon likes best. Ruckman asks Jon to describe what he likes doing, what the children's home does well, how his parents and the carers help him to feel happy, secure and safe.
2   Dream: Ruckman then uses his interpersonal skills to ask Jon to talk about the future adult life that he really wants. A future where he feels able to be successful, important, happy, secure and safe. Adapting his communication style, Ruckman takes time to encourage Jon to talk about his dream for the future, focusing on positive elements that were identified in the discovery phase.

(Continued)

3 *Design*: Ruckman asks Jon to describe the way that he thinks his dreams about his future adult life can be realised. Ruckman then asks Jon, his parents and carers to consider what change might be needed to enable Jon to achieve his dreams, support his transition to supported living and reduce the feelings of anxiety and stress that have been described.

4 *Destiny* (sometimes also called Deploy): Ruckman asks Jon, his parents and carers to consider what they now need to do to put the strategies that they have designed into action.

A common criticism of Ai is that it is difficult to apply if people are reluctant to engage with change or the social work assessment. When working with family groups, for example, the motivations and aspirations of each individual can mean that you might find it difficult to maintain consistency and continuity. Equally, a superficial understanding of the challenges being experienced (such as the example of moving from a children's home to supported living) may lead you to focus on positives, without fully exploring the practical or emotional difficulties or the ethical implications and risks associated with the decisions being made.

Main associated theory

Strengths-Based Theory

Skill category

Assessment

See also: active listening, advocacy, empathy, questioning, solution-focused practice

Further reading

Bellinger, A. & Elliott, T. (2011) What are you looking at? The potential of appreciative inquiry as a research approach for social work. *British Journal of Social Work*, 41(4): 708–725.

Cooperrider, D.L. & Srivastva, S. (1987) Appreciative inquiry in organisational life. *Research in Organisational Change and Development*, 1: 129–169.

Assertiveness is a skill that enables you to articulate your views, opinions and feelings, whilst at the same time, respecting the rights, views, opinions and feelings of others. Assertiveness skills can help you to communicate more clearly, defend your assessments, advocate on behalf of yourself and others, and build positive, productive relationships.

Being assertive also includes the ability to say no and to ask for help, support and guidance from others when needed.

Assertiveness skills are vital in social work due to the expectation that you will be able to express your feelings and concerns about issues and dilemmas in practice. They are also essential in case work management and those situations where you will be required to demonstrate the ability to work independently as well as within teams, and the confidence to assert your own initiative.

Assertiveness skills are particularly important when working with individuals, families and communities who do not agree that a social worker should be involved in their lives. In some situations, you will encounter conflict as you seek to engage other people in the social work process. As a result, you might need to assert your professional authority and your focus on individual and public protection.

When working with individuals and families it is important that you can assert your own professional authority with respectful confidence. If an individual or family questions your involvement, skills, experience and capability, it is important that you can be assertive whilst acknowledging their concerns and inviting suggestions for collaborative engagement as shown in the Skills in Action box below.

Skills in action

Assertiveness and collaborative engagement

Harry Ferguson (2011) explains that, in general, some individuals who are confused or concerned about the need for social work involvement in their lives can challenge a social worker to explain what right they have to conduct an **assessment**. He explains that being assertive in this situation is essential to maintain and uphold public trust in the services that are provided. He also suggests that a potentially useful response that you might develop in situations of resistance is:

> I recognise that you might not want social work to be involved in your life right now. However, I am here because there are concerns about … Can you tell me what you think we need to do together so that I am not involved in your life anymore?

By recognising the nature of the individual's reality, namely that they are confused or concerned, you can begin to establish your own assertiveness, stating the nature of your professional reality, namely the need to assess risk, and then invite the individual to offer suggestions for partnership working.

When working with multi-agency teams, assertiveness skills are also essential to ensure that the rights of the individuals, families and communities who you are working to support are represented and justified too. If you are advocating for the implementation of a particular action, assertiveness skills can be used to ensure that you present and defend the recommendations that you make with confidence.

When confronted with stressful experiences, being assertive means being able to stand up for your own or other people's rights in a calm and positive way, without upsetting others, and without becoming upset yourself.

Main associated theory

Psychosocial Theory

Skill category

Communication, reflection and reflexivity

See also: advocacy, challenging skills, containing anxiety, emotional intelligence, managing stress

Further reading

Phillips, A. (2013) *Developing Assertiveness Skills for Health and Social Care Professionals.* London: Radcliffe Publishing.

Assessment skills are fundamental to social work as this is *the* core activity. A holistic assessment helps you to understand people in relation to their environments and current circumstances. It is a process during which you gather information, evaluate (weigh up) that information, use it to formulate hypotheses and make professional judgements and decisions. These judgements and decisions will then inform any plan or intervention. The information that you gather should be balanced in that you should look to explore needs and risks as well as strengths and resources. Conducting an assessment is not a linear nor singular event, it is more likely to be an iterative and dynamic process especially if the situation changes, new information arises, or during the analysis and synthesis of information you realise that you need more data or data from different sources. It can be a messy and complex process!

Milner, Myers and O'Byrne (2015) identify five stages of assessment as being:

1   Preparation: to begin when you are allocated work or when you receive referral information. You will need to make some early decisions about who to speak and/or

meet with, what background information you need (for example, from existing case records or colleagues with useful knowledge).

2   Data collection: this can be gathered from individuals, families, colleagues or external agency representatives. Approach the task with professional curiosity and an investigative approach; do not be afraid to question and ask probing questions (this is the task of a social worker).

3   Apply professional knowledge: draw from theory, research evidence and practice wisdom (see the Theory Explained box below) to make sense of the data.

4   Making judgements: come to some reasoned judgements about needs, risks, strengths, care, safety, wellbeing, relationships and, importantly, capacity for change.

5   Make decisions or recommendations: you will need to reach some conclusions in order to make decisions or recommendations to inform a plan or intervention.

Theory explained

Practice wisdom

Practice wisdom can be 'slippery' as 'it has been defined in several ways' in social work literature (Rogers & Allen, 2019: 41). At times it has been described in simplistic or indistinct terms but, in essence, it is the ability to use a range of knowledge to make sound judgements and verifiable decisions. Practice wisdom relies on the combination of the 'art' of social work (the use of tacit knowledge, which is built through experience, and the ability to be creative and flexible) and the 'science' (application of research, evidence and theory). It therefore bridges the gap between theory and practice (Rogers et al., 2020). It is an advanced assessment skill and one that relies on regular **reflective practice** particularly when working with complex, uncertain and unstable circumstances.

There are many different skills involved in undertaking assessments such as **rapport building**, communicating with people from diverse backgrounds, **interviewing**, and **critical thinking and analysis** to name a few. A skilled assessor will: gather quality evidence and be thorough in doing so; gather information with sensitivity and empathy in the realisation that this may be a frightening or stressful time for the individual or family; work collaboratively with the person or family who is being assessed, considering them as the *expert by experience*, enabling them to feel empowered; employ a strengths-based and solution-focused approach rather than focusing on deficits and problems (Whittington, 2007; Rogers et al., 2020).

The purpose of assessment will very much depend on the role that you have and the remit of your team or agency. For example, if you are located in a statutory child protection team then it is likely that your assessments will be for the purpose of **safeguarding** a child or young person's safety and wellbeing. Alternatively, if you are employed in a hospital social work team, your assessments might be used to complete discharge plans for adults who are returning to their home after a period of time in hospital. The functions here vary: from a focus on the assessment of *risk* for the *protection of the individual* to a focus on the assessment of *need*. If your role involves working with people with mental health problems, then your assessment might focus on the risks to the person's safety and wellbeing as well as the public; this embeds a *public protection* function.

Skills in action

One morning Priti, a social worker in a child protection team, called into the office to collect her diary before a **home visit** and, whilst there, she quickly checked her emails. She had been allocated a referral. The information originally came from Milltown Primary School about a 10-year-old child, Paulo, one of their pupils who had been seen being collected from school by his mother who appeared to be very much under the influence of alcohol. There were concerns about Paolo's general wellbeing (appeared to be frequently tired, lethargic and unkempt). Priti was on her way to undertake a home visit in Milltown anyway and thought it would be good to 'kill two birds with one stone' and called round to Paulo's home address to visit his mother.

Stop-reflect

Think about Priti's decision-making. Return to Milner, Myers and O'Byrne's five stages of assessment and consider what you think Priti should do before a home visit to Paulo's mother. What would be considered as good practice in this instance?

There are different models for assessment and each is generally designed to meet a particular focus and purpose. Smale, Tuson and Biehal (1993) provide a popular tripartite model which can be adapted in all contexts for social work practice (whether you are working with children, families or vulnerable adults). Smale, Tuson and Biehal offer three different modes for information gathering:

- The questioning model: this can be adopted when you approach assessment with a set format of questions. It is a more structured way of gathering and evaluating data. In this approach, you (the social worker) are viewed as the expert and problem solver.
- The procedural model: this model is associated with legislation and agency policy as it is informed by procedure and agency criteria. It is these that you are concerned with when gathering data as you will need to ascertain if agency criteria are met. A limitation of this approach is that you can become overly concerned with collecting data, rather than the needs, views, rights, abilities or

strengths of the person who you are gathering data about. This can lead to a narrow focus and limited approach.

- The exchange model: in this approach, the person who is being assessed is seen as the *expert by experience* as they hold the relevant knowledge about their situation. They are able to articulate their needs, wishes and feelings and, subsequently, the experience can be empowering. The social worker helps to provide resources and seeks to maximise the potential of the service user.

Each model in Smale, Tuson and Biehal's framework requires different skills of **active listening**, **questioning**, critical thinking and recording. It is also part of your skillset in knowing which model to use and when. There are different models of assessment that are routinely found in specific areas of practice. For example, the Assessment Framework underpins many of the assessment tools found in use across children's social care, and for adults experiencing domestic violence and abuse, the DASH Risk Identification Checklist (DASH stands for domestic abuse, stalking and honour-based violence) is routinely used as a tool for undertaking a **risk assessment** to determine low, medium or high risk of harm (visit the DASH risk model website for more information www.dashriskchecklist.co.uk/).

Main associated theory

Humanistic Theory – but all actually apply

Skill category

All

See also: case recording, empowerment and enabling, evidence-informed practice, giving and receiving feedback, professional judgement and decision-making

---

Further reading

Featherstone, B., Gupta, A., Morris, K. & White, S. (2018) *Protecting Children: A Social Model*. Bristol: Policy Press.

Milner, J., Myers, J.S. & O'Byrne, P. (2015) *Assessment in Social Work* (4th edn). London Macmillan Education.

Rogers, M. (2020) Assessment skills. In M. Rogers, D. Whitaker, D. Edmondson & D. Peach (eds) (2020) *Developing Skills & Knowledge for Social Work Practice* (2nd edn). London: Sage.

B

Breaking bad news
It is vital that social workers have sophisticated inter-personal and communication skills. This is especially important when communicating complex information, explaining people's eligibility for support and, in particular, when breaking bad news. Bad news is any information that adversely impacts an individual's view or expectations about his or her future. It is, sadly, part of the day-to-day work in many areas of social work as breaking bad news is something that you may do hundreds of times during the course of your career. Despite this, the skill involved in breaking bad news and managing the situation thereafter has received little attention in social work research or literature whilst it has been recognised as a challenging, but essential skill in other caring professions, such as healthcare.

Stop–reflect

The scenarios below present some of the situations that are common to social work in which you would have to break some bad news. You might have more examples to add to the list from your own work experience. Reflect on what you might do in these circumstances to address the impact of the news when telling someone that:

- they are not eligible for any support
- you are taking their baby into care
- their teenage daughter has been the victim of sexual exploitation
- a relative has died
- the state of their mental health means that you are concerned for the safety of them and others and therefore they are going to be detained in hospital
- their birth mother/father/sibling wants no further contact with them.

You should reflect on each of these scenarios in terms of how this would make you feel and why. How would you look after yourself in these circumstances?

There is no golden handbook that offers a failproof approach to breaking bad news but it is an essential skill and one that you should actively seek to develop. This is particularly important to consider as communicating difficult information can be poorly done for several reasons including:

- insufficient knowledge of the situation and consequences of the news
- subjective views on the issue (for example, developed from personal experience)
- cultural or religious views that may conflict with the social work position
- lack of reflective ability
- burnout
- compassion fatigue.

Despite the lack of a failproof approach, there are different models that provide useful tips to enhance your communication technique in breaking bad news. One such model by Baile et al. (2000) is the SPIKES checklist, which offers a six-step protocol as an aide memoire.

S – the setting

It is likely that you will know what news you are going to break and there will, therefore, be the opportunity for an element of planning. Think about the setting and what you might need to manage in terms of the environment. For example, minimise the opportunity to be disturbed (and ensure that your phone is switched off). Have some water available and a box of tissues if you feel that the news will be upsetting for the receiver. If the setting is not the person's home, consider how they will get home safely and if they will have support there. These details will convey respect, concern and care.

P – the other person's perspective

As noted, it is important to attempt to pre-empt the response of the person who will be receiving the bad news. This is not always possible or easy; particularly if you do not know that person well. It is important to think about this so that you are in some way prepared for their response. It is also important for you to be highly attuned to the reactions of the person in order to ascertain whether or not they have understood what you have told them. It is possible that you might have to break the news over the telephone. This is much harder in terms of responding to the other person as you cannot so easily convey *empathy* over the telephone, nor do you really know how someone is receiving the information if they do not tell you or if they do not give you those cues. Obviously, if you do have to break bad news via a telephone call remember to convey empathy and concern using your tone of voice; carefully choosing the right words will help. Think about the speed at which you speak and the use of silences. You should think about the support available to the person once your call has ended; ask the person if they have someone with them, or if you can arrange for someone (a family member) to be with them.

I – invitation

Invite the person to ask you questions which will help them to understand and process the information that you have presented. At times, the limits of social work will mean that you will not be at liberty to give further detail and contextual information, but it is good practice to help someone to understand their situation as fully as possible in order for them to be able to make sense of it. So, go prepared with as much information as you can and that you are able to legally and ethically share. The person who has received the information might not have expected it. They may not have questions there and then. Ensure that you invite that person to contact you following your exchange; make sure they are equipped with information in order to subsequently access information and support.

K – knowledge

Knowledge is not limited to knowing what information you need to impart but it refers to the theoretical and empirical knowledge that you might use to underpin your communication and engagement. For example, thinking about the timing and delivery of your communication. You will need to manage the flow of information so you do not overwhelm the person receiving the news, but enable them time to absorb, process and adjust to the news. Thus, you will need to go at an appropriate pace for them (not too quickly, not too slowly). You will need to know when to talk and when to be silent. You will need to know how to convey empathy and care via **non-verbal communication**. This is skilled communication in action.

E – emotions and empathy

The need to demonstrate sensitivity and empathy is so important and cannot be over-emphasised. You will need to explore emotions with the person receiving the news and ensure that you are empathic and sensitive. Some people do not show their emotions whereas others are more open in this way. You will need to acknowledge the gravity of the news and the potential impact of this.

S – strategy and summary

When you break news, it is imperative that you end the conversation appropriately. This will rely upon sophisticated interpersonal skills and good judgement. If you can do this in a planned way (and this is not always possible) then this is the favoured strategy. It will require you to manage the time allocated for the meeting and be prepared with the information that you need and that you will need to give to the person. Arranging a follow-up visit or telephone call will convey care, sensitivity and an ethical approach centring the wellbeing of the person who has received the news.

Main associated theory

Humanistic Theory

Skill category

Communication, relational practice

See also: active listening, building resilience, challenging skills, conflict management and resolution, containing anxiety, counselling skills, dealing with hostility and aggression, dealing with resistance, emotional intelligence, grief and loss, observational skills, use of self and reflexivity

Further reading

Baile, W., Buckman, R., Lenzi, R., Glober, G., Beale, E. & Kudelka, A. (2000) SPIKES – a six step approach for delivering bad news: application to the patient with cancer. *The Oncologist*, 5: 302–311.

Building resilience Social workers frequently work with people who have experienced trauma and adversity, as well as there being concerns around welfare and safety. Some form of intervention might need to be undertaken in the immediate term, in the midst of a crisis, or in the medium or longer term. In fact, it is likely that your **assessment** will need to identify and analyse issues relating to trauma, recovery and resilience. There are many different theoretical approaches to trauma and resilience (such as psychodynamic, narrative, person-centred, or socio-ecological approaches). Each approach has a different emphasis on relational, social, psychological, structural and cultural aspects of human experience as well as divergent core assumptions about the impacts of trauma and routes to recovery and resilience (Harms, 2015).

Before we go any further, it is important that you understand the term 'resilience' as it can be rather elusive (as can the term 'recovery'). At its simplest, we consider resilience to be the human capacity to be responsive, to adapt and overcome adversity. In line with a strengths-based approach, it also includes the ability to be transformed by or build skill and strengths as a result of this experience (Grotberg, 1995). This is central to all areas of social work as it means that we can work not only to empower people with the ability to address the immediate and most pressing issue in their lives, but to equip them with the capabilities and strengths to deal with future challenges. Remember that resilience is an aspect of human capacity which is incredibly flexible and dynamic, not static. This dynamic ability is affected by a range of internal and external influences including: experiences, inner traits and environmental factors. In addition, it is helpful to consider resilience as being constituted by multiple, and often intersecting factors.

Stop–reflect

Reflect on a difficult experience that you have overcome in your personal life: for example, this may be related to bereavement, a transition or health. Think about the personal

(Continued)

traits, strengths and skills that helped you to overcome this experience. This might include qualities such as trust, patience, problem-solving skills, self-awareness and humour, as well as positive and loving relationships with others. Was there anything that you did not have access to that might have helped your levels of resilience in this instance? Did you learn anything about yourself through this experience? You might have developed new skills or qualities that you did not think you had. In the future, could you use these skills and qualities again? Are there situations in social work where you think you could utilise these skills and qualities to support others to develop and build resilience?

Research has shown that resilience has many influences at different stages of life: from infancy to adulthood (Lee et al., 2010; Randall, 2013; Raghavan, 2015). Factors affecting resilience include social characteristics (e.g. gender, ethnicity, socio-economic background, health and disability) as well as personal ones (for instance, personality, intellect, empathy with others, sense of self-efficacy, sociability, humour, self-esteem and so on). Resilience is not limited to these personal and social factors but is, of course, affected by external influences such as living in a household where there is poverty, parental mental health issues, substance misuse, or other people's violent, abusive or harmful actions. Resilience is also impacted by health, acquired injury or disability or other life transitions (such as declining mobility). As claimed above, the very notion of resilience is complex and multi-faceted! The take-away point is that social workers should be concerned with building resilience in the people that they are working with and, importantly, in themselves.

Skills in action

Shafqat is based in an adult social care team. She visits 21-year-old John who, five years prior, sustained a brain injury in a road traffic accident and has some long-lasting physical and cognitive impairments (poor short-term memory and other cognitive processing issues). He resides in supported living accommodation with 24-hour support. John wants to find a job and a girlfriend. He is prone to depression as, at times, his impairments get him down. Minor arguments with co-residents affect John and he blows them up out of all proportion. John was attending a local college for people with disabilities but, due to austerity measures, it closed. John does not have structure and purpose in his daily routine. He loves to visit his family (especially his two-year-old nephew, Jamie), but as a result of staffing shortages, there is not always a support worker to take him every week.

Stop–reflect

What should Shafqat prioritise for John? How could she encourage him to develop resilience and manage his mental health in the short, medium and longer term? Think about those factors that help to bolster people's resilience levels.

It can be demoralising when there is no purpose to your day and Shafqat might consider how to find alternative college provision for John, particularly as he aspires to finding employment. How and where could John develop skills that are suitable for work? Having a skill or talent boosts resilience. Positive relationships do too and so Shafqat may think creatively about different ways that John could see his family on a regular basis so that he has that to look forward to each week and he can still feel part of his family. The ways in which John communicates with others or problem-solves in the house might be something to consider which might help him to communicate more effectively with co-residents when things become difficult or if he is having a disagreement.

You will probably have lots more ideas.

Main associated theory

Crisis Intervention Theory, Strengths-Based Theory

Skill category

Interventions

See also: anti-oppressive practice, collaboration: working with experts by experience, containing anxiety, counselling skills, emotional intelligence, empowerment and enabling, grief and loss

Further reading

Harms, L. (2015) *Understanding Trauma and Resilience*. London: Palgrave.

C

Case recording

A case record is a form of communication and a primary means of both recording and transferring information. It is an everyday activity which takes various formats including: case notes; records of telephone conversations or messages; referral information; assessments; care plans; support plans; and records of complaints. Poor record-keeping can result in information that is inaccurate, poorly communicated, out-of-date and/or lost entirely. Poor case recording has implications for the social worker, the team and the agency as well as the people that you support.

Good record-keeping means that information is up-to-date, as factually correct as possible, holistic and comprehensive. Quality case records are critical as they can build a picture of an individual or family over time with important detail on the dynamic nature of risk, need, vulnerabilities, resilience, capacity and strengths (Rogers & Allen, 2019). There is also a legal imperative as good practice in managing information is a fundamental requirement of all agencies who should be compliant with data protection policy.

Top tips

CCCROFT

- The **3 C**'s of record-keeping help us to remember that records should be *clear, concise* and *consistent.*
- **R**eal words: don't use acronyms, shorthand (that only you can understand), abbreviations, metaphors, informal or other conversational language.
- **O**bjective language is important in order to avoid subjective, one-sided viewpoints without evidence to support what you write.
- **F**actual is best. Stick to verifiable information and try to be holistic and comprehensive (but succinct). Remember to include core information such as your name as well as the date and time of a telephone call or visit.
- **T**imeliness is critical and you should try to maintain up-to-date case records, recorded as soon as possible after the event. This is especially important if you are working within a legal timeframe; that is, producing reports or assessments as required by the court.

This list is not exhaustive but provides a solid framework for good quality case records.

A case note

12/09/2019 Home visit to Mr Mahmood Khan (DOB: 03/03/1943, preferred name 'Mo') 11 a.m. at 3 Park Ave, SS9 9SS.

Visit made following a referral from Salma Smith (practice nurse at North Ash Surgery 0113 444 5678) with concerns of self-neglect reflecting Mo's ability to self-care and current home conditions. The house was untidy and the kitchen was unclean (rubbish stacked up, dirty floors and surfaces). There was little food (just enough to last for a day). Mo stated that his daughter, Yasmeen, usually calls twice weekly to clean the house and bring shopping but she is currently in Pakistan; due back in a week. Mo said that his neighbour was due that day with some shopping. Mo said that he had been unwell with a virus, accounting for some weight loss, but was on the mend.

Action: follow up visit with Mo on 20/9/2019 as this is when Yasmeen should be back and visiting Mo. I can follow up with a conversation with Yasmeen at that time.

Michael Daniels, Social Worker, Adult Social Care team 16.30 p.m., 12/09/2019

Main associated theory

All

Skill category

All

See also: chronologies, critical thinking and analysis, ecomapping, email communication, genograms

Further reading

Healy, K. & Mulholland, J. (2012) *Writing Skills for Social Workers* (2nd edn). London: Sage.

Rai, L. (2014). *Effective Writing for Social Work: Making a Difference*. Bristol: Policy Press.

Chairing meetings
As the chair of a meeting, you should ensure that the discussion flows smoothly and involves all group members equally. During the meeting, it is your responsibility to ensure that people feel included, safe and able to contribute to the discussion. To achieve this aim, you are required to demonstrate organisational skills, **assertiveness** skills, the ability to listen and the ability to recognise and respond to **non-verbal communication**.

There is a shortage of literature on the skills needed to chair meetings in social work. Most of the advice given emerges from research undertaken in a health setting. This apparent shortage of social work specific research is quite surprising given the range and complex situations within which social work meetings take place. However, one journal article that could be used to develop a more detailed sense of the skills needed to chair a meeting has been written by Harrington (2019).

In the days leading up to the meeting, you might find it useful to ask each attendee if they have any particular items for the agenda. This initial activity will enable you to ensure that each invited person has been given the opportunity, within a suitable timeframe, to provide you with some indication of the topics that they might like to discuss. The themes that are then returned to you form the basis of the meeting's agenda. This agenda will then underpin the running order and focus of the meeting.

Structuring the meeting around a fixed agenda ensures that the discussions and focus of the meeting remain specific. The last discussion point of each agenda is usually termed 'Any other business'. It is designed to enable people to speak more broadly about topics that they feel are important but not necessarily relevant to the specific agenda.

Once attendees have contributed ideas for the agenda, it is sometimes useful if you decide how long each point should be discussed. If the meeting is scheduled to last for one hour, and there are 10 agenda items, careful **time management** will be required to ensure that all points are covered equally. When the agenda has been prepared, it is also good practice to distribute the same to all attendees a day or two before the meeting is scheduled to take place.

Top tips

In the hours leading up to the meeting, is likely that you will begin to feel anxious. Try to take some time away from the busy office to relax and prepare. Read over any previous meeting minutes. Consider the points from the previous or the upcoming meeting that might be challenged or challenging and plan how you might respond.

As the chairperson, you should not be expected to take the notes during the meeting. Therefore, ensure that you make provision to nominate a person to take notes at the start of the meeting if a minute taker has not already been agreed.

At the start of the meeting, identify whether all required attendees are present. Welcome each person and note apologies for absence. If people in the meeting have not formally met before, it is custom and practice to ask each person to introduce themselves.

Once the meeting is underway, try to ensure that the discussions remain close to the agenda. Where plans for further actions are considered, you should also facilitate a discussion about how **S**pecific, **M**easured, **A**chievable, **R**ealistic, and **T**imely (SMART) any recommended actions are.

At the end of the meeting, ensure that the action plan has been summarised and recorded by the note taker. Thank the group for their participation and ensure that the meeting minutes are circulated in good time after the meeting for verification.

Main associated theory

Ecological Theory

Skill category

Communication

See also: active listening, dealing with resistance, group work, mediation, presentation skills

---

Further reading

Harrington, A. (2019) Chairing and managing formal workplace meetings: Skills for nurse leaders. *Nursing Management*, 26(5): 36–41.

Challenging skills
Social work is often undertaken with people during the most difficult and traumatic periods in their life. These times can be punctuated with acute and/or chronic experiences of emotional, social and environmental stress (Taylor, 2011). However, it is common for the duty or responsibility of the social worker during these times to challenge people on their behaviour, inaction, attitudes, beliefs or decision-making. It may be the case that you have to challenge someone on their views about parenting, caring or discipline, for example, as these views might be based on ignorance or bias in some way. Uninformed views can lead to behaviours which are negative, damaging or even abusive. Challenging someone in relation to their views, behaviour or decision-making can be especially difficult if you know that the individual has experienced extreme or prolonged periods of adversity, discrimination, oppression and/or marginalisation. Nevertheless, as social work practitioners, we have an ethical and moral code, as well as a legal duty, that provides a mandate for professional conduct, judgement and decision-making.

There are three aspects of responsibility in relation to challenging someone (Spong, 2012). First, you should be mindful of your responsibility and/or duty to the person who you are supporting (whether this is the person you need to challenge, their carer or other close relationship). Second, you have a responsibility for self-care; that is, to look after yourself. Third, it can be likely that you have a moral or social responsibility. For example, there will be circumstances in which someone offers a view that is ageist, homophobic or reflects some other form of prejudice. This in itself does not necessarily invoke a legal duty, but presents a situation in which you feel that you have a moral duty to challenge, or it may be something that you find offensive on a personal level.

The ability and confidence to challenge another person, however, is complex and often this can be challenging in itself. Just because it is difficult, this does not mean that you should avoid it. The values of equality, social justice, dignity, integrity and **valuing diversity** underpin social work practice and should underpin your responses when faced with behaviour, attitudes or beliefs that needs to be confronted. Making judgements about how and when to challenge somebody can require careful consideration (particularly when thinking about the impact on you and the person that needs to be confronted). For example, if you are in the midst of a conversation with someone with whom you are just starting to build rapport and trust, potentially there are implications of challenging someone if, all of a sudden, they say something that you find offensive. In this instance, the communication style that you draw on will be especially important. For example, rather than taking a forthright, assertive approach, a gentler and subtle mode of challenge can be much more impactful.

Humour can be very useful as can the use of body language and gesturing (that is, **non-verbal communication**). The most straightforward way to challenge someone is to ask them in a calm, but resolute, manner to cease using offensive language or behaviour that you find to be unacceptable. The ways in which you articulate this will depend on the person that you are challenging (their temperament and mood at the time, your relationship with them, the topic, and so on).

Top tips

Be prepared with stock phrases

- I don't feel that language such as ... is appropriate and I'd appreciate it if you did not use those terms.
- I feel uncomfortable when you say ... because ...
- Please could you stop using that word as I don't think it's appropriate these days.
- I do not agree with that because...
- I don't think it is OK to label/stereotype people in that way.
- Our policy is that we respect all kinds of people and so it is not acceptable to speak in that way.
- I would ask you not to use that type of language because it might cause offence.

Main associated theory

Psychosocial Theory

Skill category

Relational Practice

See also: anti-discriminatory practice, anti-oppressive practice, assertiveness, breaking bad news, conflict management and resolution, counselling skills, dealing with hostility, dealing with resistance, emotional intelligence, giving and receiving feedback, use of self and reflexivity

Further reading

Spong, S.J. (2012) The challenge of prejudice: Counsellors' talk about challenging clients' prejudices. *British Journal of Guidance & Counselling*, 40(2): 113–125.

Taylor, B.J. (ed.) (2011) *Working with Aggression and Resistance in Social Work*. Exeter: Learning Matters.

Chronologies

A chronology is a timeline. It is a record of events presented in the order that they occurred in a person's life. Chronologies are an important part of a **case record** or an **assessment** and, as such, they are a very useful tool. They can provide a picture of significant events, transitions and interventions; all of which impact on that individual's life. To enable a holistic view, it is important to include all life events including: births and deaths; changes in family composition; changes of address; changes in schooling; illnesses or injuries; incidents of neglect or abuse; any periods of time spent in state care; any criminal activity or offences; and much more. Chronologies should contain information from any agency that has had involvement in the individual's life in order to build a holistic, comprehensive picture.

Chronologies can be particularly useful in demonstrating a pattern of repeated incidents of risk or harm, or in uncovering patterns of behaviour that may negatively impact safety, health or wellbeing. A balanced representation is needed in that both positive and negative events (illustrating risks, strengths, vulnerabilities and resilience) should be included. Chronologies are, however, only of value if an accurate and up-to-date record is maintained. As such, a chronology should be seen as a dynamic record which is revisited and updated on a regular basis. The amount of written detail should be sufficient to gain an overview but a chronology does not need the same amount of detailed narrative that you would find in a case record; a chronology complements a case record. Chronologies can assist you in the continuing assessment of needs, risk and strengths as well as during the planning, intervention and review stages of the social work process.

Danger zone

Chronologies

The value and purpose of a chronology can be undermined by the following factors:

- Out-of-date information
- Missing or inaccurate key information such as date of birth, family composition, telephone numbers of parents or carers, etc
- Writing of a subjective nature with personal opinion rather than fact and objective data.

Table C1 provides an example of an entry in a chronology for an eight-year-old child, Edith.

Table C1   Chronology for Edith

Date/ Time	Event/Service intervention	Outcome/Impact	Source of information	Action
6.1.2020 to 18.1.2020	Single assessment, Newton Child & Family team	No indications of ongoing concern following referral of domestic abuse between Edith's mum, Josie Dant, and her ex-partner (Steve Mobs). Reported incident at the school gates was a one-off, but relationship has a history of domestic abuse.	Referral by Desmond Johnson, Teacher, Newton Junior School	Assessment completed. Contact info for Newton Women's Aid passed to mum, Josie. Case closed.
28.1.2020	Edith disclosed that her mum's ex-partner (Steve Mobs) has moved back in. Home visit undertaken.	Both Edith and Josie (mum) denied that Steve Mobs had moved back in. There was no indication of his presence in the home.	Referral Lisa Latch, Safeguarding Lead, Newton Junior School	Home visit undertaken. Mum agreed to a referral to Newton Women's Aid for outreach support and to attend the Freedom Programme. Referral made and then case closed.

Main associated theory

Narrative Theory

Skill category

Assessment

See also: case recording, ecomapping, genograms

Further reading

Hardy, R. (2018) Why a chronology should be the first thing you do in an assessment. *Community Care Online.* Available at: www.communitycare.co.uk/2018/08/15/chronology-first-thing-assessment/ (accessed 25 January 2021).

Collaboration: working with experts by experience

Over recent years and particularly in the past decade there has been growing acceptance that experts by experience, specifically those people who experience social work intervention, should be involved in the making of decisions that affect them. Growing impetus has been given to the role of experts by experience by the International Federation of Social Work (IFSW, 2014). Their objective is presented within the following definition:

> Social work is a practice-based profession and an academic discipline that promotes social change and development, social cohesion, and the empowerment and liberation of people. Principles of social justice, human rights, collective responsibility and respect for diversities are central to social work. Underpinned by theories of social work, social sciences, humanities and indigenous knowledge, social work engages people and structures to address life challenges and enhance wellbeing.

In the above quotation, the term 'indigenous knowledge' is not meant to apply to the knowledge of indigenous people, but rather to the assumed fact that each individual, family or community who you work to support have their own explanation and interpretation of the challenges that they may face. As experts in their own lives, they can also provide an idea for the solution to overcome these challenges too.

The task facing you in practice, however, is to develop the relationship required to facilitate the opportunity for people to share their explanations, interpretations and solution. If you ever hope to see the world through the eyes of the people you are working to support, you must first seek out opportunities within the **assessment** to establish their views, opinions, hopes, dreams and aspirations. Recognising the influence of coercive power, collaboration with experts by experience means that you must be prepared to learn from the people you are working to support and use their 'indigenous knowledge' to share and debate ideas about the best way to deliver services.

To assist in the development of the fundamental skills needed to devise an approach to collaboration, Think Local Act Personal (2016) have developed a ladder for co-production. Representative of seven stages of engagement, the ladder describes the fundamental steps needed to achieve collaborative practice. Outlining the constituent elements for inclusion and co-production, the model can be used in many different applications from strategic action planning and service design and development to the formulation and review of individual assessments, plans and interventions (see Skills in Action box below).

Skills in action

Seven steps of collaborative practice with experts by experience

Table C2   The ladder of co-production model

Co-production. The seventh rung of the ladder encourages you to facilitate an equal collaborative relationship that can share, debate and review ideas about the best way to design and deliver services.

Co-design. The sixth rung of the ladder encourages you to include individuals and families in the assessment, planning, implementation and review process.

Engagement. The fifth rung of the ladder encourages you to facilitate opportunities for individuals and families to express their views and ideas about how best you can all work together.

Consultation. The fourth rung of the ladder encourages you to ask individuals and families what services or actions they think might be needed to influence or achieve change.

Informing. The third rung of the ladder encourages you to inform individuals and families about their rights, including their right to complain. You might also do well to explain how they will be involved in the assessment process.

Enabling. The second rung of the ladder encourages you to help individuals and families to understand the relevance and significance of your involvement.

Coercion. The first rung of the ladder represents coercive practice. At this stage you will not be taking the views and wishes of individuals and families into account.

Source: adapted from Think Local Act Personal (2016) 'Ladder of co-production' model

Meaningful collaboration with the people you are working to support requires you to listen and facilitate opportunities that can enable their views and experiences to influence change. Whilst there is plenty of focus on models of participation and co-production in theory, we feel that there is currently too little focus on ensuring that individuals, families and communities influence real change for themselves. Listening to the voices of others is only half the story; acting on what they say is what makes their involvement meaningful. If you value the indigenous knowledge offered by individuals, families and communities, you should also try to ensure that their views, hopes and aspirations are at the core of all social work assessment, planning, intervention and review processes.

There are a number of challenges to collaborative practice. Consider some of those described in the Danger Zone box below.

Danger zone

Barriers to collaboration

A number of personal and organisational constraints can hinder your ability to climb the ladder of collaborative practice that is presented in Table C2. These constraints might include feelings of fear, shame, anger, confusion or resentment. There might be a lack of capacity within services, lack of available specialist service provision, rigid threshold criteria or a lack of resources. Together with the potential for discrimination and oppression, these constraints can seriously undermine any opportunity to facilitate collaborative practices.

Main associated theory

Humanistic Theory – but all actually apply

Skill category

Anti-oppressive practice (but all others too)

See also: advocacy, appreciative inquiry, restorative practice, valuing diversity

Further reading

Think Local Act Personal (2016) 'Ladder of co-production' model. Available at: www.thinkloca-lactpersonal.org.uk/Latest/National-Children-and-Adult-Services-Conference-2016-/ (accessed 10 December 2019).

Communicating with children and young people

Throughout your social work career, you will be required to communicate with children and young people for a range of reasons. You will communicate directly with them to learn more about their views and their families' circumstances. You will also communicate with them to ascertain their views about decisions and matters that affect their lives. Put simply, you will have to be able to connect, engage, support, talk and listen to children and young people if you hope to make a positive contribution to their lives.

The key challenge that you might encounter when trying to communicate with children effectively stems from the fact that you are no longer a child. As an adult, you might have developed a more mature, formalised style of communication. The things that are important to you as an adult, might not be the same things that are important to a child. The way that you see the world might be different from the way that a child sees the world. As a social worker, who no longer communicates as a child, understands as a child or thinks as a child, the single biggest obstacle that you might have to overcome is re-learning how to value the things that a child might value.

The need to see the world through the child's eyes is set out in the United Nations Convention on the Rights of the Child. This duty provides an important legal standard for how you should consider children and young people and the significance of your communication with them. Using this legislative duty as the mandate for practice, Butler and Roberts (2003) suggest that the key question that you must be able to answer in your **assessment** is: 'How is the child?' This question is as valid today as it was all those years ago.

In order to answer this question, you have to be able to generate your answer by communicating with children and young people. Of course, children do not all communicate in the same way. Some may have their own preferred style of communication or have a particular communication need. Some might not speak the same language as you. Your skill, therefore, is not just being able to communicate across the age spectrum, but also being able to recognise that the different ages and stages of childhood might require different and varied communication methods.

Karen Winter and her colleagues usefully remind us that communication is not simply talking and listening. It also involves using a range of techniques such as touch, play, signing, body language, writing, drawing, activities, using symbols and other specialist tools to engage and communicate with children and young people (Winter et al., 2017). The importance of tailoring your approach is highlighted in the Skills in Action box below.

Skills in action

Enablers of communication

As an effective communicator you will need to ensure that you can tailor your own preferred communication style to include and account for the individual needs of the child. Most of all you will rely on time, patience, space and resources as enablers of effective communication. There are a number of core skills that could enhance your communication and Lefevre (2013) has usefully categorised them under the following four domains:

- *Doing*: whilst in practice and in training try to experiment with a variety of tools, **interviewing** techniques, listening and creative techniques, going at the child's pace, using child-centred communication
- *Being* (personal qualities): engaging and building relationships, building trust and safety, being caring, empathic, honest, sincere and warm
- *Being* (ethical commitment): eliciting children's views, providing information, maintaining confidentiality (where possible), providing uninterrupted time, being reliable, respectful and non-judgemental
- *Knowing and understanding*: having knowledge and understanding of how the social work role affects communication and how experiences affect communication and child development.

As you plan your assessments, it is important that you can devise specific ways to support and encourage children to express their views, using methods such as play, games, activity-based work and the use of creative arts. Taken together, these activities can enable children to feel more comfortable and to express and process their feelings. Activity-based work, playing games and having fun together can also enhance your relationship with a child.

For young children, activities such as games, writing and drawing help to make the process more child-friendly. To encourage young children to talk you may find it useful to have a bag containing a few toys, coloured pencils, paper, flash cards and worksheets. These methods may also be helpful when communicating with a child with a learning disability.

Older children can be reluctant to share thoughts and feelings because they fear these private things will be written down in their file and shared with strangers. A range of methods can be used to promote communication with older children, including web-based apps, camcorders, cameras, diaries and scrapbooks. Some young people find it easier to communicate whilst on the move – when walking together, for example, or travelling by car. Others use photographs and videos to give insight into their lives.

Danger zone

Some of the children and young people who you will work to engage may already have a number of other professionals involved in their lives. Whilst you might play a critical role in the work that is being provided, you must also remember that you might not be the most important professional or adult to that child. In some circumstances, it is important for you to consider how your communication with children may be mediated and supported by an adult that the child or young person already knows and trusts.

Main associated theory

Narrative and Empowerment Theory

Skill category

Communication, interventions

See also: collaboration: working with experts by experience, home visits, life story work, person-centred communication

---

Further reading

Hadfield, M., Ruch, G., Winter, K., Cree, V. & Morrison, F. (2019) Social workers' reflexive understandings of their 'everyday' communications with children. *Child & Family Social Work*, 25(2): 469–477.

Neven, R.S. (2010) *Core Principles of Assessment and Therapeutic Communication with Children, Parents and Families: Towards the Promotion of Child and Family Wellbeing*. London: Routledge.

Communicating with people with lived experience of learning disabilities

Social workers support people with lived experience of learning disabilities in all fields of practice. This includes children and families and adults in social care services, in hospital and community contexts as well as in specialist learning disability services. Whilst the generic skills described in this book provide an essential foundation to good practice, it is important to recognise that deeper knowledge and more specialised approaches are required when communicating with people with lived experience of learning disabilities.

Whilst generic social work skills are key to ensuring personalised care and support for all people, we know that people with lived experience of learning disabilities often describe encounters with inadequate and sometimes abusive institutional services (Cotterill, 2019). As a social worker, you will hold a lot of organisational power. Without careful reflection, your power can be (unwittingly) demonstrated to maintain the inadequacies that Cotterill describes. Thus, you should make deliberate attempts to ensure that your communication with people with lived experience of learning disabilities reflect the profession's values and ethics. Perhaps start this approach by considering the activity listed in the Stop–Reflect box below.

Stop–reflect

What is in a word?

Reflect on the term 'learning disability'. To whom is it referring?

Godsell and Scarborough (2006) provide a useful summary of terminology and facts related to that term:

- The term 'learning difficulty' is used in education settings to identify individuals with lived experience of specific learning needs, for example, dyslexia. Some people who are identified as having a learning difficulty may also be considered to have a learning disability, but this is not necessarily the case.
- The words 'mild', 'moderate', 'severe' and 'profound' are terms used to describe different degrees of a learning disability. A person with mild learning disabilities might communicate effectively, learn, live and work with little support. However, a person with profound learning disabilities will require support with activities of daily living, for example, communication, dressing, feeding, washing and mobility.
- A diagnosis of 'mental illness' is not the same as having a learning disability, but people with learning disabilities may have mental health issues as well.
- People with lived experiences of learning disabilities may have multiple diagnoses resulting in complex health needs.
- Not everyone with a lived experience of learning disabilities requires a social worker.

Although **active listening**, empathy and **challenging skills** are just three essential skills, social work values and ethics expect that you will be able to explain the role of the social worker within the multi-professional context and demonstrate an ability to develop a personal relationship whilst maintaining a professional identity. In all examples, professional standards also expect that you are skilful in building shared understanding and trust in working relationships, using face-to-face communications where possible, appropriate written communication styles and eliminating jargon by using language that is familiar. You should also be able to embrace approaches to an **assessment** or care planning activity that avoids a procedural assessment method or closed questions. By using conversational two-way communications that draw on the assumption of **person-centred communication**, participatory and co-produced models of assessment, you should be able to facilitate opportunities to create plans in partnership with the person, their relevant family, supporters and advocates.

The importance of **reflective practice** is also consistent with the social model of disability, which emphasises that people's experience of the world, and their opportunities to live well, flourish and have control over their lives, are determined by the opportunity to self-define their needs and strengths and express themselves in their own language and forms of communications (Stevens, 2008). Whilst good communication is central to all social work, it is important to recognise that working with people with lived experience of a learning disability often requires the use of adapted communications techniques that can optimise creative conversations, communications and partnership working.

Being flexible in your approach to communication requires you to remember that everyone is able to communicate. If someone does not communicate in a way that is generally understandable, your role is to work in partnership with the person, their relevant family, supporters and advocates to interpret the messages that you receive and consider how to make the messages that you send more understandable. Try to remember that communication is not only about verbal communication; it is also about **non-verbal communication**. For example, the use of augmentative and alternative communication systems that include sign language, Makaton, Picture Exchange Communication System and Talking Mats all represent assisted and tailored communications and technologies that can improve flexibility.

Clearly, social work terms are only beneficial if the person you are working to support understands them so, for example, **safeguarding** could be described as 'keeping a person safe from harm', but you would also need to know whether the person uses the term 'harm' to describe abuse. Use the exercise detailed in the Stop–Reflect box below to consider examples of alternative terms that are easier to understand.

Stop–reflect

Using your words to facilitate understanding

Table C3   Using your words to facilitate understanding

Social work term	What other common words could you use?	What words could you use to help support and facilitate understanding?
Safeguarding	Keeping a person safe from harm	Protecting you from people who might try to hurt you
Independence		
Person-centred plan		
Medication		
Carer		

Unless you have had previous experience of supporting people with lived experience of learning disabilities, you might, depending on your role, need to develop your confidence of using augmentative and alternative communication systems within the practice setting. However, the development of this opportunity should be underpinned by the generic capability to understand when a different form of communication may be needed, the types of communication and language aids and approaches available, and how to work effectively with **interpreters** and advocates skilled in augmentative and alternative communication systems. One skill that you can develop quite quickly is the ability to reduce the use of jargon in all of your communications with the people you are working to support.

Main associated theory

Narrative and Empowerment Theory

Skill category

Communication, interventions

See also: interviewing, observational skills, person-centred planning

Further reading

BASW (British Association of Social Workers) (2020) *Professional Capabilities Framework.* Available at: www.basw.co.uk/social-work-training/professional-capabilities-frame-work-pcf (accessed 25 January 2021).

Stevens, R.A. (2008) Social models of disability and social work in the twenty-first century. *Ethics and Social Welfare*, 2(2): 197–202.

Conflict management and resolution
Conflict is a reality of everyday life. It commonly exists when there is an interaction between two or more individuals or groups and where at least one side believes that their differences, feelings, ideas, views or opinions are not being valued or respected by the other.

Conflict in social work is a common occurrence. In some circumstances, the people who you are working to support may be suspicious of you. They might not understand why you need to be involved in their lives and they may not agree with your **assessment** of their situation. As social work is heavily invested in facilitating change for individuals, families and communities, conflict might also be common in those situations where change is perceived as being unwanted or not needed. It is widely known that most people do not like change and that they will become unwilling to change unless they can clearly see the advantage that change brings. For social work practice, this apparently natural resistance to change can lead to a number of frustrations and ethical dilemmas.

The presence of conflict in your professional career will certainly never be confined to your relationship with individuals and families. Working within multi-disciplinary teams, for example, can provide wide opportunities for conflict as the perspectives, views and opinions of different professionals will reflect their own training and philosophical assumptions. Professional debates about the most suitable approach to mental health recovery will almost certainly exhibit conflict that emerges from the competing medical and social models of practice.

Since conflict may be inevitable in social work, learning to manage and resolve it is crucial. When conflict is mismanaged, it can harm a relationship. But, when handled in a respectful and positive way, conflict provides an opportunity for growth, ultimately strengthening the bond between two people. Consider the example provided in the Stop–Reflect box below and the two separate approaches to conflict resolution.

Stop–reflect

Working together to overcome conflict

Ali and Mandeep have been asked to work together to develop a presentation to the team on the impact of parental drug use on children in their local area. At one of their planning sessions, Ali accuses Mandeep of not taking the project seriously.

Which of the following examples do you think provides the best approach to conflict resolution?

Example A:

- Mandeep dismisses Ali's concerns and tells him that he is being silly and childish.
- Ali becomes angry, leaves the office and slams the office door.
- Ali complains to his manager that he cannot work with Mandeep because she is unprofessional. He then tells the whole team that Mandeep is not a team player.
- Mandeep says that she knew working with Ali would be hard. Based on his response she tells the manager that she will never work with Ali again.

Example B:

- Mandeep asks why Ali thinks the way that he does. After a brief explanation, Mandeep explains that she is taking the presentation seriously but that she has been busy with a casework priority.
- Ali apologises for thinking that Mandeep was not taking the presentation seriously and asks her if there is anything he can do to help her with the casework.
- Mandeep asks if Ali could reschedule the planning session to later in the day so that the casework priority can be dealt with.
- Ali agrees.

When working with individuals and families, conflict can trigger strong emotions and can lead to hurt feelings, disappointment and discomfort. When handled improperly, conflict can cause irreparable rifts and resentments within the social work relationship. However, when conflict is resolved effectively, it can increase mutual understanding, build trust and strengthen relationships.

When people are upset, the words they use rarely convey the real source of the conflict. When working to engage people who may be suspicious of you or with those who might not understand or agree with your involvement, it is essential that you listen to the things that they tell you. In all circumstances, it is essential that you take any threats of violence seriously and remove yourself from the situation, and if necessary, call the police. Making an assessment to continue with a meeting, even if an individual is upset, will require you to listen carefully to what is being said whilst applying a series of key conflict resolution skills. Other key skills are listed in the Skills in Action box below.

Skills in action

Key skills

When listening to another person's point of view, the following responses are often helpful in conflict resolution. Remember, if you feel unsafe, you should leave the situation immediately.

- *Stay calm* and speak in a calm and quite manner. Do not raise your voice, and do acknowledge the person's emotions:
  - 'I can see that you are upset and I am listening to you.'
- *Encourage* the other person to share his or her concerns as fully as possible. You might say, for example:
  - 'I want to understand what has upset you.'
  - 'I want to know what you are really hoping for.'
- *Clarify* the points that the person is making, rather than making assumptions about what is upsetting them. Ask questions that allow you to assess the situation and demonstrate that you are trying to understand the situation from the other person's perspective:
  - 'Can you tell me more about that?'
  - 'What has caused you to feel this way?'
- *Restate* what you have heard, so you can demonstrate that you have heard and understood the other person:
  - 'It sounds like you were not expecting that to happen.'
- *Reflect feelings* and be as clear as possible that you acknowledge the other person's feelings:
  - 'I can imagine how upsetting that must have been.'
- *Validate* the concerns of the other person, even if a solution is not entirely clear at the time. Expressing appreciation can be a very powerful message if it is conveyed with integrity and respect:
  - 'I really appreciate that we are talking about this issue. This must be very hard for you.'
  - 'I am glad that we are working together to try and figure this out.'

Adapted from Hatiboğlu et al. (2019) and reprinted by permission of Sage Publications.

Conflict management and resolution

Main associated theory

Crisis Intervention Theory

Skill category

Relational practice

See also: active listening, emotional intelligence, empowerment and enabling, mediation, observational skills, person-centred communication

Further reading

Deutsch, M. & Coleman, P.T. (2000) *The Handbook of Conflict Resolution: Theory and Practice*. San Francisco, CA: Jossey-Bass.

Hatiboğlu, B., Özateş Gelmez, Ö.S. & Öngen, Ç. (2019) Value conflict resolution strategies of social work students in Turkey. *Journal of Social Work*, 19(1): 142–161.

Containing anxiety Anxiety is often described as a feeling of unease, worry or fear. Given the nature of complex social work practice, mild examples of anxiety can be common among social workers, particularly for those who are working to predict and manage risk when seeking to safeguard vulnerable people (Antonopoulou, Killian & Forrester, 2017).

Most social work teams try hard to support and reduce anxiety through positive organisational structures. These might include, for example, small supportive teams, staff supervision and the use of good practical support mechanisms that are designed to promote emotional wellbeing. These work-enabling conditions often establish the basis for a sense of shared responsibility and professional support for promoting mental health and wellbeing within the workplace setting.

Danger zone

Symptoms of anxiety include:

- restlessness
- a feeling of dread
- a feeling of being 'on-edge'
- difficulty concentrating
- difficulty sleeping
- irritability
- dizziness

- nausea
- heart palpitations
- sweating
- shortness of breath
- headaches.

If feelings of anxiety are regularly causing you significant distress, or if these feelings start to impact on your ability to study or practice as a social worker, for example withdrawing or avoiding contact with colleagues, feeling unable to conduct the routine practice of case work, or avoiding certain places and situations, then you may need to speak to your university tutor, practice educator, manager, doctor or health care professional.

All social workers get anxious sometimes, and learning how to manage anxiety will also be a normal part of your **professional development**. Every social worker has a different level of stress that they can tolerate, but some social workers are just naturally more anxious than others. Some may be quicker to feel unease, worry or fear, for example. The crucial thing to remember is that anxiety and feelings of unease, worry or fear do not mean that some social workers are better than others. Anxiety should never be used as a measure of capability either. However, if anxiety becomes uncontained, and the feelings of unease, worry or fear prevent the social worker from carrying out their duties, additional support might be required.

The way that you manage your anxiety may be unique to you. An example of how a social worker working in a community outreach team contains her anxiety is shown in the Skills in Action box below.

Skills in action

Candice's strategy for managing anxiety

Candice recognises that she might be struggling to contain the anxiety that she feels whilst working on placement. With the support of a more experienced colleague, Candice develops the following action plan:

1 Candice ensures that anxiety is a fixed agenda item in her supervision meeting with her manager. She finds that talking about any feelings of unease, worry or fear can help her to rationalise how her casework is making her feel. Candice finds that the experience of describing her feelings of unease, worry or fear can help her to feel better.
2 Candice keeps a reflective diary to help her recognise anxious feelings. She tries to keep an account of the situations or experiences that generate anxious feelings. As she looks back over her diary, she begins to spot patterns and

(Continued)

indicators of those occasions when she might need to ask for help and support from her team.

3   Candice accepts anxiety as being normal. She tells herself that any feelings of unease, worry or fear will pass. Candice also tries to visualise anxiety as a wave in the ocean that can swell but then gets smaller when it peaks and washes onto a beach.

4   When she notices that feelings of anxiety are beginning to swell, Candice tries to breathe deeply and slowly. She breathes in through her nose for three counts and out through her mouth for three counts. Candice tries to breathe deeply and slowly until the wave of anxiety begins to dissipate.

5   During times of anxiety, Candice tries to visualise a place where she feels relaxed and happy. She thinks about a holiday destination and when feelings of unease, worry or fear begin to grow, she tries to image that she is on holiday feeling relaxed and calm. Sometimes Candice looks at old holiday photos to visualise this calm and serene location.

6   Candice also tries to maintain a healthy lifestyle, taking regular exercise to reduce the levels of stress hormones. She tries to develop and sustain good sleeping habits and calm bedtime routines. Candice also limits her screen or computer time in the evening and she avoids work-related activity on her days off.

As you set out on your own social work journey, the experience of anxiety might be new. You might not, therefore, always recognise the signs and symptoms of anxiety, and you may find the associated symptoms frightening or overwhelming. However, with the careful application of the skills needed to contain anxiety, you should be able to manage your feelings in partnership with your manager.

Universities and workplaces are starting to invest heavily in mental health support services. If you feel that your anxiety is beginning to impact on your aspirations as a social worker try to build the confidence to make use of the support services that are available. Where possible, you might like to consider developing a discussion group that enables other social workers to talk openly and honestly about anxiety in a safe and confidential environment.

Main associated theory

Psychosocial Theory

Skill category

Relational practice

See also: challenging skills, dealing with hostility, emotional intelligence, managing stress, reflective practice

Further reading

Stanley, S. & Mettilda Bhuvaneswari, G. (2016). Stress, anxiety, resilience and coping in social work students (a study from India). *Social Work Education*, 35(1): 78–88.

Vungkhanching, M., Tonsing, J.C. & Tonsing, K.N. (2017). Psychological distress, coping and perceived social support in social work students. *British Journal of Social Work*, 47(7): 1999–2013.

Counselling skills

A tension can exist between the managerial and administrative functions of social work and the need to assess risk, reduce harm, promote independence and realise social justice. In addition to the pressure caused by this tension, individuals and families consistently say that they need to be listened to and supported to be involved in the decisions and discussions that concern them. Most importantly, they say that the administrative function of social work is beginning to undermine the ability of some social workers to treat them with dignity and respect (Riggall, 2016).

Key obstacles to providing a service that treats people with dignity and respect are found within the pressures and complexities of practice. Where relationship-based practices once existed as a gold standard, reduced resources, increased workload pressures and high staff turnover mean that the reality of practice is now more aligned to short-term, fast-paced crisis intervention models. In these examples of practice, social workers commonly and mistakenly believe that their role is to tell the people what to do.

The main problem with growing trends in procedural and directive models of casework management is that the social worker is often required to respond to situations quickly and with authority. Decisions about interventions or outcomes can be made without the full involvement or inclusion of those who are experiencing social work intervention. In some cases, social work is done to people, rather than done with people.

Where the social worker assumes expertise, and determines the actions or interventions that may be needed, the reality of the individual or family can be lost. As a consequence, where decisions are made, and the individual or family feels that they have not been listened to, supported, involved in the decisions or treated with dignity and respect, there is a high possibility that the original intention of the social worker may be misunderstood.

Current procedural and directive trends in social work practice can minimise the importance of developing empathic relationships with the people we work to support. Although the work of Carl Rogers (1951) highlights the importance of building a non-judgemental relationship, it is also known that empathic responding, unconditional positive regard and congruence are not enough to evoke change. What is needed instead is an orientation to participatory counselling methods that encourage people to talk about their lives and to establish exactly what their needs are.

The series of publications developed by Egan (2018) provide a transferable set of counselling and coaching skills that can be used to promote the principles of participation in social work practice. In contrast to crisis-driven methods of practice, Egan (2018) provides a series of techniques and models that are summarised in the Skills in Action box below to help social workers enable the people who they are working to support to take responsibility for their own decision-making.

Skills in action

An introduction to counselling skills

1   *Attending.* During an interview or **home visit**, try to give the person you are talking to your full attention. If the environment is noisy, busy or chaotic, try to find a quiet location. Ask for a television or phone to be turned off so that you can reduce distractions and focus on the conversation. Always try to allow sufficient time for the visit so that you do not feel rushed.

2   *Silence.* Silence in counselling gives the individual or family control of the content, pace and objectives. Try to recognise silence as being as important as words. Remember that silences may also facilitate the counselling process.

3   *Reflecting and paraphrasing.* Reflecting in counselling is part of the 'art of listening'. It is making sure that the person who you are working to support knows that you are listening to them. You can achieve reflection and paraphrasing by repeating and feeding a shorter (paraphrased) version of what has been said back to the individual.

4   *Clarifying and the use of questions.* Questions in counselling are classed as a basic skill. In social work, you can use open questions to clarify an understanding of what the individual is feeling. Leading questions should be avoided as they can impair the counselling relationship and the primary assumptions of person-centred practice.

5   *Focusing.* Focusing in counselling involves making decisions about what issues the individual or family want to deal with. The individual or family may have mentioned a range of issues and problems that affected them. Focusing allows you to work together with the individual to clear away some of the less important surrounding material and concentrate on the central issues of concern.

6   *Building rapport.* Building rapport with individuals and families in social work is important whatever theory or method you use. Rapport means a sense of having a connection with another person.

7   *Summarising.* Summaries are longer paraphrases. You may choose to condense the essence of what an individual is saying and feeling. The summary enables you to 'sum up' the main themes that are emerging.

8   *Immediacy.* Using immediacy enables you to reveal how you are feeling in response to the individual or family. Immediacy can be useful if the social worker is trying to challenge defensiveness and or heighten awareness.

In brief, Egan (2018) emphasises both the relationship and client action. He describes the skills that a social worker needs to find out what is currently going on in the lives of the people they are working to support. These skills include **active listening**, empathy and positive challenging. At all times the conversation is non-directive. The social worker avoids making a recommendation or a decision. Instead, the social worker uses a range of carefully selected reflective questions that encourage the individual or family to state what they want or need that might help them as they develop their own strategies and goals.

Danger zone

Transferring the counselling skills that Egan (2018) describes in social work may enable you to develop a client-centred approach by empathically responding to individuals and families, challenging them appropriately and placing them at the centre of the decision-making process. The clear danger in this transferability, however, is that you may not be employed as a counsellor. If the limitations of your own skills are not recognised, the techniques listed above might be used to encourage some individuals and families to talk about topics that you are not equipped or qualified to deal with. When applying counselling skills to the social work **assessment**, it is essential that you recognise your own limitations and the possibility that a counselling approach might cause harm. Whenever using counselling skills, it is essential that you are mindful of the principles of emotional intelligence and the relevant codes of behaviour, conduct and ethics for social work practice.

Main associated theory

Cognitive-Behavioural Theory, Strengths-Based Theory, Humanistic Theory, Empowerment Theory, Psychosocial Theory, Narrative Theory

Skill category

Communication, relational practice

See also: motivational interviewing, solution-focused practice

Further reading

Riggall, S. (2012) *Using Counselling Skills in Social Work*. London: Sage/Learning Matters.

Riggall, S. (2016) The sustainability of Egan's skilled helper model in students' social work practice. *Journal of Social Work Practice*, 30(1): 81–93.

Court skills

Court skills Court work is fundamental to social work in many areas of practice and, as such, court skills are essential. Areas of practice include: child protection social work; adoption; youth justice; disputes about 'best interests' under the Mental Capacity Act 2005; Mental Health Tribunals; or Coroner's Court; to name a few. Whitaker (2020) describes how social workers typically assume one of two main roles in court work:

> *[As] a professional witness*: usually a local authority social worker, called to provide evidence on a matter for the court, related to a case in which they have direct involvement. *[As an] independent social worker*: this may be as a children's guardian, or independent social work witness. (Whitaker, 2020: 232–233)

In both roles you would be expected to confirm your professional identity and status before describing your experience and expertise to validate your contribution in relation to the matter before the court. Your expertise and experience are not taken for granted, however, and you should be prepared to be questioned and challenged on your specialist knowledge. This requires you to maintain a certain level of confidence in your own expertise. Concerns in relation to this, and the 'preparedness' of social workers for undertaking court work, have been frequently reported (Lewis & Erlen, 2012: 3). It is undeniable that court work can be daunting, but it is of critical importance that the performance of social workers is flawless in the court environment as what they *say* and *do* can have significant and wide-ranging implications.

Written evidence

If you are required to prepare a court report, take a look at some exemplars completed by colleagues. Your employer might have a document or protocol to guide you in terms of the content and required format. Moss (2012) argues that there are four aspects of **report writing** that are important in the preparation of documents for court. These are that: writing is relevant and concise; facts are clearly distinguished from opinion; an informed opinion and recommendations are made which are legally appropriate and draw on relevant research and professional knowledge; and the writing should be accessible using objective and neutral language so that the person who is the subject of your report can easily read and understand it (Moss, 2012).

There are, of course, some additional conventions to bear in mind such as presentation needs (pagination and numbered paragraphs with section headings to ensure a professional produced report which is easy to navigate). A professionally produced final report will rely on careful proofreading to ensure that there are no spelling or grammatical errors. In terms of finalising your report, you must ensure that it is finished by the set deadline and that you include any standard requirements such as your name, date and signature.

Your time in court

Before you are required to undertake court work, it would be helpful to shadow an experienced colleague through their pre-court preparation and during their time in court. The court system in the UK might seem antiquated at times, but it is a well-established institution with deeply embedded traditions and expectations. For example, the requirement for formal dress persists (that is, no dayglo colours, outlandish patterns or casual daywear please) and you should bear in mind the saliency of symbolic communication (that is, things that we give meaning to and that can represent a message or attitude, such as clothing or the physical environment). It is imperative, therefore, to comply with court etiquette. The use of language and modes of address are very important to court etiquette: Table C4 provides a summary in terms of forms of address in different types of court.

Table C4 Formal court etiquette

Court	Form of address	Physical movement
In all courts	You should address the magistrate or judge, *not* the person that asks you the questions.	Ask the usher or clerk of the court where to sit. This will depend on your specific role, and may alter as you undertake different roles in the proceedings.
		Always stand when the magistrate or judge enters, rises or leaves the court room.
		In more formal courts, you will be asked to give an oath (*swear on a holy text*) or affirmation (*make a solemn promise*) that you will be truthful.
		Witnesses often stand when giving evidence (unless it is in the family court).
Magistrates Court	Collectively as 'Your Worships' or as 'Sir' or 'Madam' individually	
High Court	'My Lord' or 'My Lady'	
Family Court/ County Court	'Your Honour' in the County Court or 'Sir' or 'Madam' (unless it is the Family Division of the High Court)	
Tribunals	'Sir' or 'Madam'	

(Continued)

Table C4 (Continued)

Court	Form of address	Physical movement
Crown Court	'Your Honour' unless in the Old Bailey, then 'My Lord'	
In all courts	Solicitors and barristers refer to each other as 'learned friends'. Other professionals refer to barristers as 'counsel'.	
	The clerk to the court is usually referred to as the 'the learned clerk'.	
	All other participants in the court process should be afforded the courtesy of Mr, Mrs, Miss or Ms followed by their surname.	

Source: Whitaker, in Rogers et al. 2020: 237. Reprinted by permission of SAGE Publications.

If you are required to give direct evidence, the same protocols apply in relation to good report writing; that is, that you are honest, clear and concise in your communication and that you try to speak in a measured way. If you are struggling to control your nerves or find yourself getting flustered, try to slow down and regain that measured composure. Remember that talking slowly and deep breathing both help to contain nerves. Remain neutral and focused upon commenting on matters that you have expertise or direct knowledge of. Similarly, answer the question that you are asked and do not offer additional or superfluous information. Importantly, you should be able to substantiate your evidence and recommendations and if you know that you can, this can boost your confidence and help you to feel in control of your responses.

It is generally acknowledged that 'in the moment' it is difficult to recall all relevant information and it is acceptable to use notes where necessary whilst being mindful that these can be shared with all relevant parties. In considering your response, it is important that you follow the court's instruction, so if you find that you are unclear about what is being asked, or you are unsure about how to respond, always seek clarification; do not try to mask your uncertainty with comments that have not been thought through or that might appear to be defensive, rather than measured and objective. It is very helpful if you have prior warning of any issues that may arise (for example, more detailed information than is given in your report) and the legal representative from your agency should be able to identify this. In all cases, however, try to remember that as the social worker assigned to the case, you probably know more about the individual or family than anyone else in the court, except for the individual or family concerned.

Danger zone

Cross-examination: giving evidence in court

Cooper (2014) comments that trying to guess what the legal advocate is going to ask is pretty difficult as 'it can be as long and short as a piece of string' and is not necessarily limited to the content of your report. Cooper warns to watch out for:

- the use of leading questions: questions that suggest a preferred answer
- the attempt to control the witness: the legal advocate knows the answer before asking it
- the 'tell – don't ask' technique: the legal advocate uses action to prevent the witness's account.

Finally, it is widely recognised that attending court and giving evidence is not easy; confidence does come with time and experience. If you are well prepared, understand the process and etiquette and can retain your composure, then you should make a credible witness and offer substantiated evidence and recommendations that the court will take notice of.

Main associated theory

Psychosocial Theory

Skill category

Communication

See also: active listening, assertiveness, critical thinking and analysis, evidence-informed practice, presentation skills

Further reading

Cooper, P. (2014) *Court and Legal Skills*. Basingstoke: Palgrave Macmillan.

Johns, R. (2017) *Using the Law in Social Work* (7th edn). London: Sage.

Whitaker, D. (2020) Court skills. In M. Rogers, D. Whitaker, D. Edmondson & D. Peach (eds) *Developing Skills & Knowledge for Social Work Practice* (2nd edn). London: Sage.

Critical incident analysis
There are various models and frameworks that can guide a practitioner through a reflective process. This chapter explores critical incident analysis as a model for reflection. First, it is helpful to consider what constitutes a 'critical incident'. The notion of a critical incident first arose to assist the investigation of mishaps, or 'near misses', in the field of aviation (Flanagan, 1954). The emphasis on analysis in this instance was to analyse and evaluate a procedural failure (or human error) with the aim of reducing future risk.

A critical incident is now understood, more broadly, to be an event or situation that has some consequence. The 'critical' in 'critical incident' is, however, a misnomer as this type of occurrence does not have to be a dramatic or extraordinary event, but an event or situation that marks a significant turning point or change in your life. It might be the sort of event or situation that has prompted some reflection of particular aspects of your life; for example, in questioning your beliefs, values, norms and behaviour. It may also be an event or situation that has resulted in some form of personal or professional discovery and learning. As such, the 'critical' reflects the process of critical thinking and analytical skills, rather than the pivotal nature of the event.

Critical incident analysis has developed as a tool to aid **reflective practice** in social work (and other disciplines such as health and education). It was influenced by the work of Tripp (1993). Tripp (1993: 24–25) describes critical incidents as 'commonplace events that occur in routine professional practice […] which are rendered critical through analysis'. In a practice setting, a critical incident could be related to:

- an aspect of your work that was particularly successful
- an aspect of your work that proved challenging or resulted in a less successful outcome
- an incident involving positive feedback of your practice
- an incident involving criticism of your practice
- a piece of work with an individual, family or group that you found particularly demanding
- a piece of work with an individual, family or group that increased your awareness or position in relation to an ethical or social justice issue (such as equality or inclusion)
- an incident involving hostility, aggression, conflict or resistance.

Critical incident analyses have been used widely in social work education and practice. It has varied uses as a learning tool, as a form of **assessment** and as a tool for critical reflection with particular worth in an examination of ethics, values and **anti-oppressive practice** (Thomas, 2004). See the Top Tips box for a comprehensive framework that you can employ as an alternative model of reflection.

Top tips

A critical incident analysis framework

1 Account of the incident
- What happened? Where and when? Who was involved? What was your involvement?
- What was the context of the incident? For example, was there previous involvement of yourself or the agency? What was the purpose and/or focus of your involvement/intervention?

2 Initial responses to the incident
- What were your thoughts and feelings at the time of the incident?
- What were the responses of the others involved in the incident? If unknown, what do you think these might have been?

3 Issues and dilemmas highlighted by the incident
- What practice dilemmas, values and ethical issues were identified as a result of the incident?
- Are there implications for inter-disciplinary or inter-agency collaboration which you have identified as a result of the incident?

4 Learning
- What have you learned: for example, about yourself, your relationships with others, the social work task/intervention, agency and its policies or procedures?
- What theories or research have (or might have) helped your understanding about the incident or some element of it?
- How might an understanding of the legislative, organisational and policy contexts explain some element of the incident?
- What future learning needs have you identified as a result of this incident and how might you achieve these?

5 Outcomes
- What were the outcomes of the incident for different participants?
- What are your thoughts and feelings now?
- Has this incident led to changes in how you think, feel or act in particular or future situations?

Source: adapted from Green Lister & Crisp, 2007: 49–50. Copyright © 2007 British Association of Social Workers, reprinted by permission of Informa UK Limited, trading as Taylor & Francis Group, www.tandfonline.com on behalf of British Association of Social Workers.

Stop-reflect

Can you identify an event or situation in your life in recent years that was significant in terms of having a turning point? This could be an example from your personal or professional life. Now work through the different stages of the critical incident analysis framework to reflect on why this was a significant event which led to change or learning. For example, it could be a notable life event such as a birth or death, a personal achievement (such as gaining a qualification) or a professional win (such as a promotion or some form of award). It could also be a seemingly insignificant event, such as a telephone call or a singular conversation, but one that had considerable impacts.

As alluded to in the framework detailed above, a critical incident analysis is not just a reflection model, it can also be a useful learning aid. As such, this is an adaptable tool which will be of value through social work training and into practice.

Main associated theory

Crisis Intervention Theory

Skill category

Critical thinking and analysis

See also: critical thinking and analysis, reflective writing, risk assessment, use of self and reflexivity

---

Further reading

Green Lister, P. & Crisp, B.R. (2007) Critical incident analyses: A practice learning tool for students and practitioners. *Practice*, 19(1): 47–60.

Critical thinking and analysis In social work discourse, the capacity for **reflective practice** is often mooted as the cornerstone of best practice, but without the ability to think critically and analytically, the process of reflection is not possible. As such, we argue, the processes of critical thinking and analysis represent the cornerstone of best practice in social work. Critical thinking can be defined as:

> [...] the ability to analyse information objectively and make a reasoned judgement. Effective critical thinking involves the ability to evaluate sources of knowledge, such as law, policy, research and theories, to draw and articulate reasonable and verifiable conclusions. It also requires an ability to discriminate between useful and less useful information to solve problems and to make decisions. (Rogers & Allen, 2019: 19)

Critical thinking and analysis are skills that can be learned and developed and are fundamental to the process of integrating knowledge, skills and values in social work practice. When put to good use, these skills enhance social work and result in the promotion of social change, social cohesion and problem-solving as well as the empowerment and liberation of people who might have experienced substantial levels of adversity, discrimination, oppression and marginalisation. As such, the centrality of critical thinking to the primary goals of social work is hard to ignore.

In addition, the capacity for critical analysis is a crucial aspect of social work education and practice. In England this ability is measured against the Professional Capabilities

Framework (PCF) (BASW, 2020). The PCF is the framework used to assess all social workers in England and has nine domains (one being critical reflection and analysis albeit the capacity for critical analysis underpins each domain).

Danger zone

Knowledge and critical thinking

Knowing a lot of 'stuff' in social work is not enough. Put another way, having knowledge of the laws, policies, theories and research that are applicable to the endless scenarios that social workers find themselves amidst is not sufficient. You need to employ a critical understanding of that knowledge and be able to use it judiciously and be able to articulate its limitations and weaknesses as well as its value and strengths. You need to be able to articulate those times when law or policy (or research or theory) is not helpful in shining a light on a particular course of action to counter a complex ethical dilemma or when different pieces of legislation (or research or theory) conflict. Thus, a critical understanding and application of knowledge is vital.

Unquestionably, developing and utilising skills in critical thinking and analysis can be cathartic and empowering, but simultaneously this process can be challenging as you are required to turn a mirror onto yourself and onto your own practice. Engaging in critical analysis requires you to carefully examine the ways in which aspects of yourself (your experiences, background, norms and values) impact upon your practice (that is, the way that you 'do' social work and the way that you 'think' about people and their situations). In addition, as noted above, critical thinking requires you to examine other sources of knowledge and influences, such as law, policy, research and theories to make sense of the ways in which *you* use this knowledge and the efficacy of your practice as a result. The way in which you use this knowledge is never going to be the same as the way in which your colleagues and peers use this knowledge and these differences in approach and application are affected by the fact that you come from different social locations and backgrounds and have different experiences, norms and values.

Skills in action

Mohammed

John is a social worker in a transitions team working with young people with disabilities who transfer from child and family services to adult social care services. In the preparation and planning for his first visit to Mohammed, a young person with physical impairments and mild learning disabilities, John spoke to Mohammed's existing social worker from child and family services. The social worker was extremely helpful, explaining what

(Continued)

was hoped for Mohammed in this transition in terms of staying in the family home and continuing to go to college; that is, making the transition with little disruption to existing arrangements.

John went to the first meeting with Mohammed and his parents with relevant information about continuing transport support for college. After introductions, John explained to Mohammed's parents that the transition from one service to another should involve as little disruption as possible to Mohammed's existing routine. Mohammed's parents agreed with John that the best plan was to continue the arrangements for college and to stay living at home where Mohammed was loved and cared for by his immediate and extended family. Mohammed was very quiet, and John could sense from his body language that Mohammed was unhappy and angry even.

Stop-reflect

What do you think might be happening? What do you think John might be thinking when he noticed Mohammed's body language? John might have thought, 'I've come at a bad time. Mohammed isn't in a good mood today'. He might be right. John might have thought, 'There is something going on between Mohammed and his parents'. Again, John might be right. John might also think, 'Mohammed is a moody young man. I'm not going to make much progress here'. Yes, he might be right about that too.

However, rather than attribute Mohammed's **non-verbal communication** to Mohammed's mood or predisposition, it would be more useful for John to take a critical stance and reflect on his own practice since entering the family home; that is, he should turn that mirror onto himself and onto his practice. He might then consider the way in which he interpreted the social worker's information as categorical. He might consider the way in which he sought the agreement of Mohammed's parents, rather than of Mohammed himself. He might also consider and acknowledge his lack of person-centred practice in that immediately after everyone had introduced themselves, John did not then consult Mohammed on: 1) what he would like to be the outcome of his engagement with John and the transitions service; 2) what Mohammed would like to discuss during that initial meeting; nor 3) what Mohammed considered to be his short- and medium-term wishes, desires and goals during the transition period.

If John had centred the discussion on Mohammed, he might have found out that Mohammed was unhappy at college and was hoping that the transitions service, and his move to adult social care services, would help him to access life skill training, to build the confidence and ability to move towards supported living, as Mohammed felt more than ready for a planned move towards greater independence.

It is important to remember that the 'critical' in critical thinking does not mean being negative. It means to question, examine and evaluate. This means not taking things at face value. Critical thinking relies on engaging in a process of evaluation, analysis and synthesis. This is central to best practice in social work. You should read this chapter in combination with those areas identified in the Skill Category box below; this will help you to gain an in-depth understanding of critical thinking and its application in relation to knowledge, skills and values.

Main associated theory

Humanistic Theory – but all actually apply

Skill category

Critical thinking and analysis

See also: assessment, critical incident analysis, emotional intelligence, evidence-informed practice, professional judgement and decision-making, reflective writing, use of self and reflexivity, valuing diversity

---

Further reading

Mathias, J. (2015) Thinking like a social worker: Examining the meaning of critical thinking in social work. *Journal of Social Work Education*, 51(3): 457–474.

Rogers, M. & Allen, D. (2019) *Applying Critical Thinking and Analysis in Social Work*. London: Sage.

Cross-cultural practice
Immigration, resettlement and factors such as globalisation have resulted in greater cultural diversity across the globe. The implication for social work is that the body of people that we work to support and empower is constituted by a diverse mix of ethnicities, cultures, religions and experiences in addition to characteristics and social locations pertaining to socio-economic status, sex, gender identity, sexuality, health and physical ability, immigration and asylum status, and so on. Indeed, the backgrounds and experiences of those people who make up the social work profession are diverse too; albeit there is a long-standing gender bias with more female social workers in practice. Diversity means that social workers need to be confident and competent in cross-cultural practice.

It is helpful to think about culture as the values, norms, traditions, communications and actions characteristic of a social group. It is imperative that you do not ascribe those aspects of culture associated with a particular group to an individual by making assumptions. Put another way, do not presume someone's cultural identity and practice merely from the cues given by their name, skin colour or style of dress. In addition, remember that culture is not homogenous and be aware that when culture is referenced, it is commonly those values, norms, traditions and communications of a dominant culture that are invoked (Morton & Myers, 2016).

Stop-reflect

When someone avoids eye contact, what assumptions do you make? Do you think that the person must be shy, lacking in confidence, or even guilty, shifty and lying?

These are cultural interpretations that are commonplace in white British culture. Conversely, in other parts of the world, avoiding eye contact is a marker of respect or sexual modesty (Lishman, 2009).

In social work assuming someone's culture reflects those values, norms, traditions and communications that are dominant in that particular societal and community context can lead to attitudes that are problematically broad-brush in approach. For example, this type of approach reflects such views that in order to work with Asian communities it is imperative to understand Asian culture, or in order to support gay or lesbian people it is important to understand gay culture (Yee & Dumbrill, 2003). This attitude is highly problematic as it assumes a fixed, universal culture and thus the complexities, nuances and diversities of people and communities go unrecognised, and instead shared character-istics, values and traditions are presumed to exist.

Stop-reflect

The diversity of culture

Reflect on the term 'Asian community'. To whom is this referring?

In actuality, you could include people who identify as Indian, Pakistani, Bengali, Chinese, Tibetan, Muslim, Hindu, Buddhist and more. The values, norms, traditions, communications and actions that are characteristic of any of these social groups will be rich and extensive in variation. Take India, an expansive country with a large population and many varieties of cultural identities and patterns. Across India there are many different languages, creeds and customs. The first census conducted in 1961 recorded 1,652 different languages and dialects in India and the latest census completed in 2011 recorded 19,569 'mother tongues' (defined as the language spoken in childhood from a mother to a person) (Government of India, 2018). When classified into distinct languages, there were 121.

The term 'cross-cultural' refers to any sort of interaction where more than one culture is involved. This is open to a narrow interpretation which relates merely to national cultures (e.g. English, American, European) but a broader interpretation will embed an appreciation of any type of cultural difference (e.g. ones that are regional, generational or emerge from a community of people with shared social locations). An understanding of cross-cultural practice is important to social work and underpins an approach that is respectful, inclusive and ethical. Cross-cultural practice can integrate different approaches and there are two which we consider to be fundamental to a cross-cultural approach: cultural humility and cultural competence.

C

Cultural humility is the inclination and ability to suspend what you know, or what you think you know, about a person, family or community particularly when this knowledge is based upon culture-based generalisations and typecasts. Instead, what you learn about the culture of a person, family or community emerges from your interactions with them as they clearly indicate or state what is an important part of their sense of self and everyday life.

Stop–reflect

In order to practice in a culturally competent way, you need to adopt cultural humility. Why?

Cultural competence is the explicit ability to consider a person, family or community's social characteristics and backgrounds (for example, socio-economic status, sex, gender identity, sexuality, health and physical ability, immigration and asylum status, and so on) (Birkenmaier, Berg-Weger & Dewees, 2014). This informs your interactions and your sense-making processes in terms of an analysis and evaluation of their responses, experiences and situation. The process of cultural competence means that you avoid pathologising or analysing a person, family or community from your own social location and by drawing from dominant cultural norms, traditions and communication forms. Sue (2006) recognises four components of cultural competence: becoming aware of one's own assumptions, values and biases about human behaviour; understanding the worldview of culturally diverse people; developing appropriate intervention strategies and techniques; and understanding organisational and institutional forces that enhance or negate cultural competence.

Stop–reflect

Making assumptions (from Allen and Riding, 2018 and reprinted with permission of ERRC)

Case study: An Irish Traveller talking about an application for a Special Guardianship Order:

Getting the Special Guardianship Order* was a terrible experience for me. I have buried three of my own children, experienced domestic abuse and now live away from my family and community because that is what the social worker said I would

(Continued)

have to do if I wanted to look after my Grandson. But, when I applied for Special Guardianship, the Local Authority initially refused because I am an Irish Traveller.

The social worker said that my Grandson 'was not meeting his cognitive potential because he was living in an Irish Traveller culture' and that I was 'oppositional and unable to support the development of my Grandson because I am an Irish Traveller'. After a week's long court hearing, my barrister challenged all the negative reports about me. I was awarded the Special Guardianship Order, but nothing has ever been done about the racist things that the social worker said about me.

Thinking about the real-life example above, what might you need to do to ensure that you become more capable of cross-cultural practice?

* A Special Guardianship Order is a legal order appointing one or more individuals to be a child's 'special guardian'. It is an order made under the Children Act 1989 and is intended for those children who cannot live with their birth parents but who would benefit from a legally secure and permanent placement.

Main associated theory

Humanistic Theory – but all actually apply

Skill category

Anti-oppressive practice

See also: advocacy, anti-discriminatory practice, anti-oppressive practice, critical thinking and analysis, empowerment and enabling, ethical practice, use of self and reflexivity, valuing diversity

Further reading

Gottlieb, M. (2020) The case for cultural humility framework in social work practice. *Journal of Ethnic & Cultural Diversity in Social Work*. DOI: 10.1080/15313204.2020.1753615.

Harrison, G. & Turner, R. (2011) Being a 'culturally competent' social worker: Making sense of a murky concept in practice. *British Journal of Social Work*, 41(2): 333–350.

Mlcek, S. (2014) Are we doing enough to develop cross-cultural competencies for social work? *British Journal of Social Work*, 44(7): 1984–2003.

Morton, J. & Myers, S. (2016) Identity, difference and the meaning of 'culture' in health and social care practice. In A. Ahmed & M. Rogers (eds) *Working with Marginalised Groups: From Policy to Practice*. London: Palgrave.

D

Dealing with hostility and aggression
Hostility can be directed towards social workers, other professionals, family members and/or other members of the public. It is, however, important to remember that the relationship between a social worker and the person they are supporting is not typically characterised by hostility, but social work is an emotive business and hostility can result from fear and anxiety as well as anger and frustration. Hostility can result in situations where there has been poor communication, a lack of consultation or when interventions are experienced as punitive, discriminatory or oppressive.

Where hostility and aggression ensue, social workers can be faced with: aggressive language (shouting, swearing and verbal abuse); aggressive behaviour (physical assault, injury); threatening or intimidating behaviour (making threats verbally or in writing, invading personal space, preventing a person from leaving). Working with people to address their aggressive or violent behaviour can be an aspect of the social work task.

Hostility and aggression can be frightening. Some people have grown up with such behaviour; for instance, growing up in a home where there was domestic violence and abuse. Most of us will be able to describe an experience of violent or aggressive behaviour to a certain degree; think about childhood bullying or conflict, road rage incidents, frustration and 'sounding off' with partners, siblings, call centre workers or cold callers. Notwithstanding, being faced with aggression and hostile behaviour can still be frightening and it is important to develop the skills and ability to avoid responding to aggression and hostility with aggression and hostility, or in some other provocative way which can escalate the situation.

Skills in action

Jasmine

You are on duty and take a call from a health visitor, Sheila. Subsequently, you need to undertake a visit to Su-Pei and Martin Long and their four-month-old baby, Jasmine, that day. Sheila stated that she is concerned about Jasmine. She reported that the family's flat was in a poor state of cleanliness with minimal furnishing and a lack of basic baby equipment. More concerningly, she noted Jasmine's poor level of hygiene and some marks on her arm that she thought could be grab marks. Su-Pei and Martin have been together for two years. They live in a one-bedroom flat on an estate where they have no family or other forms of support. Su-Pei has mental health needs and has previously been

(Continued)

dependent on alcohol, although she has been abstinent for two years. Su-Pei had a baby removed from her care five years ago.

Martin has a learning disability and has also had prior involvement with social care. During his previous relationship it was known that there were high levels of domestic abuse (perpetrated by both Martin and his partner at the time, Tanya). There were ongoing concerns for Tanya's three children, from a previous marriage, which primarily centred on Tanya and Martin's ability to provide basic care, routines and concerns about physical chastisement. It was written in the previous case record that Martin had an 'anger management issue'. He had previously been aggressive and made threats to the former social worker.

Stop–reflect

Each time you plan a **home visit**, what do you need to be aware of in terms of personal safety? We would argue that you need an awareness of the potential reaction of the people with whom you are going to visit. For example, visiting to discuss the adoption of somebody's child is vastly different from visiting a person to discuss the care needs of their elderly parent.

You will also need an awareness of the family (are there any other family members who are frequently in the home?) and the environment (are you going to visit a three-bedroom detached house or a studio flat on the tenth floor of an apartment block?). You will need to think about your own reactions to people who are hostile. How will you respond if Martin becomes aggressive? You need to think about how to cope emotionally in this scenario and what skills you will need to defuse the situation.

You might also think about practical factors such as whether you need to undertake a joint interview with a colleague. Once at the property you will need to ensure that you are seated near an exit if you feel that you may need to leave quickly. Think about home visiting policies: does someone know when you are leaving, where you are going and when you are due to return to the office?

However, it is incredibly important that you do not visit the family with a firm vision of what might happen based on what you have read in case records, heard from colleagues or based on stereotypes or other unverifiable information. Be open-minded, non-judgemental and go with the attitude that you are visiting for the first time to initiate a positive working relationship with the family.

Defusing a situation that has become heightened is a skill that can be enhanced with some thoughtful communication. The Top Tips box offers some tips in relation to verbal and **non-verbal communication** techniques to defuse, not inflame, a tense or hostile situation.

Top tips

Defusing a hostile situation

- Be cognisant about both the pitch and volume of your voice in a stressful situation. Introduce or maintain calm by using a steady voice. When your voice rises in pitch and in volume it suggests that you are under stress and lacking control.
- Try not to use accusatory language and continuously make 'you ...' statements.
- Consider when, and if appropriate, diversion (and in some occasions, humour) might help to dispel some of the tension.
- Think about your facial expression: keep your face relaxed and maintain eye contact. Do not smile as it might be construed as mocking the aggressor.
- Maintain a non-confrontational stance and posture. Do not cross your arms or point your finger; both can antagonise a person who is already showing hostility or aggression.
- Maintain a safe and reasonable distance: too close and you can feel intimidated and vulnerable, too far away and you might appear aloof and disengaged.
- Control your breathing; consciously think about having relaxed and slow breathing.
- Try to demonstrate receptivity through gestures and head movements (for example, nodding). Hand movements should be slow, gentle and convey reasonableness (not surrender or aggression).
- Prioritise your safety and wellbeing and therefore if nothing works and you need to leave, do.

Main associated theory

Humanistic Theory and Crisis Intervention Theory

Skill category

Communication, interventions

See also: assertiveness, challenging skills, conflict management and resolution, containing anxiety, critical thinking and analysis, dealing with resistance, setting and maintaining professional boundaries

Further reading

Taylor, B.J. (ed.) (2011) *Working with Aggression and Resistance in Social Work*. Exeter: Learning Matters.

Dealing with resistance Not all people who are involved with
social workers are willing receivers of the support or intervention. Sometimes
people have social work intervention as a result of statutory duties (for example,
as a result of a court order). Resistance to engaging with social workers is not
uncommon and practitioners should view resistance as a 'normal' aspect of the
social work environment. Resistance occurs when people feel unwilling to engage
with you or they feel coerced into doing so. The important point to remember is
that we should not label people as 'resistant', but we should focus on how we can
work with that resistance.

There is value in trying to understand some of the reasons for resistance as it can inform
how you progress. Egan (2013) offers some explanations for resistance as:

- seeing little reason for social work presence or intervention
- feeling fear, shame or uncertainty about what will happen
- feeling anger or resentment about the referral and information source
- seeing no reason for change
- when change begins, seeing there being more detriment than benefit
- being reluctant to change as it comes at a cost by, for example, admitting failure or
  inadequacy.

Stop–reflect

Reflecting on resistance

Think about a situation where a person that you were working with was resistant or you
perceived them to be resistant.

What do you think were the reasons for this?

Was there anything about your approach that you would do differently if you
encountered a similar situation?

The different reasons for resistance require a sensitive and considered approach. For
example, it is more helpful to acknowledge feelings of resistance rather than ignore or
deny their validity. Remember that you need to accept, respect and work around resistance. It is important that you do not view resistance as 'ill will' or a 'personal rejection'
(Lishman, 2009). Instead, consider why there is resistance and what incentives there
might be to help people not to feel and enact resistance.

You should also remember that resistance is not necessarily a one-way phenomenon
in that social workers are not immune from negative emotions that can be directed

towards or result from our interactions with people that we are working with. You should reflect upon your own response, resistance and defensiveness and on how you respond to resistance; that is, do you respond in a similarly defensive or hostile manner? This is extremely important as you should strive to be mindful of your use of professional power, especially if the reason for social work intervention has resulted from a statutory duty. Gaskell-Mew and Lindsay (2016) list six core skills that are required in order to work positively with resistance.

D

Top tips

Skills for dealing with resistance

- **Motivational interviewing** (Miller & Rollnick, 2013): based on a premise that an empathic, person-centred approach is effective despite initial resistance whilst using a readiness ruler, that is, measuring when a person is ready and willing to make changes.
- The ability to develop a trusting, respectful and 'authentic' relationship: an approach that is supported by a wealth of research evidence to support its efficacy (Ruch, 2010).
- The maintenance of clear boundaries with transparent use of professional power: again, there is evidence to suggest that the effectiveness of relationship-based practice relies significantly on transparency about the power invested in the social worker's role from the outset (Ruch, 2010).
- Building strengths: there is evidence to show that people appreciate and respond positively to the approach of social workers who outline their strengths (as well as their deficits) (Smith et al., 2011). Further, whilst strengths-based approaches such as motivational interviewing and **solution-focused practice** have been criticised in their failure to assess risk, when applied properly such approaches do require *authentic* feedback supported by tangible evidence.
- Using supervision for reflection, **assessment**, support and self-esteem: again, there is a research base that illuminates the benefits of reflective supervision and the space for social workers to reflect on decision-making and the emotional labour of social work in a supportive environment (Ruch, Turney & Ward, 2010).
- Practising de-escalation micro-skills: these are core skills that need to be embraced as essential to a practitioner's toolkit. The ability to be professionally assertive is essential in order to not aggravate those negative emotions (including anxiety, fear, confusion and anger) that can fuel resistance.

Adapted from Gaskell-Mew and Lindsay, 2016: 206–210.

Main associated theory

Humanistic Theory, Crisis Intervention Theory

Skill category

Communication, interventions

See also: active listening, anti-discriminatory practice, anti-oppressive practice, containing anxiety, critical thinking and analysis, emotional intelligence, empathy, reflective practice, use of self and reflexivity, using humour

Further reading

Taylor, B.H. (ed.) (2011) *Working with Aggression and Resistance in Social Work*. Exeter: Learning Matters.

Ecomapping Ecomaps were developed by Ann Hartman in 1975 as a means of providing a graphic representation of an individual's support network, or their 'ecological system' (in this sense, 'ecological' refers to the social environment). An eco-map centres the individual and aims to represent the quality and significance of their formal and informal relationships with others (family, friends, colleagues, neighbours, relevant professionals or agencies). The map illustrates the social connections for an individual in a particular time and place. It provides a 'snapshot' of that time as ecomaps are not fixed and constant, but subject to flux.

The process of completing an ecomap can be therapeutic; it should be led and owned by the individual; that is, the expert by experience. The task of constructing an ecomap is relatively straightforward (see Figure E1 for an example). Place the individual or family at the centre of the map and by using symbols and/or colour, you can illustrate the quality and strength of a relationship with the individual or family member. You can show the reciprocity of relationships in terms of a positive and/or negative connection. It is useful to create a key to show to others what your symbols mean as the ecomap should form part of the overall case record for a person or family and can therefore be accessed by any relevant professional.

In terms of the use of symbols or colour, it is useful to follow some conventions. For example:

- thicker, darker lines represent a strong and positive connection
- broken lines represent a weaker or negative connection
- jagged or 'lightning' lines mean that the relationship is a stressful one
- arrows pointing to the service user mean that the person/organisation primarily influences them
- arrows pointing to the person/organisation mean that the service user primarily influences them
- arrows pointing in both directions depict a reciprocal flow of influence.

In deciding what information to include, reflecting on what is relevant and useful, you should be led by the expert by experience as they should have the overall say in what is included in their ecomap; that is, use ecomapping as a person-centred tool. If used in a person-centred approach, the process of completing an ecomap can be of benefit in build-ing rapport as the discussion that you have is led by the person, not you, and can indicate to that person that you are interested in them as an individual (and you are not primarily focusing on the 'problem' to be assessed). You might want to include more personal information about the connections (such as ethnicity or age). If you use abbreviations, remember to include a key.

The ecomap for Len Riding represents a simple representation of Len's social network, but you can see that a great deal of information is contained within the map itself.

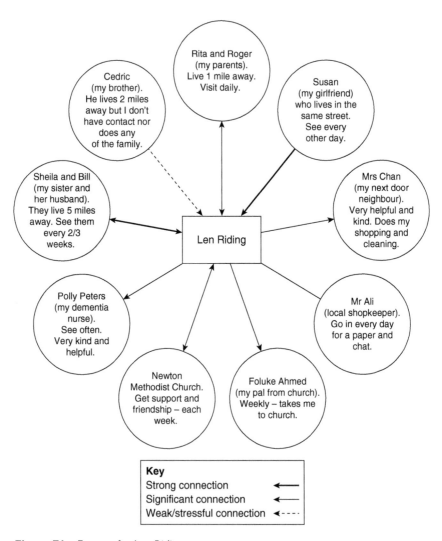

Figure E1   Ecomap for Len Riding

Produce a fictitious ecomap or a template, with the key included, to be used as an aide memoire. Keep it in your diary, ready to use with individuals whenever this tool may be appropriate.

Main associated theory

Ecological Theory

Skill category

Assessment

See also: active listening, chronologies, genograms, life story work, person-centred communication, person-centred planning, systemic practice techniques

Email communication
Communicating by email is an everyday activity and email is a useful communication tool because of its reach and speed. Always take time to think about your message before you write it, then draft and redraft until you are certain that the message is accurate and fitting; try not to send an email in haste. Think about purpose, audience and desired outcome. Ineffective emails are usually long-winded, disorganised, repetitive and/or are crafted with a tone that is inappropriate. In contrast, effective emails are: brief; contain enough context; use structure (paragraphs and bullet points can be effective in helping to separate out information); have a clear purpose and state the desired outcome, that is, if you need a response then let the reader know or state the next steps (e.g. 'I will let you know how the meeting goes in the next day or so').

Table E1   Examples of good and bad practice in email communication

Poor communication	Good communication
	Hi Dan
	I hope that this email finds you well.
Hi Dan, r we mtg in ur office? Cu l8r. Thx, M	Are we meeting in your office today?
	Much appreciated
	Michaela

(Continued)

Table E1 (Continued)

Poor communication	Good communication
	Dear Sarah
	I hope that this email finds you well.
WHEN is the meeting with Allen Daniels?	Could you please let me know when the meeting is due to take place with Allen Daniels?
	Many thanks
	Michaela
Michaela	Dear Michaela
I'm writing to you as support worker for Frank Mbeki. When are you going to contact my client? He's been waiting for weeks.	I'm writing to you in my position as a support worker for Frank Mbeki. It would be very helpful if you could let me know when you are planning to visit Frank as we're currently planning a trip away in between his college commitments.
Dan	Much appreciated.
	Best wishes
	Dan

Table E1 provides some examples of poor writing practice in email communication whilst the Top Tips box below offers more specific tips detailing appropriate writing practice and good habits to get into.

Top tips

Good practice in email communication

- Wherever possible respond immediately so that you do not overlook the email or forget to reply.
- Make good use of subject lines: this is the first thing that the receiver reads (as well as your email address).
- Keep messages clear and succinct.
- Be polite: use appropriate salutations ('Dear ...', 'Hello ...') and a name if you have it, and sign off politely too ('Best wishes', or 'Warm regards' if you are more familiar with the person).
- Check your tone and style: do not use text speak or informal/colloquial language and be very careful about the use of capitals to emphasise the point that you wish to make (it can be read as shouting and aggressive).

- Try to think about how the person might receive and respond to the written content of the email as this is especially important as they do not have the communication cues that are available when you communicate with someone in person (that is, the intonation of the spoken word, paralanguage ('ums' and 'ahs'), body language, facial gestures).
- Proofread, proofread, proofread!

Lastly, do not forget that your email is a lasting record and as with reports, plans and other written documents, your email communication might be filed away and included in a person's case record. It might even be used as evidence in court. Remember, an email is never private and confidential!

Main associated theory

Humanistic Theory and Psychosocial Theory

Skill category

Communication

See also: case recording, interprofessional practice, report writing, respecting confidentiality

Further reading

Healy, K. & Mulholland, J. (2012) *Writing Skills for Social Workers* (2nd edn). London: Sage.

Emotional intelligence
As shown throughout this book, social work demonstrates a central commitment to relationship-based practice. In those relevant chapters, we recognise that the absence of a positive relationship (with the self and others) can lead to an absence of proactive engagement and change. It is the central focus on relationship-based practice that highlights the importance of emotional intelligence.

If relationships, developed through the careful application of interpersonal and intrapersonal skills, define the social work process, it naturally follows that emotions and feelings present as equally important. Social work does, after all, comprise so much emotional labour. If these emotions and feelings are not carefully managed, they could easily threaten and undermine the profession's values and ethics.

Although written over two decades ago, Goleman's (1995: xiii) definition of emotional intelligence remains one of the most definitive. For him, the key skill can be shown in the ability to:

motivate oneself and persist in the face of frustrations; to control impulse and delay gratification; to regulate one's moods and keep distress from swamping the ability to think; to empathize and to hope.

The focus on the control of emotion, and the ability to ensure that feelings or emotional reactions do not direct social work action emerges as a clear message for emotional intelligence. However, the importance of emotional control or restraint can only be fully considered if it is contextualised first by the emotional distress and trauma that can accompany the social work interaction.

In each social work interaction, there are likely to be accompanying emotions. Whilst some of these emotions can be used to advocate for services that are designed for the betterment of individuals, some of these emotions can also be used to the detriment of individuals. Consider, on one hand, the possibility that some of the people who you work to support remind you of a friend, your children or a close relative. In these situations, you might experience feelings of compassion, sympathy or even affection. On the other hand, you might also work with people who remind you of situations and behaviour that you do not like. In these situations, you might experience feelings of disgust, loathing and embarrassment. The point that we are making is that in both examples, you might, if you are not careful and reflexive, potentially use these feelings and emotive responses to determine and justify social work action or inaction.

Consider the example that is described in the Stop–Reflect box. Consider how Jimmy's emotions might be impacting on his professional judgements.

Stop-reflect

A friend or a professional helper?

An early career social worker called Jimmy is working to support Sunita. Sunita is a former schoolteacher who is living with an acquired brain injury after being involved in a road traffic accident. Sunita's husband, Ranjit, has been her main carer for two years. Jimmy and Ranjit have a good relationship. They support the same football team and like the same music.

During a scheduled **home visit**, Ranjit tells Jimmy that he is paying a company based in Holland £270 a week for a new medication that will make his wife better. He shows Jimmy a website advertising the medication as the 'miracle cure' and explains that although the medication that he is giving to his wife gives her diarrhoea and makes her vomit he is keen to continue using it because it can take up to six months to take effect.

During the home visit, Jimmy feels sympathy for Ranjit. He feels sorry for him and his situation, but Jimmy is worried and begins to feel stress. He does not want to jeopardise his good relationship by pointing out the fact that Ranjit is being exploited and that he is potentially poisoning his wife. As Jimmy feels sorry for Ranjit and Sunita he says that he also hopes that the 'miracle cure' medication will work.

In taking this action, why might Jimmy be failing in his basic duty as a social worker?

Emotional intelligence accepts the cognitive behaviourist argument that there is a connection between our thoughts, feelings and behaviour. For this reason, the way that you perceive, think, feel and behave towards the people and situations that you are working to support becomes important. As a large proportion of your time is likely to be spent assessing, analysing and debating situations that may be complex or unfamiliar to you, you may also begin to experience feelings of stress that can reflect your developing confidence to cope.

In another publication that warrants inclusion here, because of its influence on social work thinking, Lazarus and Folkman (1984) suggest that if you feel able to cope with your encounters and interactions, you might begin to experience positive stress and a sense of competence. Conversely, if you feel unable to cope, then you might begin to experience negative stress and a sense of incompetence. Importantly, the separation between positive and negative stress should not be viewed as opposing. The aim is not to reduce feelings of negative stress by seeking to substitute them for feelings of positive stress. The aim is to achieve a position where you feel able to cope with your encounters and interactions without feeling stress at all. It is the ideological absence of stress that makes emotional intelligence a difficult concept to achieve.

Although emotional intelligence can be considered as the absence of stress (Lazarus & Folkman, 1984), it is essential that you do not associate your own stress, feelings and emotional reactions with a lack of emotional intelligence or competence. Indeed, to work with compassion requires a degree of emotion. Remember, then, that the connection between the way that you perceive, think, feel and behave towards the people and situations that you are working to support is important. However, to ensure that you are not relying on feelings or intuition to determine social work action, or inaction, you must be able to discuss your emotions and stress openly and honestly in reflective supervision, and if appropriate, with the multi-agency team.

The aim of reflective supervision is to provide you with an opportunity to talk about your self-awareness, self-regulation, professionalism, motivation, **empathy** and social work skills. It can help you to develop your emotional intelligence by increasing your chances of accurately perceiving emotions in the self and others, and developing a reflective rather than impulsive style of practice. As emotional intelligence is an essential skill that you need to develop and maintain through self-awareness and critically **reflective practice**, do not overlook the value of effective supervision.

Main associated theory

Psychosocial Theory and Cognitive Behaviour Theory

Skill category

All

See also: anti-discriminatory practice, anti-oppressive practice, assertiveness, building resilience, professional challenge, safeguarding

Further reading

Morrison, T. (2007) Emotional intelligence, emotion and social work: Context, characteristics, complications and contribution. *British Journal of Social Work*, 37(2): 245–263.

Stanley, S. & Mettilda, G. (2020) Professional competencies in social work students: Emotional intelligence, reflective ability and empathy-a comparative and longitudinal analysis. *Social Work Education*. DOI: 10.1080/02615479.2020.1724933.

Empathy involves being able to see the world from another person's perspective.

It enables you to understand their opinion and sometimes gain a deeper understanding of their experiences. Kadushin and Kadushin (2013: 129) also describe the ability to see the world from another person's perspective before meeting them as 'anticipatory empathy'. This skill is particularly important when you are planning a first visit or if you are meeting somebody for the first time.

The skills associated with empathy require you to anticipate another person's emotions (such as anxiety, fear, confusion, grief or resistance) and pre-empt their responses or behaviour. Crucially, they require you to begin to understand how perspectives or emotions might result in certain types of behaviour. In this way, being empathic enables you to set aside judgements about perspectives, emotions and behaviour and it enables you to communicate a readiness to understand. Being empathic in everyday practice is a key skill that enables you to approach each example of work in the same ethical, person-centred and humanistic way.

Skills in action

Irene had been supporting the Moorhead family for six months and was due to visit them. Three-year-old Suki Moorhead had been recognised to be a child in need. Her parents, Ishmael and Judith (both 20 years old), were struggling with parenthood and the family lived in abject poverty. Ishmael had worked on a building site, but during the COVID-19 pandemic, he'd lost his job. Judith had a mild learning disability, had never worked and had disengaged with education when she became pregnant at 17 years old. Nine months after the start of the pandemic Ishmael was struggling to find work. Both had amassed a significant debt with a local loan shark and it was suspected that Ishmael had returned to previous behaviour of heavily smoking cannabis. Irene was in her office preparing for the **home visit**. Irene said to her colleague, Winston, 'I feel so sorry for this family with the global pandemic, Ishmael losing his job, but I did tell him he needed to get a different job because he was working on the side, you know, with a cash in hand arrangement. He's going to find it hard to get another job unless it's back to the old one with the dodgy cash in hand arrangement, and I saw his former drugs worker at a meeting the other day. She had heard that Ishmael had weakened, was hanging out with his old crowd and had gone back to using drugs. I do feel sorry for them, but he needs to sort this out and quickly.'

Stop-reflect

Do you think that Irene is being empathic? Or is she being sympathetic?

There is a distinction to be made between empathy and sympathy. Sympathy is different in that it is an emotion that results from a feeling of sadness about someone's situation or misfortune. It does not necessarily mean that we understand that person's situation or misfortune. Moreover, when feeling sympathetic, we can still pass judgement on the reasons for the current circumstances.

In some ways, empathy builds on our feelings of sympathy as it requires us to more fully understand the reasons for the lead up to the situation and a non-judgemental stance. As noted above, it requires us to stand in someone's shoes and engage with a deeper sense of what is going on for that individual or family.

Whilst empathy is a key skill in communication, it is not always easy if the circumstances of the person that we are working with are far removed from our own experience of the world. For example, Irene is a 51-year-old white British woman who enjoys a stable marriage to a 50-year-old white British man, Jim, who enjoys his employment as a teacher. Irene and Jim have two children who are happy and successful in their endeavours. Irene grew up in a household with parents who both enjoyed continuous employment (her father was a professor of history at the local university and her mother was a neurologist at a nearby hospital). Irene has never experienced racism, poverty, unemployment, nor the everyday difficulties that these things bring.

Having lived experience that is radically different from another person does not mean that a person cannot be empathic or develop empathic communication. In fact, it is important to do so, as a lack of empathic communication can prevent a person from feeling understood and accepted. It can then impede relationship-based practice between a social worker and the person that they are working to support. Moss (2012) argues that empathy is not a skill in the strictest sense of the word, but a quality. Empathic communication, however, is a skill that can be practised and developed and, more importantly, the outcome of empathic communication is especially important in developing positive partnership working.

Top tips

- Practise 'empathic attunement' (Koprowska, 2020: 48) which is the ability to actively listen to another person to hear what is significant, picking up on non-verbal signals and 'tuning' into their experiences or perspectives.
- Acknowledge both these verbal and non-verbal cues so that you communicate your understanding to the other person.
- Give carefully crafted responses and use sensitive **questioning** to probe further to understand what is going on and why.
- Use mirroring to convey rapport and understanding. Do so by adjusting your posture, gestures and tone of voice to mirror those of the other person.
- Reflect on the careful and considered use of touch. A light touch of a person's arm can convey care, understanding and 'empathic attunement', but always consider cultural practices and boundaries in relation to the appropriateness of touch.
- Finally, remember that being empathic not only benefits you and your working relationship with another. The value of empathic communication is that it can also be beneficial for the other person and can help them to make sense of their emotions, experiences and needs.

Main associated theory

Psychosocial Theory and Cognitive Behaviour Theory

Skill category

All

See also: active listening, anti-discriminatory practice, anti-oppressive practice, containing anxiety, counselling skills, critical thinking and analysis, emotional intelligence, person-centred communication, professional values and ethics, use of self and reflexivity

Further reading

Howe, D. (2008) *The Emotionally Intelligent Social Worker*. Basingstoke: Palgrave Macmillan.

Empowerment and enabling

The profession of social work is primarily concerned with supporting individuals, families and communities who are at risk. The overriding goal of social work activity is to enable people to overcome the risks by responding to structural inequalities that can deny the rights and privileges that many others can take for granted. By tailoring intervention in the transaction between individuals and their environment, social work activity has traditionally been directed by **systemic practice techniques,** relationship-based practice and the central assumption that inequality is embedded within the social context.

The breadth of such intervention has created a great disparity in the knowledge, values and skills that inform social work practice. Specifically, within the picture that is created by the historical and traditional ambitions of social work, there emerges a picture of an entire group of powerless individuals, families and communities who are calmly waiting for a social worker to lead them to a better life. Not only is this image condescending, it also assumes that individuals, families and communities lack the resources, capacity, capital and power to help themselves. Whilst it is important to recognise that many of the people who social workers aim to support experience a deep sense of powerlessness, it is also important to recognise that this deep sense of powerlessness has a cause.

For some, powerlessness emerges from socio-economic deprivation, marginalisation and stigmatisation. For others powerlessness emerges from a sense of insecurity, a lack of opportunity, social injustice, and an abusive family or peer group system. However, in all cases, the art of supporting others to manage and overcome the root cause of their powerlessness is central to the premise of empowerment and enablement (Love & Lynch, 2018).

Both terms, empowerment and enablement, require you to recognise that you are not the expert in the lives of the people you are working to support. Instead, you should seek to use your skills to support individuals, families and communities to become strong enough to influence and change the events and systems that are affecting their own lives. In this respect, the aim of empowerment relies on your ability to facilitate opportunities for people to gain particular skills and knowledge. As shown in the Skills in Action box below, the aim of enablement relies on your ability to support people to exercise their own power to influence change in their lives and in the lives of those who they care about.

Skills in action

Empowering and enabling with the social model of disability

At the onset of the disability rights movement in the 1970s, social workers often controlled the lives of people with a lived experience of a disability (Baker et al., 2004). Today, the advancement of the social model of disability enables social workers to empower people with a lived experience of a disability to select, commission and manage their own

(Continued)

support services. In the United Kingdom, The Netherlands and Canada, for example, social workers support people with a lived experience of a disability to hire their own personal assistants.

Guided by the principle of empowerment as a process and an outcome, a social worker's role has changed from being the expert in the life of the person with a lived experience of a disability to being more of a broker of services and facilitator of self-advocacy. By enabling a person with a lived experience of disability to control the services that they receive, the social worker is also able to facilitate opportunities for people to gain new skills, knowledge and sufficient power to influence their own lives.

An important strategy aimed at the promotion of social change requires you to empower people to become their own resource in managing and improving their own lives. Once you transfer this power to the individual, family or community, you are working to support enablement by identifying opportunities to build on individual strengths, whilst, at the same time, providing people with the means, ability, and opportunities to overcome the challenges that they face. Individuals, families and communities who have received empowering and enabling services benefit through improved self efficacy resulting in improved social outcomes and quality of life (Baker et al., 2004). Social workers who facilitate empowerment and enablement have a sense of achievement, confidence in the therapeutic relationship and improved job satisfaction (Fleming & Ward, 2017).

The skills associated with empowerment and enablement centre around the notion of self-help. Although a social worker might work with an individual, they might also help to facilitate self-help groups, peer support groups, network building, education groups and social action groups. Once a group is established, the social worker would slowly withdraw their support until such time as it might be needed again. The value of achieving empowerment and enablement through peer support, as shown in the social model of disability (McLaughlin, 2016), is the opportunity for collective action, critical thinking knowledge, skill building and peer support, which enables those living with a sense of powerlessness to overcome adversity and create and sustain their own change.

Main associated theory

Humanistic Theory – but all actually apply

Skill category

Anti-oppressive practice, assessment, communication, interventions, relational practice

See also: advocacy, ecomapping, group work, mediation, radical social work

Further reading

Adams, R. (2008) *Empowerment, Participation, and Social Work* (4th edn). New York: Palgrave Macmillan.

Fleming, J. & Ward, D. (2017) Self-directed groupwork – social justice through social action and empowerment. *Critical and Radical Social Work*, 5(1): 75–91.

Love, J.G. & Lynch, R. (2018) Enablement and positive ageing: A human rights-based approach to older people and changing demographics. *International Journal of Human Rights*, 22(1): 90–107.

Endings

Attachment theory highlights many things including the important contribution that stability, security, permanence and consistent close relationships make to human growth and development across the life course (Walsh & White, 2019). In recent years, attachment theory has gained great prominence in social work; a prominence that we believe is warranted for a number of valid reasons. However, whilst attachment theory can only be safely and ethically used by those with the requisite qualifications and experience, it can be used more readily to guide and inform the way that we manage relationships and endings with the people we are working to support.

When working to support people, social workers understand the importance of consistency, honesty, transparency and trust. We work hard to keep our appointments and to do the things that we say we will do. We are reliable and dependable. We let people know how they can complain about the service we provide. We try to include people in the decision-making process, recognising that they are the expert in their own life, and try to enable and empower people to achieve their full potential. We do all of these things because of attachment theory. For this reason, we also know that the ending, along with **emotional intelligence**, is an important part of the helping relationship. In the Skills in Action box below, the actions of a social worker to support an ending are described.

Skills in action

Supporting an ending

After working with a family for six months, Abebe is getting ready to close a case. He decided to write the family a letter to say goodbye. Within the letter, Abebe summarised the reasons why he was saying goodbye and described the things that the family had achieved since he had known them. Abebe gave examples of work that he had enjoyed, and listed the support that might be available to the family, if needed, in the future. Then, during the last home visit, Abebe thanked the family for all of their hard work and asked them if they had any questions about what would happen now that he was no longer involved in their lives. Before saying goodbye, Abebe then handed over the letter that he had written and wished them the best for the future.

The ending represents the skill of facilitating disengagement from the helping relationship. Whether you facilitate a last **home visit**, write a letter or speak over the phone, the ending is where you say goodbye.

Usually ending skills are demonstrated when goals are reached, when the specified time for working has ended, when work is reallocated or when the person being supported is no longer interested in continuing the work.

Main associated theory

Humanistic Theory – but all actually apply

Skill category

Interventions, relational practice

See also: appreciative inquiry, person-centred planning, professional values and ethics, valuing diversity

---

Further reading

Huntley, M. (2002) Relationship based social work – how do endings impact on the client? *Practice*, 14(2): 59–66.

Ethical practice is an integral part of social work. On a daily basis, social workers are faced with a range of ethical dilemmas that require them to apply **critical thinking and analysis** skills. The term 'ethical dilemma' is used to describe the experience of having to make a choice between two actions based on conflicting personal and professional values. It is the feeling of uncertainty that can create the dilemma for the social worker.

As a profession, we have come to appreciate uncertainty and ambiguity. However, we do not treat uncertainty or ambiguity lightly. Although social workers are faced with a range of ethical dilemmas, they also make a commitment to act ethically because ethical and humanistic practice is an essential aspect of the quality of the service that is offered.

Respect for human rights and a commitment to promoting social justice are at the core of social work practice throughout the world and the British Association of Social Workers (BASW, 2014: 5) reminds us of this fact:

> Social work grew out of humanitarian and democratic ideals, and its values are based on respect for the equality, worth, and dignity of all people. Since its beginnings over a century ago, social work practice has focused on meeting human

needs and developing human potential. Human rights and social justice serve as the motivation and justification for social work action.

Contained within the ambition to meet, promote and develop human need, ethical and humanistic practice requires social workers to act in good faith and with a genuine desire to work in the best interests of all. However, as social workers grapple with ethical issues, the professional codes of practice that guide and inform social work actions are crucial.

Ethical practice is a key component of social work. On a daily basis, you will be presented with situations that require you to resolve ethical dilemmas. Whilst these dilemmas will be personal to you, Doel (2016) suggests that they may pertain most specifically to questions about self-disclosure, personal and professional boundaries, privacy and confidentiality and conflicts of interest. Where these or any other ethical dilemmas arise in practice, we would encourage you to engage in a process of critical reflection by asking yourself the following questions:

- Am I placing the person who I am working to support first, or are my actions being motivated by my own needs, thoughts and feelings?
- Could my actions challenge professional boundaries and undermine the social work code of conduct?
- Am I blurring the boundaries between my personal and professional life?
- Would I consider it to be reasonable for another social worker to make a similar decision given the facts and circumstances?

Reflecting on the answers that you give to these questions, you may be in a more suitable position to make a judgement about your use of **emotional intelligence** and your ethical practice. Consider the example in the Skills in Action box below and how Miguel managed to demonstrate ethical practice skills despite feeling anxious and worried.

Skills in action

Ethical practice in action

A student social worker called Miguel had planned to visit a man living with an enduring mental health difficulty in his home. The man had a reputation for being rude and aggressive towards social workers. As Miguel approached the man's house, he began to feel anxious. Miguel realised that he did not want to see the man who was reported to be rude and aggressive. He thought that he could easily go back to the office and say that the man was not home. However, before returning to the office, Miguel began to critically reflect on the way that he was feeling.

Miguel recognised that by feeling anxious and by thinking that he could lie about the man not being at home, he was not placing the needs of the man first. He realised that his behaviour was being motivated by his own negative thoughts and feelings of anxiety.

(Continued)

Miguel began to consider how his own professional boundaries were being challenged by the situation. He understood that he needed to visit the man and that by falsifying a report that the man was not home he would breach his professional code of conduct.

Miguel then considered how his behaviour, negative thoughts and feelings of anxiety were being created by an ethical dilemma between his personal and professional life. Miguel considered himself as a person who would avoid conflict. He did not like to hear people arguing and did not like the sound of raised voices. Worried that the man might shout and become aggressive, Miguel felt unsafe. However, as a social worker, Miguel knew that it is important to separate people from their behaviour. Miguel had a duty to visit the man and for this reason had a duty to listen to the things that the man had to say.

Miguel then thought about what another social worker might do in the same position. He quickly realised that he would not consider it reasonable for another social worker to lie about the man not being at home. Under similar circumstances Miguel assumed that another social worker would visit the man and be clear in their boundaries with him.

As Miguel's work was guided by a professional code of ethics, and because he recognised his duty to visit the man, he decided that he had to knock on the door. He also knew that he had to act ethically because he remembered that ethical practice is an essential aspect of the quality of the service that is offered.

In addition to engaging in the process of critical reflection, you can also seek out opportunities to talk about practice dilemmas through action learning sets, peer consultation and supervision. You should also seek out opportunities to resolve dilemmas by seeking out evidence informed practice that includes the local policies of the organisation that you represent.

Main associated theory

Humanistic Theory – but all actually apply

Skill category

All

See also: anti-discriminatory practice, anti-oppressive practice, building resilience

Further reading

Bell, L. & Hafford-Letchfield, T. (2015). *Ethics, Values and Social Work Practice*. Maidenhead: Open University Press.

Doel, M. (2016). *Rights and Wrongs in Social Work: Ethical and Practice Dilemmas*. London: Macmillan Education.

Evidence-informed practice underpins the way that you seek to develop and enable better outcomes and opportunities for the people you are working to support. Put plainly, the term 'evidence-informed practice' is used to describe the way that bringing together the best available evidence from research, policy, theory, supervision and the views and wishes of the people you work to support will improve service delivery and the outcomes that it generates. The main challenge that you might face in practice is deciding what type of evidence should inform practice.

E

Without venturing into a philosophical debate about what constitutes knowledge, which we would, of course, encourage you to do independently, it is important that you recognise the difference between reliable and unreliable evidence. In the main, reliable evidence used to inform social work practice comes from empirical research. Research that draws conclusions and advances recommendations based on verifiable observation or experience rather than tacit knowledge or opinion.

As you read through the example illustrated in the Skills in Action box below, consider how evidence is used at each stage to inform the approach that is taken by the doctor.

Skills in action

An evidence-informed approach in Accident and Emergency

Kehinde is seven years old. She attends Accident and Emergency with her mum because she has injured her arm. Kehinde's mum tells the doctor that Kehinde hurt her arm falling down the stairs. The doctor considers the mother's explanation, verifies it by asking Kehinde what happened, and believes that the account of the event provides evidence that is consistent with the injury. Recognising that Kehinde is in pain, the doctor prescribes a course of analgesics (pain management medicine) because she knows from clinical research that pain relief can ease the discomfort of people with a physical injury.

Drawing on clinical guidance, the doctor also knows that before Kehinde's arm can be treated effectively, an X-ray is required to reveal and verify the full extent of the injury.

When reviewing the X-ray, the doctor, being aware of clinical research on orthopaedic conditions, sees that Kehinde has suffered a spiral fracture. The doctor knows, therefore, that a spiral fracture, also known as torsion fracture, could only have occurred if Kehinde's arm had been violently twisted. Therefore, the research suggests to the doctor that she might expect to see this type of injury for people who play contact sport, but not for people who fall down the stairs.

(Continued)

85

The doctor uses the clinical research as the evidence to inform her treatment of Kehinde's arm. However, given the inconsistency in the evidence provided by Kehinde and her mother about how the accident happened, the doctor also raises a concern to the hospital social work team because she is worried that Kehinde has suffered a non-accidental injury. At each stage, the doctor's actions have been informed by evidence.

In social work, your ability to draw on research, in the same way that doctors might during their clinical examinations, is essential to ensure that your conclusions and actions are supported and informed by evidence. Consider, by way of example, research undertaken with the people you are working to support. The evidence constantly shows that social workers need to involve people in decisions that affect them and treat them with courtesy and respect (Laitila et al., 2018). Due to this evidence you should be working hard to plan ways to ensure that your practice is informed by that ambition. The point that we are trying to make is that research evidence, professional codes of conduct and statutory guidance form the bedrock of information that should inform the way that you do social work. The key challenge, as recognised in the chapter on **appreciative inquiry**, is that where there is limited research and no clear evidence of the 'right way' to act, your ability to draw on evidence-informed practice can be limited.

By way of solution, the International Federation of Social Work (IFSW) provides us with a clue on how to proceed in their definition. The IFSW reminds us that social work is underpinned by evidence that extends to and includes indigenous knowledge. To reiterate the point that we made earlier, the term 'indigenous knowledge' is not used to refer to indigenous people, it used instead to refer to the knowledge that exists inside us all. Use the activity shown in the Stop–Reflect box below to consider how indigenous knowledge can be used to support practice alongside research, law and social policy.

Stop–reflect

What counts as evidence?

When considered carefully, indigenous knowledge can be a useful source of evidence that can help to inform your **assessment** of risk. If we consider the Skills in Action box above, we can assume that the twist fracture was not caused by the act of falling down the stairs. Instead the injury that has been sustained is non-accidental, in other words, it was done on purpose.

- What does the initial evidence provided by Kehinde and her mother (that the girl had fallen down the stairs) suggest to you?
- How might the evidence presented by the fracture type determine your assessment of risk?

- What other evidence might you require and how might you go about collecting it?
- How might the evidence that you gather inform your actions?

Recognising the assumption that the people you work to support are experts in their own lives, and are as such able to provide the evidence to inform practice, you should seek to gain knowledge from the people who you work to support at all times. Your supervisor, practice educator and university tutor are all available to provide you with evidence, advice and guidance.

Social work colleagues and other professional agencies can also help to provide evidence to inform your practice. For this reason, if you ever feel that there is limited research and no clear evidence of the 'right way' to act, remember that you work within an incredible multi-agency team that includes the people you are working to support. By drawing on their advice, experience and support, you can begin to gain a more confident understanding of the research, policies and statutory guidance documents that inform your practice. As you develop your own experience in social work, you will also develop your own empirical evidence base of what works, and perhaps, one day, you will also be able to share your experience with others.

Main associated theory

Humanistic Theory – but all actually apply

Skill category

All

See also: active listening, assertiveness, questioning, observational skills

Further reading

McLaughlin, H. & Teater, B. (2017) *Evidence Informed Practice for Social Work*. London: McGraw Hill Education.

G

Genograms are a practical tool that can help you to explore and record the relationships that the person you are working to support has with different people across time. Typically, genograms illustrate familial relationships through at least three generations.

Similar to a family tree, the information that the genogram provides can enable you to work in partnership with individuals and families as you seek to understand relationship dynamics and gather information about family functioning and process.

Genograms can be created by hand using paper and pencil. They can also be computer-generated through online software-based genogram tools. Genograms use a complex combination of symbols, shapes, colours, lines and captions to depict family information. As shown in the Skills in Action box below, circles are traditionally used to depict females and squares are used to depict males. Other shapes are available to depict individuals who do not identify with sex and gender binaries. The name and age of each individual is then written within the shape. Relationships between each family member are depicted using the appropriate line. For example, a solid horizontal line denotes marriage, solid vertical lines denote parentage, dotted lines illustrate non-married relationships. Once individual family members and their basic connections have been added to the genogram, you can use the visual illustration to talk to the people about the specific details of each individual and relationship and identify other family members who might be relevant to your **assessment**.

<hr>

Skill in action

A very basic genogram

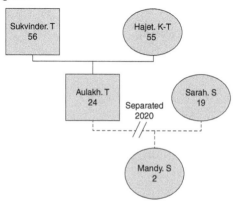

Figure G1   The T family genogram

Main associated theory

Systems Theory, Ecological Theory

Skill category

Assessment, interventions

See also: ecomapping

Further reading

G

McGoldrick, M. (2016) *The Genogram Casebook: A Clinical Companion to Genograms: Assessment and Intervention.* New York: W.W. Norton.

Giving and receiving feedback Throughout your social work

career, it is important that you know how to provide feedback to others, effectively and constructively without causing offence. There will be many opportunities in your career for providing others with feedback, from commenting on the way that your colleague has carried out a task, to discussing care plans with the people who you are working to support.

Giving feedback is not disapproval, criticism or a personal attack, it is a way to let people know how effective they are in what they are trying to accomplish. It provides a way for people to learn how they affect the world around them, and it is intended to empower and enable others to become more effective. When feedback is constructive and consistent, and is given by someone in an informed position, it can be very useful (Ion, Sánchez Martí & Agud Morell, 2019). How can you make sure that your feedback is effective?

1   If you are giving feedback to somebody about something that they have done, or not done, try to ensure that your comments focus on the behaviour, not the person. When giving feedback it is important that you are clear in your message and that you remember not to comment on an individual's personality, or other personal characteristic.

2   Try to ensure that your feedback is delivered in a supportive, blame-free and non-threatening way. If you are giving feedback that could be perceived as negative, try to develop your **breaking bad news** skills and perhaps start off the conversation with something positive. Starting with a positive point might help the person to feel at ease. Always try to end on a high note, discussing the things that are going well, which can help reduce feelings of despondence and guilt.

3   Try to explain that your feedback is intended to be of value to the other person. Presenting feedback that is helpful makes it much easier for the recipient to hear

and accept it, even if you are giving negative feedback. Try to talk about specific occasions, and specific behaviour, and point to exactly what the person did, and exactly how it made you feel. The more specific the better, as it is much easier to hear about a specific occasion than about 'all the time'.

4   Try to pick an appropriate time to provide feedback. Try to be aware of the emotions and feelings of others. If, for example, a person is angry or frustrated, they may be less inclined to accept your support. Wait until they have calmed down and given consent to your offer of feedback.

When giving feedback that might be perceived as negative, remember that some people will feel that you are being critical of them, even if that is not your intention. If people do think that you are being critical, they may be less inclined to hear or remember the things that you say. For this reason, try to pay attention to things that are positive as well. As shown in the Skills in Action box it is important that you try not to limit your feedback to negative behaviours. If someone does something that you think is positive, feed back your thoughts and opinions on that too!

Skills in action

The power of positive feedback

Rhonda is constantly aggravated by colleagues who leave their dirty cups and plates in the shared office kitchen sink. She feels frustrated because she is constantly giving negative feedback to her team about their behaviour. One day, Rhonda decides to change tactic. Instead of giving negative feedback to people who leave their dirty cups and plates in the kitchen sink, she decides to give positive feedback to the people who always wash their cups and plates and put them away. By giving praise to those who are behaving in a considerate manner, and by ignoring those who behave in a selfish manner, Rhonda soon beings to notice that more and more people are keeping the office kitchen area tidy. Rhonda realises that her colleagues much prefer positive feedback and sees a change in the behaviour of some people who like to attract her positive attention.

If giving feedback requires you to be specific, sensitive and supportive, it is also important to think about what skills you need to receive feedback, especially when the advice is unwanted. Developing you own skills when receiving feedback will undoubtedly help to develop your skills when giving feedback.

I   Try to be open and receptive to feedback. In order to hear feedback, you need to listen to it. Try not to be defensive or to think about what you are going to say in reply to the speaker, just listen. Pay attention to **non-verbal communication** as well, and listen to what your colleague is not saying.

2   Practise your skills of **questioning, reflective practice** and **active listening** to ensure that you have fully understood all the information that is being given and avoid misunderstandings. Use different types of questions to clarify the situation, and reflect back your understanding, including your emotions. Try to ensure that your reflections and questions focus on behaviour, and not personality. Even if the feedback has been given at another level, you can always return the conversation to the behavioural, and help the person giving feedback to focus on that level.

3   **Emotional intelligence** is essential. When receiving feedback, you need to be aware of your emotions to be able to manage them.

As with any new skill, the act of giving and receiving feedback takes practice. Giving and receiving feedback can be difficult or uncomfortable for some people at first, but as long as you follow the guidelines for giving and receiving feedback, and the motives behind the feedback are positive, you will soon start to see a change in your own behaviour and that of others as a result.

Main associated theory

Empowerment Theory, Humanistic Theory

Skill category

Reflection and reflexivity

See also: dealing with hostility, empathy, group work, interviewing, person-centred communication

Further reading

Rogers, M., Whitaker, D., Edmondson, D. & Peach, D. (2017) *Developing Skills for Social Work Practice*. Los Angeles: Sage.

Grief and loss
Most people associate grief and loss with encounters involving death and dying. However, grief as a response to loss permeates all facets of our lives. We experience loss not only through death, but also through changes that we encounter throughout our life course. Working with and recognising grief and loss, which may manifest in many different forms, has long been identified as one of the core skills of social work practice (Goldsworthy, 2005). Although all of us experience loss as part of our lives, it is clear we do not experience the same amount of loss. Neither do we perceive loss in the same way.

Clearly, a prime example of loss is death – the loss of life itself. But there are other examples of loss too. Consider the factory worker who has lost their job due to the mechanisation of industry. Consider the family who have lost their home due to flooding. Consider the individual who has lost their health due to illness or disease, or the person who has lost their religious freedoms and human rights due to systematic oppression. Consider the child who has lost their birth family because they were raised in state care or the grandmother who has lost her family due to immigration. In all of these examples, loss can define that person's lived experience. The grief that they feel because of that loss can be devastating and long lasting. The way that you acknowledge and respond to grief and loss is going to be important. Currer (2010) reminds us that because you will be working within multi-agency teams, it is important for you, as a social worker, to be clear about your own role and skills.

For some people, counselling can provide a useful opportunity to discuss thoughts, feelings, and behaviours associated with the experience of grief and loss. Although social workers received rudimentary training in counselling techniques, social workers are not counsellors. Therefore, any attempt to engage a person using skills associated with social work theories should be undertaken with extreme care, taking in to account the tenets of **ethical practice** at all times. The danger of encouraging people to talk about their feelings of grief and loss without sufficient training or experience is that you may do more harm than good. Sometimes it is more ethical to encourage people to self-refer to health-based or charitable organisations that are specifically designed to provide counselling.

The skill of encouraging people to self-refer for counselling does not mark the end of social work practice. Remember that social work is a relationship-based activity. At all times, this relationship, and the skills that you demonstrate, can provide the important stability, security and reliability that people need as they navigate their way through the complex experience of grief and loss. Some of these skills are listed in the Skills in Action box below.

Skills in action

Supporting people who experience grief

Key skills that you can demonstrate to support people who experience grief include:

*   Being ready to apply your knowledge, skills and values to recognise that people might be experiencing the effects of grief and loss.
*   Recognising the impact of people's values and beliefs, including their own, on the feelings associated with grief and loss and committing to the principle of living well until you die, whatever that means for someone.
*   Valuing people as individuals, and ensuring their wishes and needs are respected at all times.

- Ensuring that people who are experiencing grief and loss, especially those from marginalised or disadvantaged groups, can empower themselves and be enabled to get the support they need.
- Being aware of the impact of loss, including the physical impact that it can have on people. Know how to use law, evidence and systems to support and protect people from the effects of loss.
- Being able to judge when specialist support is needed for people and when you yourself may need additional support.
- Engaging with people who experience grief and loss and those close to them to ensure they have the practical, emotional, psychological and spiritual support they need. This includes working with individuals, groups and communities.
- Accessing advice, information and input from others within the multi-agency team.
- Reminding others of the need to recognise and respond effectively to people who are experiencing grief and loss, acting as a mentor, and sharing your learning. This includes advocating for people's rights and supporting them to access the information and help that they need.

Source: adapted from the Association of Palliative Care Social Workers, 2016.

Typically, social workers do not like to witness suffering. As a helping profession, which subscribes to high ethical standards, social workers seek to identify and reduce suffering in all of its manifestations. There are times, however, when we must accept grief and loss and suffering as a part of the human experience and recognise that our ability to create change can be limited.

When working with people who are experiencing grief and loss, there may be times when you feel powerless to help. You might also feel inadequate, incompetent and embarrassed. However, as shown in the Stop–Reflect box, it is important that you recognise that the skills you demonstrate in **active listening** and **empathy** can sometimes make a significant and powerful difference to the lives of the people who you are working to support.

Stop-reflect

The importance of self-care

Self-care is essential when working in any practice area, but even more critical when working in settings where grief and loss are common.

- What strategies do you think will be important for you to keep yourself emotionally healthy in your professional practice?
- What systems of support are available to you as a social worker?

Main associated theory

Empowerment Theory, Humanistic Theory, Psychosocial Theory

Skill category

Assessment, relational practice

See also: emotional intelligence, using humour, valuing diversity

Further reading

Currer, C. (2010) *Loss and Social Work.* Exeter: Learning Matters.

Group work Social work has a long tradition of applying different theories, methods, tools and skills to empower and enable people to overcome adversity and create and sustain their own change. Much of this work is carried out with individuals and their families. It is essential, therefore, that you are confident to use **person-centred communication** skills with individuals of whatever age. Likewise, family approaches, including those skills applied to **systemic practice techniques** and **chairing meetings**, must be a part of every social worker's tool kit. However, group work skills are also essential if social workers hope to intervene with various populations in multiple settings (Skolnik, 2019).

The value of group work skills, and opportunities for community development work more generally, are central to the concept of social action. Not only can your group work skills increase the capacity for change, they can be used to promote peer support networks and participation.

In social work, the word 'group' refers to three or more people. Members of the group usually depend on each other, know something about each other, they might work together, and they might share ideas and a commitment to common goals and a common purpose. In practice, these groups can represent families, communities or individuals with shared experiences. Groups can also represent multi-agency teams that include the people you are working to support directly or indirectly.

There are many skills associated with the facilitation of group work. The ones that we will focus on here relate to Tuckman's (1965) 'forming-storming-norming-and-performing' model of group development (See Skills in Action box). Although the original concept is over 50 years old, it continues to provide a good introduction to group work skills. Recently developed to include two other stages, 'adjourning and transforming', it is one of the better-known team development theories and has formed the basis of many further ideas since its conception.

Using skills to apply Tuckman's (1965) model today

Aiden, a student on placement, was asked by his manager to organise and manage a mental health support group for men who are foster carers. He uses Tuckman's (1965) model as the basis for his **evidence-informed practice**.

Forming: Aiden recognised that the men who would be invited to attend the group might not want to attend because they do not know him. He also recognised that for the men to come to the group they would need to feel safe. For this reason, Aiden wrote a letter to all of the men being supported by his agency and included a colourful advert for the new men's group. He listed the broad aims and objective of the group and then summarised the group's commitment to confidentiality. During the first meeting, Aiden organised several 'icebreaking' and 'getting to know you' activities because he knew that initial impressions of group members would be important to the sustainability of the group.

Storming: Over the period of four weeks, as the group progressed and as people became more familiar with one another, Aiden facilitated a series of discussions about how the men wanted the group to run. He was flexible and listened to their suggestions. He tried to ensure that each person was able to participate in the development of the group identity and the formulation of the group's collective goals. Aiden realised that some people took on different roles in the group. Some appeared to be supportive, some appeared to be negative, and some appeared to sit back and listen. Aiden realised that he needed strong leadership skills, effective communication skills and the ability to compromise to manage group discussions inclusively and effectively.

Norming: After a further three weeks, once the group had agreed their identity and the formulation of collective goals, Aiden saw that the group were starting to work in harmony. They chose a group name and designed a group logo. Aiden began to feel that his role in the group was changing. During the 'forming' and 'storming' stages, Aiden felt like he was the group leader. Now, as the group was beginning to self-manage, he felt more like an equal partner who had the respect and trust of the men who attended. As the group began to work together, Aiden was worried that the focus on mental health was being lost. For this reason, he worked with the group to agree that each session should start with a conversation about wellbeing.

Performing: Aiden realised that the men's group had reached the performing stage when it became independent, self-sustaining and self-sufficient. The group began to recruit more male foster carers without Aiden's support. The effects of the team were being spoken about very positively within the fostering community and the mental health of male foster carers was seen to be improving.

(Continued)

Adjourning and transforming: As Aiden's placement ended, he recognised the importance of **endings** and the impact of loss. He asked the men's group if he could attend one of the meetings to say goodbye. He thanked the group for their hard work and summarised the things that he had enjoyed about the journey that they had been on together before saying goodbye and introducing the group to the person who would be taking over his role.

Although Tuckman (1965) provides a useful introductory understanding of group skills, it should be noted that the group relationship can return to any phase within the model as it experiences change, for example, a review of the reasons why the group was established or when there is a change in team composition. Whilst changes to the dynamics of a group and resistance may be common, it is important that you remain flexible and committed to deploying your skills to facilitate opportunities for group members to reach the performing stage as far as possible.

Main associated theory

Systems Theory, Ecological Theory

Skill category

Interventions, relational practice

See also: assertiveness, conflict management and resolution, cross-cultural practice, rapport building, risk assessment

Further reading

Crawford, K., Price, M. & Price, B. (2014) *Groupwork Practice for Social Workers*. Los Angeles: Sage.

Tuckman, Bruce W. (1965) Developmental sequence in small groups. *Psychological Bulletin*, 63: 384–399.

H

Home visits are very often essential and are incredibly useful as the home is a place where you see individuals or families in their everyday environment. During a home visit, a person's or family's behaviour is likely to be more natural and you will get the opportunity to witness people's interactions. Home visits, therefore, enable you to use **observational skills** as part of the **assessment** process. This means making note of what you see, hear, smell and touch: for example, you will see the way in which the house is organised and maintained. Your sense of smell can be of value as Trevithick (2012: 190) notes ('the smell of poverty is unique and deeply memorable'), but it is also critical that you do not jump to assumptions or make judgements with only basic information (the smell of poverty alone is not enough and as ever, ensure that any hypothesising or decision-making is based on full and verifiable evidence).

Stop–reflect

Small gestures

When you arrive at someone's house, are there any gestures that enable you to convey respect (in that you are entering their home) and which help to build trust and rapport?

Perhaps you might ask if the resident wishes you to take your shoes off. Think about what this gesture conveys to the other person.

What do you do if you are offered a cup of tea? Some social workers might always say no (whether or not they actually would like a cup of tea). Consider what this refusal means to the other person. It is traditional and customary to share a cup of tea with someone and it is a leveller in that it is something that most of us do (whatever our background and social location).

Do you always ask about the other person and enquire after their family? As the social worker you should know something about the other person. Do they have grandchildren? If they do, would you ask after them? If not, why not? Asking about a person's grandchildren communicates a great deal; it is a respectful, person-centred and humane action.

All these points should be considered within the context of person-centred, relationship-based practice (Toner & Black, 2020).

The purpose of a home visit will dictate how you then prepare for that visit. For example, you might be visiting a parent to complete an initial assessment following a referral from nursery, or you might need to undertake a review with an adult who is in receipt of community-based treatment for a mental health condition. Notwithstanding, there are some fundamental principles that you should apply when you conduct your first (and indeed subsequent) visit; for example, ensure clarity and transparency in your verbal communication; avoid technical language and jargon (even the words 'referral' and 'assessment' can mean different things to different people). Be prepared with all the information that you may need including options for moving forward from the visit. Do not assume that the individual or family will understand the reason for your visit or involvement, so be open, honest and transparent. Ensure that the individual or family has your contact details when you leave and that they understand what will happen next.

Stop-reflect

Home visits and risk assessments

Each agency that you work for should have a Lone Working Policy. This contains protocols to ensure your safety and accountability when you are working away from the office. What do you think should be included in a Lone Working Policy? Here are some examples:

- There should be a system for recording the address of the home visit as well as the time that you leave the office and the approximate time when you anticipate returning to the office.
- If your visit is at the end of the day, there should be a system to notify a colleague or manager once you have finished your visit and you are safely on your way home.
- If you need to report information 'out of hours' (that is, outside of the core hours of working e.g. 9.00 a.m. to 5.30 p.m.) there will be a duty line to telephone or some other reporting system.
- A **risk assessment** protocol should be in place so that if an individual is known to be hostile or aggressive, no one undertakes a home visit alone.

Main associated theory

Humanistic Theory

Skill category

Assessment, interventions, reflection and reflexivity

See also: active listening, emotional intelligence, empowerment and enabling, interviewing, non-verbal communication, questioning, setting and maintaining professional boundaries, use of self and reflexivity, valuing diversity

Further reading

Winter, K. & Cree, V.E. (2016) Social work home visits to children and families in the UK: A Foucauldian perspective. *British Journal of Social Work*, 46(5): 1175–1190.

H

Interpreters Social workers are frequently tasked with communicating with people from ethnically and linguistically diverse communities. Working with interpreters is not uncommon although the use of interpreters in social work has received little attention in social work research or literature. However, researchers and practitioners have collectively identified problems associated with interpreter-mediated sessions (Westlake & Jones, 2018) with the primary message that these problems can lead to poorer services for individuals and/or families (Kriz & Skivenes, 2010). Notwithstanding, interpreter-mediated communication can serve a number of functions such as ensuring that communication is effectively conveyed and received by both you (the social worker) and the person that you are working with.

Some people may wish for their friends, family or neighbours to act as the interpreter, but you should avoid this wherever possible; only use friends or family as a last resort in situations where information is not of a confidential nature. The requirement for a professional interpreter is vital for many, important reasons including:

- the need for the interpreter to understand their role and remit
- the need for the interpreter to understand any technical information that needs to be conveyed
- the need for the interpreter to be comfortable (not embarrassed or uneasy) in discussing sensitive or taboo subjects
- the social worker's need to have confidence in the right information being translated appropriately and effectively (that is, avoiding any bias, misrepresentation or inaccuracies) ensuring that cultural nuances are dealt with in the process of translating information
- the need for confidentiality, which is particularly important if you are undertaking statutory interventions (for example, you are undertaking an **assessment** under a court's direction) and in light of data protection legislation.

Arranging for a professional interpreter communicates to the individual or family that you respect and value the ethnic, cultural and language diversity of that individual, their family and/or community. It also signifies the emphasis that you place on ensuring comprehensive and effective communication as a two-way process in order to ensure the best outcomes for that individual or family.

Arranging interpreter-mediated communication

- Before you begin, ensure that the interpreter and the individual/family speak the same language/dialect.
- Clarify the purpose and focus of the conversation.
- Involve the individual/family in 'chit-chat' to build rapport.
- Frequently check understanding and always clarify misunderstandings.
- Listen and attend to both the interpreter and the individual or family.
- Observe the eye contact and **non-verbal communication** of the interpreter as well as the individual or family to identify any misunderstanding or points of confusion.
- Use clear and simple language (avoid jargon and technical language where possible), and ensure that the interpreter understands key terms and relevant concepts.
- Where there are family members with differing levels of language proficiency, conduct the conversation entirely in the native language.
- Ensure open questions and reflections are interpreted.
- Try to work with interpreters who are experienced professionals who convey empathy and a non-judgemental attitude.
- Try to work with interpreters who demonstrate a strong commitment to confidentiality and **ethical practice**. (Moss, 2012; Birkenmaier, Berg-Weger & Dewees, 2014; Westlake & Jones, 2018)

Main associated theory

Empowerment Theory

Skill category

Assessment, interventions

Further reading

Westlake, D. & Jones, R.K. (2018) Breaking down language barriers: A practice-near study of social work using interpreters. *British Journal of Social Work*, 48(5): 1388–1408.

Interprofessional practice
Effective interprofessional practice is central to the provision of high quality **person-centred planning**, service delivery and review. Uncoordinated or divided teamwork can reduce the quality of services and may potentially result in further marginalisation.

The needs of the people who you are working to support will vary. They will almost certainly be complex. For this reason, effective social work often requires the integrated services of a range of professionals who can demonstrate a diverse range of knowledge, values and skills. It is very rare that one single professional discipline delivers the comprehensive package of care that many people might require.

Interprofessional practice provides a basis for establishing an integrated approach to social care and health. It can be defined as a collaborative process involving two or more professionals who can draw on their complementary knowledge, values, skills and expertise to work together effectively to assess, plan, implement, review and evaluate the support that is being provided.

When applied effectively, interprofessional practice can promote and maintain the wellbeing and welfare of individuals, families and communities whilst improving the effectiveness of social work support services (Crawford, 2012). However, research frequently shows us that interprofessional practice remains a challenge when interprofessional relationships, including teamwork, building collective knowledge, interprofessional documentation, communication and team relations, are not fully considered (Kelly et al., 2020).

Most importantly then, interprofessional practice depends on high-performing professional teams. However, teamwork is not an automatic process. As shown in Tuckman's (1965) theory of **group work** development, every effective team needs to establish mutual interest in the quality and efficiency of practice performance and task orientation, which includes clarifying the roles and responsibilities of team members. Meaningful attempts to include team members should focus on shared decision-making, efficiency, person-centred approaches to practice and organisational efficiency. Inconsistent attitudes to treatment among team members may result in anxiety, defensiveness, confrontational relationships and a culture of blame (Kelly et al., 2020) that might lead to reduced **collaboration**.

To aid an equitable approach to interprofessional practice, it is common for partnerships to be guided by a written plan that outlines the team's goals, aims and objectives. This document might be a 'Care Plan', a 'Care Pathway', a 'Protection Plan', a 'Terms of Reference' or any other formal plan that seeks to organise the roles and responsibilities of team members. Whatever the nature of the plan, the overall aim will be to ensure that the most appropriate management occurs at the most appropriate time and that it is provided by the most appropriate person. Often implemented to introduce and support best practice, the written plan can also enable and monitor high performance work systems that reflect the views, wishes and expectations of the person being supported as well as improving organisational performance, strengthened relationships and coordination among team members. The main limitation of the written plan is that it does not account for or address any stereotypes, hostility or prejudice that might exist with the interprofessional team. In other words, that assumption that you could do the job better than anyone else.

In health, social work, criminology and education the contact hypothesis has been described as an important way to improve interprofessional practice (Allport, 1954). The basic assumption of Allport's theory is that interpersonal contact between professional groups is one of the most effective ways to reduce hostility and prejudice. By taking the opportunity to actively communicate with other professionals and consult them on their views, **assessment** or opinion of a situation, you are more likely to understand and appreciate different points of views and different ways of working. As a result, issues of stereotyping, prejudice and discrimination can be reduced as opportunities to foster positive and collaborative action can be increased.

Whenever you are engaged in interprofessional practice, try to get to know the people who you are working with. Ask them about their role, how long they have been working in that role and engage them in general conversation. As relationship-based practice is an essential social work skill, remember that it extends to the relationship that you have with other professions as well as the people you are working to support. With a good relationship, a clear written plan and a list of shared aims or objectives, you will be in a stronger position to provide high quality person-centred planning, service delivery and review. Other Top Tips are listed below.

Top tips

Skills for interprofessional practice

- When you set out to develop an effective team, try to start by supporting personal interaction between team members. Spend time planning ways to promote informal, personal interactions that can enable people to learn about one another and facilitate opportunities for professional relationships to occur.
- Once team members appear to be relaxed in the company of the group take time to include them in an exercise that defines the team goals. Outlining common goals can aid the development of a team vision, establish mutual interest in the task, contribute to person-centred planning and aid organisational efficiency.
- Once you have defined team goals, spend some time clarifying the roles and responsibilities of team members. A clear written plan, or terms of reference, can provide each member with a clear understanding of their role including what is expected of them.
- Remember, the written plan can be a really useful document that can help you to determine shortfalls in service provision or resources. It can also help you to promote accountability and shared responsibility.

(Continued)

- Try to schedule planned review meetings where you can discuss the goals and evaluate progress. The participation of the whole team in the review process is important if you want to enhance team cohesiveness and enable team members to commit to decisions and action.
- When considering how to overcome a specific challenge, shared decision-making facilitates the opportunity for team members to develop trust in and respect for each other's knowledge, values and skills.

Main associated theory

Systems Theory, Ecological Theory

Skill category

Relational practice

See also: chairing meetings, collaboration: working with experts by experience, cross-cultural practice, dealing with resistance, endings, managing stress, professional values and ethics, task-centred work, valuing diversity

Further reading

Allport, G.W. (1954) *The Nature of Prejudice*. Cambridge/Reading, MA: Addison-Wesley.

Crawford, K. (2012) *Interprofessional Collaboration in Social Work Practice*. Los Angeles: Sage.

Interviewing
Barker (2003) describes an interview as a conversation that is undertaken or designed to meet a specific purpose. Indeed, there are particular models of interviewing (see chapter on **motivational interviewing**). Interviewing is a core aspect of social work as it enables information to be collected, checked, analysed or conveyed. The need for an interview might result from a new referral or it might be necessary as part of ongoing casework. You may be required to interview a child, adult, family member or another professional. You might not call the conversation 'an interview' *per se*, but it is likely that you will plan for or hold a conversation that is intended to meet a specific purpose (Barker, 2003). A great number of chapters in this book are strongly associated to the theme of this one – interviewing – and should be read in addition to this (see the end of this chapter for further signposting).

Top tips

Good practice principles for interviewing

- Before you undertake an interview, prepare and plan to ensure that you are very clear and knowledgeable (as far as you can be) about the situation (which may be complex, distressing or contentious) and about what you wish to achieve.
- Similarly, think about the people who are going to be present and how they may be feeling (anxious, fearful, angry, evasive, hostile or a complex mixture of these emotions).
- Consider any communication needs: such as learning disability, sensory impairment (hearing or sight loss), cognitive impairment (e.g. resulting from a brain injury, stroke or dementia), English being a second language and support that may then be needed (e.g. the use of an **interpreter**).
- Think about the setting and any environmental factors that might impact the interview.
- At the start, aim to establish rapport, trust and convey respect: this can facilitate a relationship-based approach.
- Likewise, aim to build a partnership to empower people.
- Wherever possible aim to include people in decision-making by asking for a person's wishes, feelings and opinions; do so according to their age and ability.
- Do not use jargon, acronyms or technical language; ensure that your role, remit, the concerns or issues, and any plan or future actions are clearly communicated and understood. (Moss, 2012; Henderson & Mathew-Byrne, 2016; Rogers, Whitaker, Edmondson & Peach, 2020)

In addition to the good practice principles summarised above, and the art of **questioning**, there are a number of micro-skills that underpin effective interviewing. These are outlined here.

Active listening: the art of **active listening** can enable a social worker to show that the individual speaker is the central focus of the conversation and that they are committed to facilitating the space for the speaker to tell their story in their own time. By helping to promote a person-centred approach, active listening assumes that the social worker is prepared to listen more than they speak and that they will attempt to avoid forming opinions and judgements before appropriate to do so. Active listening requires you to be patient, accepting of short periods of silence, and ready to ask questions that enable the speaker to describe the detail of their situation, thoughts and feelings in their own time.

Clarifying, reflection and paraphrasing: again, these are tools needed for active listening. The act of clarifying a speaker's account is important in order to avoid misunderstanding. The art of reflecting back what you hear enables you to demonstrate that you are listening, hearing and understanding the speaker. This can be achieved in different ways by either using the speaker's own words and repeating what you heard, or by paraphrasing. To paraphrase is the skill of reflecting what you heard by putting this into your own words. For example, Czech-born Mr Adámek says:

I miss bramboráky [potato pancake] like my mother used to make, with pivo [beer]. That's the Czech way. It's not the same when Petra makes it. She's not Czech; it's not the same. I haven't spoken to her, my mother, for weeks. It is too expensive to telephone.

You could paraphrase by saying:

I'm sorry to hear this, Mr Adámek. It sounds like you are very homesick and that you are missing your mother. It must be hard not to speak to her for such a long time.

Paraphrasing is a very useful tool to help you to check the accuracy of your understanding and interpretation.

Summarising: ending the conversation by summarising all that you understood from the speaker's story is beneficial. This helps you to check your understanding, but also to check that you gleaned all the points that are important to the speaker.

Main associated theory

Humanistic Theory – but all actually apply

Skill category

All

See also: challenging skills, critical thinking and analysis, giving and receiving feedback, interpreters, non-verbal communication, professional judgement and decision-making, rapport building, use of self and reflexivity

Further reading

Kadushin, A. & Kadushin, G. (2013) *The Social Work Interview*. Columbia: Columbia University Press.

L

Life story work (LSW) is a social work intervention which is used in a range of settings with different groups of people such as children and young people, people with learning disabilities and older adults. When utilised with children and young people, LSW is predominantly employed in fostering and adoption. When used with adults, LSW has value as a reminiscence therapy or during life history projects. For older adults, LSW has value for people with memory problems (e.g. with people who have suffered a stroke, traumatic brain injury or who are living with dementia). LSW embeds a narrative approach and is designed to recognise an individual's or group's past, present and future. There are various methods and techniques for completing LSW and just a few are covered here.

Life story book: life story books are often used in adoption and fostering. In this instance, a life story book is written with or for a child resulting in a child-friendly version of their life. It includes information about the involvement of social work services including the reasons that they were removed from their parents' care. Whether fostered or adopted, the story will include details of those people caring for the child (that is, foster carers or adopters) and the child's life with them. In general, LSW should assist a person to make sense of and manage the feelings that are associated with their past. A life story book does not necessarily have to involve the person and can be completed by others; this is especially the case when the book is constructed by social workers before placing a child for adoption. There is a risk that a child who does not fully understand their history and reason for being removed from their birth family can develop an imagined story of fictional family members and events. Over time, this can result in emotional difficulties (for example, anger and resentment) and lead them to develop a misplaced sense of identity. Life story books can be complementary to or seen as an end product of LSW.

Later life letters: another technique to use with children is a later life letter (LLL). This is a letter written to a child intended for them to open at a future date (usually around their eighteenth birthday). An LLL has utility for children who might be too young to understand their life story book or when there have been significant, sensitive and/or contentious issues that led to their removal that are simply not suitable for children to hear about at a young age (Cooper, 2020). The LLL would then contain a more detailed and age-appropriate account of events (their removal and relevant social work intervention) including the steps taken to provide a permanent alternative solution for them. If you write an LLL it is important to remember that this will be your version of events and that the birth family will have their own version, which might contrast and conflict with yours. As such, it is helpful to add a sentence making it clear that this is your understanding and interpretation of what happened.

Reminiscence work: LSW with older adults is often centred around memory loss and is gaining popularity as a useful intervention in supportive work with people living with dementia. Used in this way, LSW can have a number of positive outcomes including: improving care for the person with dementia; enhanced family support; enabling a reflection on services received; and hearing the voice of the person with dementia (Kellett et al., 2010; McKeown et al., 2015). A very specific form of LSW, reminiscence work, or reminiscence therapy, uses life histories (written, spoken or both) to improve wellbeing and can be used individually or collectively with a group of people. Whilst research into LSW with older adults does suggest many positive outcomes of reminiscence work, there are potential drawbacks such as the possibility of upsetting memories being aroused or the potential for LSW to problematically locate the person in the past. However, to date, few challenges of undertaking LSW specifically with people who have dementia have been found.

Skills in action

Annabelle

Jamie, a 28-year-old social work student, was embarking on his first professional work placement. Jamie had previously worked as an actor, but decided to train in social work after enjoying a couple of years of working in an arts-based charity delivering theatre workshops in the community. Jamie had relevant personal experience as he was adopted into his family as a young child. Jamie began his placement with a local charity that delivered various services for older adults including a day centre. After shadowing Jan, who ran the arts and craft sessions, Jamie decided to do something different. He took his guitar into the day centre and introduced a reminiscence group. Jamie played and sang songs from the 1950s, 1960s and 1970s, encouraging people to join in.

Annabelle, a 75-year-old who had dementia, attended all of Jamie's session. The effects of dementia meant that Annabelle spoke infrequently, using one word at a time to communicate. To the delight of Jamie, the group and her carer, at Jamie's fourth session, Annabelle broke out into song, joining in with a rock and roll classic from the 1960s. It is important to remember that it is not only words or actions that can invoke memories in people, music can have a significant therapeutic effect, triggering memories and emotions that can help soothe people and transport them to a different place.

Main associated theory

Narrative Theory

Skill category

Interventions, relational practice

See also: advocacy, building resilience, empowerment and enabling, evidence-informed practice, grief and loss, group work

Further reading

McKeown, J., Ryan, A., Ingleton, C. & Clarke, A. (2015) 'You have to be mindful of whose story it is': The challenges of undertaking life story work with people with dementia and their family carers. *Dementia*, 14(2): 238–256.

Walker, S. (2012) *Effective Social Work with Children, Young People and Families: Putting Systems Theory into Practice*. London: Sage.

Managing stress The practice of social work brings about both rewards and challenges. Some of the challenges you will encounter during an average working day (managing high caseloads and the demands of administrative work) may invade your personal life (bringing the need to complete those administrative tasks during evenings or at weekends). Others are less tangible (for example, the emotional content of social work and the impact of working with others who are under significant stress). Without adequate management strategies, individually or combined, these pressures can cause stress to build whether you are a social work student or an experienced practitioner. Developing the skills to manage stress during your social work training is important in enabling you to enjoy a long and rewarding social work career.

The qualities that enable professional resilience are similar to those qualities that you should encourage in the people that you are working to support (see chapter on **building resilience**). Research has shown that resilient professionals have a number of qualities including:

- self-awareness, self-confidence and a strong sense of identity
- a positive concept of self and **emotional intelligence**
- enhanced social skills and the capability to forge effective relationships
- the ability to set and maintain boundaries and limits, whilst also having the capacity to be flexible and adapt to change
- the ability to draw on a wide range of coping strategies
- critical thinking and creative problem-solving skills
- the ability to identify and draw on internal and external resources
- persistence in the face of adversity, challenges and setbacks
- a sense of purpose and the ability to derive a sense of meaning from difficulties and challenges
- the ability to reflect and to learn from experience. (Grant & Kinman, 2012)

Stop-reflect

Skills for managing stress

Consider each of the qualities and skills summarised by Grant and Kinman (2012). Which do you think you already have? Can you identify any that you think you will benefit from developing? How will you approach developing those skills and qualities?

Often it is the more contentious or sensitive aspects of social work that can cause stress, e.g. the forthcoming meeting with the individuals who have been angry or hostile with you in the past, or the visit during which you will have to break some news that the family will find very difficult to hear. What could you do to develop resilience when having to manage these types of situations? Role playing or practising difficult conversations can help (you can do this alone in your car if that helps). Rehearsing **breaking bad news** or your ability to be assertive helps to build confidence whilst also helping you to be empathic in an attempt to think through how the information might be received.

Another tip is to make good use of supervision by exploring the more challenging scenarios that you have to face in a critical reflective discussion. Talking through the different ways in which you might approach challenging scenarios can enable you to find your own solutions or learn from your supervisor. Similarly, peer supervision can be informative, as asking colleagues how they might approach a particular situation can offer insights that you might not have arrived at on your own. Overcoming specific challenges or tackling complex scenarios enables you to build resilience and enhances your ability to cope with stress through the development of skills.

Main associated theory

Psychosocial Theory

Skill category

Reflection and reflexivity

See also: assertiveness, critical thinking and analysis, managing supervision, reflective practice, use of self and reflexivity, using humour

Further reading

Kinman, G. & Grant, L. (2011) Exploring stress resilience in trainee social workers: The role of emotional and social competencies. *British Journal of Social Work*, 41(2): 261–275.

Managing supervision The benefits of good supervision cannot be underestimated. However, the critical factors of quality and quantity can impact on your experience of supervision. For supervision to be effective, it should be regular and long enough in duration to give you time to step back and reflect on your practice and allocated work. Supervision can serve several functions including:

- the provision of time and space to enable critical reflections and discussion about your practice with the individuals and families that you are working to support
- the provision of a context in which you are supported and encouraged, as well as focusing attention on the development of your knowledge and skills, identifying any

training needs for your continuing professional development (CPD)
- an accountability function to ensure that your decision-making and interventions are appropriate, timely and evidence-based
- an administrative checking function to ensure that your practice is aligned with the agency role, remit, thresholds and priorities
- a regulatory function to ensure that you are working to the standards of your regulatory body (in England this is Social Work England).

The most common scenario for supervision is when it takes places between a social worker and their line manager, but it can also take place between colleagues and in groups (known as peer or group supervision).

Stop–reflect

Good and bad supervision

Think about experiences that you have had of supervision; whether on a one-to-one or group basis. Use these experiences to reflect on what constitutes 'good' and 'bad' supervision. Put another way, what are the barriers to and what enables effective supervision? Think about different aspects of supervision such as communication, relationships, power differentials, the physical environment or practical arrangements.

In the Stop–Reflect activity you might have focused on the other person (that is, the supervisor) rather than yourself. It is, however, critical that you take responsibility for the quality and effectiveness of the supervision that you receive. You can do this by: being well prepared and knowing what issues you would like to discuss; being on time and appropriately equipped (if you are going to take notes for example); if relevant, taking responsibility for the physical setting (ensuring space, light and quiet); being assertive but also being open, honest and receptive to constructive feedback.

Despite paying attention to all these, supervision also relies on the behaviour and attitude of the supervisor and issues can arise where you might feel short-changed, criticised or blocked in some way. There can be personality clashes and, you might feel, a lack of meaningful reflective discussion (rather there is an over-emphasis on getting the job done with little regard for reflection on your personal development and wellbeing). There are things that you can do to mitigate these potential difficulties. For example, in the session itself try to be assertive and raise the concerns that you have or, if this has the potential for more challenges in your relationship, raise the issue with a member of the senior management team. To ensure that your expectations are realistic, you should be very clear about the supervision policy and practice of your agency (revisit your job description and the agency policy in this regard).

Skills in action

Using supervision

Sarah was completing an **assessment** after a teacher had made a referral of concerns about 14-year-old Emily. Sarah was doing her best despite difficulties in forging a relationship with Emily's mother, Kim. In fact, Sarah found Kim to be incredibly difficult to engage with, obstructive and even aggressive, both in person and over the telephone. Over the course of one week, Sarah avoided telephone calls from Kim as during the previous telephone call Kim had been loud, almost to the point of shouting, and not listening to what Sarah was trying to tell her.

Sarah had supervision with her line manager, Ambrose. Ambrose listened to Sarah's account of Kim. Ambrose then repeated back to Sarah what he had heard, which was the action of a mother (Kim) who was scared, in uncharted territory having never had social care intervention before, and who was confused about what was going to happen next. By engaging in a critically reflective discussion with Ambrose, Sarah was able to see how her responding to Kim in a defensive and avoidant manner had led to an escalation of Kim's anxieties. Sarah was also able to see Kim's anxieties affected her behaviour. Kim also acknowledged that by labelling Kim as one thing (aggressive), rather than another (worried and fearful), she had created a barrier to using more advanced communication skills to engage Kim.

Sarah made contact with Kim, apologised for not returning her calls in a timely manner and acknowledged that Kim must be frustrated and anxious about what was going to happen next. She arranged to meet with Kim and at that meeting Sarah was able to use skilled and open communication, along with a more relational approach, to get her relationship with Kim onto a more positive footing.

Main associated theory

Task-Centred Theory

Skill category

Critical thinking and analysis, reflection and reflexivity

See also: assertiveness, building resilience, critical thinking and analysis, giving and receiving feedback, managing stress, reflective practice, time management

Further reading

Beddoes, L. (2010) Surveillance or reflection: Professional supervision in 'the risk society'. *Journal of Social Work*, 40(4): 1279–1296.

Rogers, M. (2020) Maximising supervision. In: M. Rogers, D. Whitaker, D. Edmondson & D. Peach (eds) *Developing Skills & Knowledge for Social Work Practice* (2nd edn). London: Sage.

Mediation As shown in the various chapters of this book, social work skills are often underpinned by principles of empowerment, enablement, self-determination, social action and a commitment to social justice. Where principles have been described, they are often accompanied by the notion, which is either implicit or explicitly expressed, that you should be active in the engagement and achievement of social change.

The concern that we have with this notion is that many of the people you will work to support were able to live their lives without your involvement. There does not exist a community of people waiting patiently out in the world for you to come and rescue them. Of course, some people do find themselves in crisis and value your involvement, because of the services that you are the gatekeeper of, but in the main you will find that people will not welcome you into their lives unless they have good reason to.

In our collective experience, one of the main barriers to overcome relates to trust and power. Smith (2013) provides an excellent explanation of power, its causes and effects, so we will not dwell on that topic too much here. Instead, we will highlight the importance of trust and your potential to be a facilitator of change, rather than an active agent of it, through the concept of mediation.

Mediation is frequently utilised in social work, yet, with the expectation of criminal or restorative justice (see for example Bradt & Bouverne-De Bie, 2009), there has been surprising little research written about it.

When engaging in interfamilial topics associated with divorce and separation, ageing, mental health, relationships and adoption, any initial ambition to implement an action-oriented approach to practice might be constrained. Equally, when engaging in community-based matters that might be found in the workplace, such as criminal justice, social policy or interprofessional **collaboration**, your influence to create change through action might be limited too. For those of you who are determined to transfer your knowledge of critical and **radical social work** theories to direct action-orientated practice, the challenges that you might face in this endeavour could take an increasing toll on your energy and spirit.

We know that a single focus on an action-oriented approach to change is not sustainable unless you are privileged enough, and yes, we mean that word quite seriously, to receive the trust of the people and communities who you are working to support. Unless you plan how to develop trusting relationships, even in the most complex casework examples, any enthusiasm for social work involvement or change will quickly wear out.

Mediation can be a good enabler of trusting relationships. Unlike traditional approaches to empowerment, enablement, self-determination and social action that require you to engage in action-orientated practice, mediation focuses you towards person-centred perspectives. Rather than seeking to find the solution or develop directive approaches to social work, which might be appropriate in some situations, mediation skills require you to develop trust and engage the people who you are working to support in the process of consensual joint decision-making.

Once consent for mediation has been given, you then draw on the value base of social work as you exercise impartiality and assist those in dispute to work together to reach their own mutually acceptable agreements, as shown by Roberts (2014). By focusing on person-centred perspectives, your main role, like that of Namazzi shown in the Skills in Action box below, is to facilitate and support an unbiased conversation between people who you might not know to identify and enable opportunities for change.

Skills in action

Facilitating and supporting an unbiased conversation

Namazzi is working at a drug and alcohol service. She has been working to support a young person whose father is dependent on alcohol. During one of the planned support sessions, the young person tells Namazzi that she loves her father but wishes that he would stop drinking alcohol. Namazzi asks the young person if she has ever told her father about how she is feeling. The young person says no, but that she desperately wants to.

With consent from both the father and the young person, Namazzi organises a mediation session, using the following framework:

1 *Preparation.* On the day of mediation, Namazzi talks to the father and the young person about the ground rules for the mediation. All three agree that one person should talk at a time, and that whilst one person is talking the others listen in silence. They agree that there will be no shouting and swearing and that the role of the mediator is to be impartial.
2 *Understanding the problem.* Namazzi then asks the young person and her father to talk about why they are attending the session and what they would like to achieve by the end of the discussion.
3 *Exploring agreement and disagreement.* During the discussion, Namazzi begins to highlight topics of conversation that the father and young person agreed or disagreed with. Moving towards a person-centred perspective she asks them both to focus on the future and to talk about what their life would be like if there was no alcohol.
4 *Developing a plan.* After facilitating the discussion detailed in step 3, Namazzi incites the father and young person to take a short comfort break. When they return, Namazzi asks them to consider what they could do together. Namazzi then helps them to create a specific, measurable, achievable and realistic plan that could provide a solution to the problems that they are experiencing.
5 *Formalising the plan.* At the end of the mediation, Namazzi thanks the father and the young person for their hard work and commitment to overcome the challenges that they are experiencing. Namazzi then writes down the plan that the father

(Continued)

and young person have agreed before summarising it back to them. Concluding the session, Namazzi reminds the father and the young person about the support services that are available to them and invites them to consider attending a further mediation session to consider and review the progress of the plan.

Framework adapted from Roberts, 2014.

Main associated theory

Empowerment Theory, Humanistic Theory, Psychosocial Theory, Cognitive Behavioural Theory

Skill category

Intervention

See also: active listening skills, emotional intelligence, empathy, giving and receiving feedback, non-verbal communication, observational skills, questioning, solution-focused practice

Further reading

Roberts, M. (2014) *Mediation in Family Disputes: Principles of Practice* (4th edn). Farnham: Ashgate Publishing Ltd.

Motivational interviewing
The skills associated with motivational interviewing have been developed from the work of Miller and Rollnick (2013). Originally developed to support people living with an addiction to substances, it has become an approach to practice that is used in a wide variety of settings and circumstances.

The primary skill associated with motivational interviewing is the ability to adapt your communication style and the way that you have been socialised to engage in conversation. For example, imagine that you are talking to a friend or family member. After a short time, they begin to tell you that they are frustrated about a challenge or difficulty that they are experiencing. Due to your relationship with that person, you might attempt to alleviate the frustration that is being described by providing suggestions for a solution. These suggestions emerge based on your relationship and reflect your own experiences or opinion. The friend or family member might welcome that advice and use it to resolve the matter that they have described

In social work, and following the principles of motivational interviewing more specifically, offering advice or recommending a solution to a person you are working to support is not the same as offering advice or a solution to a friend or relative. As a social worker, you have a quite different relationship, which some people who you work to support might resent. If you offer advice to somebody in a professional capacity, and the advice does not achieve the desired effect or outcome, confidence in your ability could be undermined.

So, how can you bring about change, alleviate frustration, challenges and difficulties that another person is experiencing without offering advice or solutions? The answer, of course, is through motivational interviewing.

One of the main aims of motivational interviewing is to build a relationship with the people you are working to support. The following Stop–Reflect box summarises the skills that might help you achieve this ambition.

Stop–reflect

OARS

Rosengren (2018) explains that the key skills needed to build a relationship using motivational interviewing can be remembered through the acronym OARS:

O = Open questioning. An open-ended question is a question that cannot be answered with a 'yes' or 'no' response. 'Are you happy with your situation?' is a closed question. 'What do you think about your situation?' is an open question.

A = Affirming. Confirming something to be true. For example, 'You are very brave for talking to me about your situation.'

R = Reflective listening. Showing that you understand and have listened to the other person by asking a clarifying question. For example, 'You have said that you think your current situation is difficult to manage; am I right to think that you would like this situation to change?'

S = Summarising. Summarising the main points of the speaker. For example, 'You have said that you think your current situation is difficult to manage, and that you would like to change the challenges that you face by talking to your partner.'

Why do you think OARS is recommended to build a relationship using motivation interviewing?

The core skills required to develop motivational interviewing techniques reflect the principles of **empathy**, dignity, respect, individualisation, vision, strengths, participation, self-determination, and **empowerment**. Put plainly, motivational interviewing requires you to believe that the person who you are working to support is the expert in their own life. To bring about the change using these skills, you must first believe, and have an uncompromising faith, that the person who you are working to support is able to create the change themselves. See how Mollie attempts to achieve this change in the Skills in Action box.

Skills in action

An example of uncompromising faith

Mollie is working at an agency that supports people to find employment. She has been working with a person called Ryan who is at risk of becoming homeless. Mollie is aware that there are four key processes of motivational interviewing and tries to apply them with Ryan.

1   *Engaging.* Mollie focuses on building a relationship with Ryan. Without adopting a formalised approach to **assessment** and without engaging Ryan in small talk, she tries to use her rudimentary **counselling skills** to show Ryan that she is genuinely interested in him and his unique situation.
2   *Focusing.* Recognising that Ryan's situation is unique, and conscious of the effect of potential power imbalance, Mollie avoids setting an agenda for the meeting. Instead, she asks Ryan if there is anything that he would like to discuss. Mollie also encourages Ryan to focus on the matter of unemployment and potential homelessness.
3   *Evoking.* Once Ryan has outlined his concerns about unemployment and potential homelessness, Mollie begins to evoke change talk in the questions that she asks. In one example, Mollie asks Ryan to consider a future where he might be employed. She asks him to identify and list the things that he might need to do to achieve that goal.
4   *Planning.* Now that Ryan has identified his goal, Mollie begins to encourage him to explore the realistic nature of the plans. Mollie uses positive reinforcement to support Ryan's commitment to change and enable him to move from discussion to action.

The main challenge to motivational interviewing is time and your ability to reposition yourself in a professional helping relationship. Many students tell us that they have come into social work to help others, to make a difference in people's lives and to protect those who are most vulnerable. We have to reflect on this motivation.

As you start out in practice, you will be eager to demonstrate the contribution that you can make to the lives of others. However, if you attempt to help others by offering advice, comparing their life to your own, or others, and set out to rescue people because you feel sorry for them, you could be working close to the line of oppressive practice. A further challenge to motivational interviewing may be encountered when you are asked to respond to crisis or risk. Taking emergency action to protect a child or vulnerable adult, for example, may mean that motivational interviewing is a less effective skill to employ.

Always starting from a position where the person who you are working to support is the expert in their own lives is a core social work value. A skill associated with motivational interviewing that remains constant in all aspects of practice, regardless of context or complexity, is the focus on empathy, dignity, respect, individualisation, vision, strengths, participation, self-determination and empowerment. To be successful you should try to limit the amount of pressure that you put yourself under by recognising that you do not have all of the answers, and that some people do not want your advice. Instead, recognise that the people who you are working to support want you to listen. They want you to recognise the uniqueness of their situation, the specific challenges that they face and the answers that they have, as experts in their own lives, to overcome their difficulties that they face. If, after the encouragement that you provide to people to identify solutions, facilitated through the skills of person-centred practice that draw on the principles of empathy, respect, honesty and congruence, you are unable to make progress, then you can substantiate a conclusion in your assessment that an alternative approach to motivational interviewing might be needed.

Main associated theory

Empowerment Theory, Humanistic Theory, Strengths-Based Theory

Skill category

Communication, relational practice

See also: active listening, non-verbal communication, observational skills, person-centred communication

Further reading

Boyle, S., Vseteckova, J. & Higgins, M. (2019) Impact of motivational interviewing by social workers on service users: A systematic review. *Research on Social Work Practice*, 29(8): 863–875.

Non-verbal communication

Social work is a profession that is built on the skills of excellent communication. Whilst verbal communication is an important method to convey meaning, often achieved through a variation of tone, pitch, volume, pauses, fluency and speed of speech, non-verbal communication, such as body language, can convey meaning too.

As you engage in the **assessment** of individuals, families and communities, you will rely heavily on your communication and analytical skills. By making sense of the things that you hear, see, smell, touch and taste (sometimes your own adrenalin), you will take meaning from the way that people communicate verbally and non-verbally. However, as communication is a method to convey information, it is also important that you seek to minimise the potential for variability in meaning.

Your assessment of others, and the sense-making activities that you engage in, require the utilisation of skills that will be developed over time. Like any other skill that we have introduced in this book, we encourage you to consider your own communication skills before assessing the communication skills and meaning of others. In this chapter, that skill pertains to non-verbal communication.

When we hear the words non-verbal communication, we might think about body language. Whilst body language is recognised as a method to convey meaning, we should also consider other factors that might influence or impact on practice. These might include, for instance, the layout or decoration of a room, clothing or appearance, punctuality and human agency, power and professional authority. All of these factors can communicate meaning. If you attend a meeting at the time that has been agreed dressed in an appropriate manner and well prepared to facilitate the conversation, you might communicate a message that you are interested and professional. If, on the other hand, you are late for the meeting, unprepared and nervous, you may communicate the opposite message. Although body language is one aspect of non-verbal communication, there are many other ways that you communicate meaning, status and power to the people you are working to support. Tops tips to support non-verbal communication skills are listed in the box below.

Top tips

Observing non-verbal communication

- Wearing an identity badge on a lanyard can be a convenient way to show the person who you are working with that you are who you say you are. However, consider how wearing a lanyard as you walk to a property might be perceived by the person in the house and their neighbours.

- At all times, try to be mindful of your posture. Research on non-verbal communication suggests that poor posture, such as slumped shoulders or slouching in a chair, can convey a meaning of low confidence. If the people who you are working to support perceive you as having low confidence your professional credibility could be undermined.
- Try to use positive body language to convey a meaning of confidence and professionalism. Smile when greeting someone, make appropriate eye contact and lift your head up. Try to avoid crossing your legs when sitting down or folding your arms, as this action can convey a meaning of hostility or defensiveness.
- When facilitating a meeting in an office, try to promote a pleasant environment. You might work with the office manager, for example, to improve decoration and room layout.
- During meetings, avoid glancing at your watch, your phone or towards the door as it conveys a meaning that you are not interested in the conversation.
- During a **home visit**, remember social etiquette and ask the homeowner if you should remove your shoes. Avoid putting your workbag on the furniture and always wait to be invited to take a seat before sitting down.

If you are talking to a person who crosses their legs or folds their arms, do not assume that they are hostile or defensive. Instead, ask them what they are thinking or how they are feeling.

Egan (2018) provides the useful acronym SOLER to help guide our approach to non-verbal communication. Assuming that the meeting space has been designed to facilitate a conversation with chairs positioned at a slight angle opposite one another, SOLER stands for:

S: Sit SQUARELY to the person who you are working to support.

O: Maintain an OPEN posture at all times, not crossing your arms or legs, and place your hands on your knees.

L: LEAN slightly in towards the person.

E: Maintain EYE CONTACT with the person but do not stare.

R: RELAX. If you relax the person who you are working to support might begin to relax too.

SOLER is an integral part of the non-verbal communication strategy. It requires you to assume a posture that can minimise the transmission of unintended meaning.

However, SOLER and the broader concepts that Egan (2018) describes are not without limitation. In addition to concerns that include equality and cultural sensitivity, students regularly tell us that assuming the SOLER model during a conversation makes them feel uncomfortable. Students complain that the posture that the model encourages feels awkward or unnatural and that the act of placing their hands on their knees, when they might sooner cross their legs, makes them feel vulnerable. The point that we always emphasise to encourage the inclusion of the model into the praxis of non-verbal communication is that whilst SOLER might feel uncomfortable to you, it might not be uncomfortable to the person who you are working to support.

Main associated theory

Psychosocial Theory – but all actually apply

Skill category

Communication

See also: active listening, communication with children and young people, communication with people with lived experience of learning disabilities, counselling skills, dealing with hostility, emotional intelligence, giving and receiving feedback, presentation skills, rapport building, valuing diversity

Further reading

Egan, G. (2018) *Student Workbook Exercises for Egan's the Skilled Helper* (11th edn). Melbourne: Brooks/Cole.

Observational skills
As a social worker, you will be required to assess and understand complex situations. You will be expected to gather information from multiple sources and develop an accurate and holistic understanding of the circumstances and conditions within which people live.

Throughout this book, we have introduced the various ways in which you can gather information from people using procedural, participatory or co-produced methods of **assessment**. Perhaps employing communication skills that align to the principles of restorative justice, ecological perspectives, motivation or strengths-based practice, you will be seeking to understand the experiences and realities of others by interpreting the information that is being verbally communicated to you. However, by combining the principles of **anti-discriminatory** and **anti-oppressive practice** that have been presented, it is possible to shed some light on the limitations of verbal communication too.

People are not always able to communicate in a way that is generally understood. The things that they are thinking about, the way that they are feeling or the things that they want may not be clear to everyone. Some people might try to hide things from you because they are worried about the consequences of being honest. For this reason, observing people in the environments within which they live can also help you to gather information.

Recognising the importance of observation highlights the relevance of tacit knowledge. In other words, the filter or lens through which you interpret the information that you acquire throughout the assessment process. When conducting an assessment, you will be required to make a judgement about the things that you see. A judgement that will form the basis of risk. The main challenge is to ensure, as far as possible, that your observation of a situation is accurate and not skewed by personal bias. In the following reflection shown in the Stop–Reflect box, the circumstance of an 'untidy house' highlights our point perfectly.

Stop–reflect

What do you mean the house was messy?

Grace and Kitty were planning a joint **home visit** to conduct an assessment on a person who had been referred to their agency by a community nurse. The community nurse highlighted a concern that the person's health was deteriorating due to self-neglect. The referral cited an 'untidy house' as a **safeguarding** risk.

(Continued)

After the assessment, Grace and Kitty returned to the office to de-brief one another and plan the conclusions for the report. However, they could not agree about the alleged safeguarding risk. Based on her observations, Grace believed that the house was untidy. She also concluded that the person might be a hoarder and saw a safeguarding risk. Kitty, on the other hand, agreed that the house was cluttered, but explained her observation that the clutter was organised and not untidy. Kitty did not see a safeguarding risk.

- Why do you think that Grace and Kitty have these two differing opinions?
- How could Grace and Kitty resolve the differences in their observations and opinions?

The potential for variability in observation in a social work assessment means that the skills associated with its use must extend to inform the assessment process and be considered in supervision, peer support and casework discussions. As the conclusions drawn from observation can be subjective, it is important that you seek to verify the accuracy of your interpretation at all times.

As the assessments that are written about the people whom you are working to support become formal documents that can form a part of their history, it is equally important to qualify the observations from which conclusions are made. For this reason, it is important that you avoid labelling your observations. Rather than saying that 'a house is untidy', describe the things that you observe. Rather than saying a person's behaviour is 'challenging' or 'confrontational', explain the detail of behaviour that you have seen. If you take time to explain and understand the detail of your observation, you may be better positioned to use the assessment process, supervision, peer support and casework discussions to verify your understanding of the circumstances and conditions within which people live.

Main associated theory

Psychosocial Theory

Skill category

Assessment

See also: active listening, case recordings, cross-cultural practice, communication with children and young people, communication with people living with experience of learning disabilities, non-verbal communication, report writing

Further reading

O'Loughlin, M., O'Loughlin, S., Ryden, N. & Hughes, J. (2014) *Effective Observation in Social Work Practice*. Los Angeles: Learning Matters.

Person-centred communication

The skills associated with communication represent the cornerstone of social work practice. Without these skills, your ability to understand, represent and then advocate for the people you are working to support will be limited.

As an adult, it is likely that you have developed a number of sophisticated communication skills. These skills enable you to build and maintain relationships with others and they enable you to indicate your preferences, likes and dislikes. However, as you are taking your steps towards professional practice, it is important to reflect on the way that you communicate in your existing interpersonal relationships in order to develop the ability to transfer your skills to the task of social work.

The skills associated with person-centred communication are based on the person-centred approach developed by Carl Rogers (1980). Highlighting the need for you to accept other people, be empathic towards their situation, understand and find congruence (agreement) with their point of view, person-centred communication centres around the confidence, competence and capability to demonstrate genuine positive regard for others.

Where a genuine positive regard is present in your work, person-centred communication becomes the foundation from which you can begin to develop interpersonal relationships, facilitate growth and enable change. Whether you are communicating by phone, email, text or face-to-face the person-centred approach requires you to consider and tune into the thoughts, feelings, motivations and situations of others.

Without the ability to demonstrate genuine positive regard, the opportunity for person-centred communication and the development of interpersonal relations can become lost. If you do not have the time or the inclination to spend time with others to develop a mutual understanding of a situation, if you are quick to devalue another person's opinion and if you are unable to empathise or seek agreement whilst being mindful of other people's feelings, you may struggle to promote person-centred communication in social work practice.

Other factors can challenge your ability to demonstrate person-centred communication. Crisis intervention and **task-centred practice**, which can sit within a model of procedural **assessments**, high caseloads, pressure and stress mean that the time needed to develop person-centred communication can be lost too.

Being aware of the challenges to person-centred communication, and the solutions needed to overcome them, is an important step towards achieving this skill. By seeking to develop a facilitative relationship you may be in a better position to reflect on your inherent communication skills, strengthen your attitude towards the people you are working to support and evaluate the influence that you can have. Consider the two examples in the Stop–Reflect box below. Analyse how each person demonstrates the skill of person-centred communication.

Stop–reflect

Placing the person at the centre of the conversation

Theo is talking on the phone to a young person who has recently left foster care. The young person is living in a flat on the outskirts of town. A summary of the conversation is below.

Young person: I hate this flat. I can't stand it here. I want you to help me get a new flat. If I continue to live here, I don't think I'm going to be able to keep my job.
Theo: Ahh, don't say that. You love living there. I know that what you are going through is hard, but I work with loads of people like you who struggle at first, but with perseverance and hard work they always get by. Anyway, I have to go. Stop worrying about the flat. You will be fine.

In the above example, Theo has tried to use the skills of **active listening** but he has ignored the young person's perspective. He has not accepted the young person's point of view; he has not shown **empathy** towards the situation, sought to understand or agreed with the young person's concern. Instead, he has dismissed the concern, compared the young person to others and suggested that the young person is not persevering or working hard.

In another office, Shabs is talking on the phone to another young person who has recently left foster care. Like Theo, this young person is living in a flat on the outskirts of town. A summary of the conversation is below.

Young person: I hate this flat. I can't stand it here. I want you to help me get a new flat. If I continue to live here, I don't think I'm going to be able to keep my job.
Shabs: Ok, I can hear that you hate the flat. How long have you been feeling like this?

In the above example, Shabs' response seeks to accept the young person's point of view, demonstrate empathy, understanding and concern. By asking a series of follow up questions, Shabs might also begin to agree a plan of action consistent with the person-centred approach to communication.

Imagine that you were the young person calling their social worker and answer the following questions:

I   If you were a young person, who would you prefer to speak to, Theo or Shabs?
2   What is the reason for this choice?

How could Theo and Shabs improve their approach to person-centred communication?

As person-centred communication requires you to demonstrate congruence, acceptance, empathy and understanding of each person's unique situation, it is likely that you will demonstrate this skill with great variance. What we mean is that the skills needed to apply person-centred communication with one person may not be the same skills that you apply when working with someone else. However, if you remember to tune into the thoughts, feelings, motivations and situations of others using **active listening** skills, whether you are communicating by phone, email, text or face-to-face meeting, your path to person-centred communication will significantly enable the realisation of that goal.

Main associated theory

Empowerment Theory, Humanistic Theory, Narrative Theory, Psychosocial Theory, Strengths-Based Theory

Skill category

All

See also: appreciative inquiry, counselling skills, cross-cultural practice, empowerment and enabling, motivational interviewing, person-centred planning, solution-focused practice, valuing diversity

Further reading

Storlie, T.A. (2015) *Person-centered Communication with Older Adults: The Professional Provider's Guide.* London: Academic Press.

Person-centred planning The skills associated with person-centred planning relate primarily to the accessibility of public services. If individuals are unable to access services, due to eligibility criteria, entitlement, funding and resources, service availability or individual choice, person-centred planning is hardly going to be achieved.

Assuming that a public service is available to meet an assessed need, person-centred planning requires you, and the organisation within which you work, to be responsive, capable and flexible enough to deliver individualised services in response to that assessed need. However, for you to ensure that person-centred planning extends to include and promote growth and individual change, you, and the organisations within which you work, must recognise the need for wider systems links that might include, for instance, effective multi-agency **collaboration** with health, education and employment plans, communication plans, care management services, care commissioning and welfare rights agencies. It is only by working to ensure that systems are working well, and implementing change effectively, that individualised approaches to person-centred planning can be achieved.

The first skill of person-centred planning requires you to recognise that **assessments**, plans, methods for intervention, reviews and evaluations cannot be conducted in isolation. By facilitating opportunities for participation and co-production, you should seek to include the person who you are training to support and all other relevant organisations that provide an individual service to meet, share information and plan the person-centred initiative. By being highly organised, you would also be a capable leader who can negotiate effectively, advocate honestly, communicate inclusively, schedule work carefully and risk assess confidently. You should be competent in the skills associated with **assertiveness** and **collaboration** and be proficient at **chairing meetings**.

The second skill reflects your ability to promote inclusive conversations that maintain a central focus in the views and wishes of the people who you are training to support. You should be committed to an outcome that leads to improvements in people's quality of life, and builds self-esteem, life satisfaction and self-determination, consistent with the philosophy of social role valorisation (Wolfensberger, 1983) described in the Theory Explained box.

Theory explained

Social role valorisation

The philosophy of social role valorisation was formulated by Wolf Wolfensberger (1983). It assumes that people are much more likely to experience equal opportunity and social justice if they hold valued social roles in society.

The goal of social role valorisation in person-centred planning is therefore to create valued social roles for devalued people, with the primary aim of supporting people to access equal opportunity and social justice.

Although the language that Wolf used to describe people who do not hold valued social roles in society has changed over the last four decades, the central premise of his philosophy remains as valid now as it did then.

Being committed to an outcome that leads to improvements in people's quality of life, you should be better equipped to demonstrate the third skill of person-centred planning; namely, to maintain a faithful view of an individual's positive social image and personal competencies.

Facilitating a relationship that promotes an individual's positive social image and personal competencies, you may also be more likely to support opportunities that enable people to develop their skills and advance their own solutions. By shifting the focus of power and expertise from the professional, you can begin to support people by providing the services that they want and need to enable the change that they believe is important. As bureaucracy and service inaccessibility can marginalise some of the people you work to support, the clear advantage that this third skill could bring to the person-centred planning is in the ability to organise more effective service delivery, **interprofessional practice**, and **advocacy**.

When applied effectively, the three skills that we have suggested to underpin person-centred practice can begin to enable you to consider the aspirations and capacities that are expressed by the people you support, or those working on their behalf, rather than their needs, limitations or deficiencies. The emphasis on the authority of 'voice' can help you to locate and advocate for service provision.

The three skills that we have introduced could also help you to incorporate a person's family and wider social network in plans for service provision. Being mindful of the interest that friends and family members have, you can seek to broaden your awareness of resources and ideas that might be available.

Finally, these three skills could promote the importance of person-centred planning that is based on providing support to enable people to achieve their own goals, rather than limiting the goals of people based upon the limited access to services, eligibility criteria, entitlement, funding and resources or service availability.

Main associated theory

Humanistic Theory

Skill category

All

See also: active listening, appreciative inquiry, counselling skills, cross-cultural practice, empathy, empowerment and enabling, motivational interviewing, person-centred communication, solution-focused practice, valuing diversity

Further reading

Sanderson, H. & Lewis, J. (2012) *A Practical Guide to Delivering Personalisation: Person-centred Practice in Health and Social Care*. London: Jessica Kingsley.

Presentation skills are vital as a means of communication that can be

adapted to various speaking situations, such as talking to a group, addressing a meeting or briefing a team. The social work contexts in which you might be required to demonstrate competent presentation skills can occur from your point of entry into social work training, when applying for jobs and then in practice contexts (e.g. when requesting resources from a panel, delivering training to colleagues or during court proceedings). Whatever the situation, being articulate (that is, presenting information clearly and effectively) is a key communication skill. Some people take this in their stride, others find it much more challenging, particularly if the context is of a formal nature (e.g. during court proceedings) or if you are tasked with presenting to a large group (e.g. during a conference). Therefore, we include some hints and tips that will help whatever the situation.

Top tips

- *Prepare, prepare, prepare.* If you do not prepare, it will be very apparent to the audience. Being prepared enables you to feel confident. This does not necessarily mean that you have written out and rehearsed a speech word-for-word (although this works for some people). It does, however, mean that you have all the information that you need and that you can be confident that you are saying the right thing, in the right way, and can answer any questions that may arise.
- *Know your audience.* During your preparation, you will need to consider the audience as you need to select the right information, consider any message that you wish to convey and understand the right pitch and level for transmitting that information or message. For example, if you were tasked with making a presentation to an audience that includes professional colleagues and experts by experience, then you would need to ensure that you do not include technical language, jargon and acronyms: whilst your professional colleagues might understand this, experts by experience may not. So, think about accessibility and the appropriateness of content and language.
- *Keeping time.* In certain circumstances (e.g. during a conference, or resources panel) it is likely that you will be allocated a time slot. You should not overrun. In fact, being short and to the point is much more effective.
- *Non-verbal communication.* Remember that the majority of our communication is unspoken. Try to remember the following: stand tall (with uncrossed legs); make eye contact and smile (despite any nerves) to be engaging and build rapport (unless the circumstances are not appropriate e.g. during court). Body language to avoid includes crossing your arms, keeping your hands in your pocket or behind your back, looking down, strutting or pacing around.
- *Verbal communication.* The tone of your voice and the speed at which you speak are important factors in communication. Using your tone and pitch to emphasise points will help the audience to receive and understand the information or message.

In addition, using a slower pace will enable you to feel in control and more effectively hold the attention of the audience.

- *Coping with nerves.* Breathing is important, or more specifically, how you breathe is important in helping you to control your nerves. Try to consciously regulate your breathing; slow it right down and focus on taking full and deep breaths. This will automatically help to control your nerves and enable you to feel more relaxed.
- *Using slides.* Avoid 'death by PowerPoint'! Use up to 10 slides for a short presentation and try to limit the amount of text that you include on each. Do not fill all the space. Use pictures and animations to add interest, but do not add so many that it is overly gimmicky and distracts the audience from the points that you are making. Use one colour for the background; do not use overly colourful and patterned backgrounds as this can obscure the text and make the slides difficult to read. Think about accessibility; using a coloured background helps people with dyslexia. Also, make sure that the font size is big enough to read at a distance (use a font size of 24 point and upwards).

Skills in action

Overcoming nervousness

Jasmeen applied for a secondment to a newly created team that had been set up to address the high rates of child criminal exploitation (CCE) in the town. She had to do a presentation as part of the selection process. Jasmeen was nervous at the thought of it. She did some research and found some tips for how to overcome nerves. In addition to lots of preparation and several rehearsals, Jasmeen remembered the following:

1 The audience are just people, like you and me.
2 The audience are supportive of you and want you to do well.
3 Being aware of breathing and pace can help (nerves can make our breathing shallower, and make us speed up when talking, so make a conscious effort to breathe deeply and talk slowly).
4 Focus on the topic, not the audience.
5 Have water on hand (a remedy for dry mouth syndrome).

On the day Jasmeen remembered all the strategies that she had learned. She had rehearsed with her partner on several occasions (and alone in the car on the journey home from work). Success! Jasmeen was offered the secondment.

Finally, it is useful if you can do some 'disaster planning' to have a back-up plan in case something goes wrong. For example, what would you do if you are tasked with delivering a PowerPoint presentation and technology does not work on the day? You should take handouts (for the audience members and one copy for you with your notes). Also, think about how you will manage audience members who are silent, challenging, too talkative. It is likely that you will draw on existing skills in communication that you use in everyday practice.

Main associated theory

Psychosocial Theory

Skill category

Communication

See also: court skills, group work, non-verbal communication, use of self and reflexivity

---

Further reading

Trevithick, P. (2012) *Social Work skills and Knowledge: A Practice Handbook*. Maidenhead: McGraw-Hill Education.

Professional challenge In social work you will come into contact with a range of different professionals and agencies from health, housing, education, criminal justice and the women's sector to name a few. Within each there are a range of sub-sections (e.g. in the field of criminal justice there is youth justice, the police, the courts, the probation service, witness protection and legal advisory bodies). Agencies offer services to a wide variety of communities such as refugees and asylum seekers, children and young people, older adults and homeless people. This diversity makes social work stimulating and rewarding, but it can also be challenging as working across disciplines and agencies can result in cultures, structures, orientations and approaches that contrast and conflict. These cultures, structures and approaches can lead to everyday assumptions, goals and practices that can end in professional disagreement.

Stop-reflect

Case study: Domestic violence and abuse

In her influential article, Hester (2011) noted how there had been increasing recognition in both policy and practice of domestic violence and abuse (DVA) as a **safeguarding** issue for children. Policy and practice developed to reflect this, with emphasis on multi-agency approaches and responses. In her article, Hester outlined her model of the 'three planets' as a way of conceptualising what was happening for frontline practitioners. Hester reflects on the three planets of DVA, child protection and child contact, identifying each as having contrasting approaches including cultures, objectives, decision-making protocols and, importantly, differential thresholds for defining 'harm' or providing intervention.

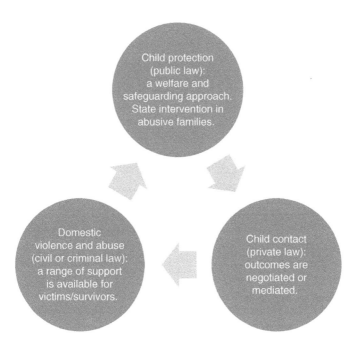

Figure P1 The three planets of domestic violence and abuse, child protection and child contact

Source: adapted from Hester, M. (2011) The Three Planet Model: Towards an Understanding of Contradictions in Approaches to Women and Children's Safety in Contexts of Domestic Violence. British Journal of Social Work, 41(5): 837-53. Reproduced by permission of Oxford University Press

Agencies located on the 'DVA planet' include refuges and providers of **advocacy** that specifically support the victim/survivor as well as those criminal and civil justice agencies that intervene with DVA perpetrators. Work on the 'child protection planet' is primarily concerned with safeguarding the child. However, the 'child contact planet' involves a different approach as Family Court Advisors and other relevant professionals are centred on the needs and wishes of parents and their residence and contact arrangements in relation to the child.

Do you think that the perspectives of these three planets are balanced and holistic? What happens when these three perspectives come together?

Think about the DVA practitioner's perspective that the male partner is violent, abusive and harmful and views a criminal justice approach as the appropriate response. How does this align with the child protection practitioner's view that the father is abusive *but* the mother also has responsibility for safeguarding and in living with an abusive partner,

(Continued)

she has failed to protect her children? How does the child contact practitioner's view, which considers that the father is good enough to have contact, coexist with the DVA practitioner's perspective that sees the father as a risk in relation to violence and the potential of harm to safety and wellbeing?

There are many grounds on which professionals can disagree including: eligibility thresholds being too low or too high; case management decisions, planning and intervention; perceived capacity for change; and perceived level of improvement or change. It is important to avoid silo working and to discourage a blame culture. In striving to achieve this, there are some good practices to adopt such as:

- open, regular and timely communication
- information-sharing within the realms of data protection and confidentiality protocols
- using negotiation and **mediation** skills
- using language with other professionals that avoids jargon and acronyms that are social work specific
- attempting to understand the position of professional others
- the ability to flex and adapt in response to professional disagreements or the confidence to stand firm when necessary.

Professional disagreement is not always a negative thing as studies on task-related conflict have demonstrated that reasonable levels of conflict can actually stimulate creativity and innovations and result in better quality decision-making (De Drue, 2007). It is important to remember that challenging other professionals in the pursuit of sound decision-making, planning and intervening should be rooted to good practice and reflects professional standards. For example, Professional Standard 3, 'Be accountable for the quality of my practice and the decisions I make', detailed in the Professional Standards from Social Work England (2020) (the regulatory body in England) specifically requires practitioners to:

3.6 Draw on the knowledge and skills of workers from my own and other professions and work in collaboration, particularly in integrated teams, holding onto and promoting my social work identity.

3.7 Recognise where there may be bias in decision-making and address issues that arise from ethical dilemmas, conflicting information, or differing professional decisions.

These standards act as a reminder to engage in **collaboration** and interprofessional practice, but to maintain social work values, ethics and priorities as well as challenging other professional decision-makers where necessary. This makes it clear that professional challenge is not an imagined or desired practice, but a professional requirement.

Main associated theory

Psychosocial Theory

Skill category

Communication

See also: assertiveness, challenging skills, conflict management and resolution, dealing with hostility, dealing with resistance, interprofessional practice

---

Further reading

Barnes, V. (2016) Skills for inter-professional practice. In K. Davies and R. Jones (eds) *Skills for Social Work Practice*. London: Macmillan Publishers Limited.

Professional development
Once you qualify as a social worker, your training and professional development does not end there. Being a social worker requires you to engage in a career-long process of reflection and growth. In most countries this will be officially recognised by the professional standards and frameworks through regulation and ethical codes for practice. It is useful to draw on England as a case study as the set of standards from its professional body, Social Work England (SWE) (2020), includes one dedicated to 'maintain[ing] my continuing professional development' (see Top Tips box below). SWE requires all registrants to meet its standards for continuing professional development (CPD) by providing evidence and critical reflections on your professional developmental activities captured within an online portfolio. SWE undertakes an annual audit of randomly selected portfolios. This standard is aligned with quality measures and workforce benchmarks in terms of knowledge and skill.

Top tips

Professional Standard 4: Maintain my continuing professional development

4.1 Incorporate feedback from a range of sources, including from people with lived experience of my social work practice.

4.2 Use supervision and feedback to critically reflect on, and identify my learning needs, including how I use research and evidence to inform my practice.

4.3 Keep my practice up to date and record how I use research, theories and frameworks to inform my practice and my professional judgement.

(Continued)

4.4 Demonstrate good subject knowledge on key aspects of social work practice and develop knowledge of current issues in society and social policies impacting on social work.

4.5 Contribute to an open and creative learning culture in the workplace to discuss, reflect on and share best practice.

4.6 Reflect on my learning activities and evidence what impact continuing professional development has on the quality of my practice.

4.7 Record my learning and reflection on a regular basis and in accordance with Social Work England's guidance on continuing professional development.

4.8 Reflect on my own values and challenge the impact they have on my practice.

© Social Work England, 2020. www.socialworkengland.org.uk/cpd/the-cpd-standard/ (accessed 25 January 2021)

Another development across England in recent years has been the provision of CPD, which has been addressed regionally by the development of teaching partnerships between local authorities (employers) and higher education providers (HEPs). Such partnerships were anticipated to enable localities to commission CPD that reflects workforce needs. In reality, workforce planning is incredibly challenging and a review of the impact of teaching partnerships showed mixed results (Baginsky, Manthorpe & Hickman, 2019). It is, therefore, important that from the beginning of your journey into social work training you adopt a view that your professional training and development is something that you need to take responsibility for.

Stop-reflect

My developmental needs

Think about completing an audit of your existing knowledge and skills and those that you would like to develop in order to expand your capacity for excellent practice. Ask yourself:

- What is my level of knowledge/skill in [e.g. law/communication/theory on human development]?
- What can I do to enhance my level of knowledge/skill in [e.g. law/communication/ theory on human development]?
- When should I complete this work? [e.g. build yourself a timetable for learning activities]
- How will I know when I have developed my level of knowledge/skill in [e.g. law/ communication/theory on human development]?

The last question is important as you need to have some kind of benchmark or idea of how to measure your development. You might then realise that you have more learning to do, or you might decide that your level of knowledge or skill is more than adequate and so you consider other learning needs to focus on. You might wish to complete a formal training needs audit; you should be able to find a template freely available on the internet.

What constitutes CPD is wider than that which is provided by HEPs or in-house via employers, as self-directed learning is just as important. Therefore, a broad range of activities can constitute CPD including participation in webinars and other online/offline training sessions, reading research reports or theoretical papers, attending subject-specific meetings (e.g. a public meeting on austerity measures and the local impact) and many more.

It is important that you frequently reflect on your practice in order to feed into a plan for professional development. Supervision is the ideal structure to support a reflective discussion. Reflective supervision functions not only to support your **critical thinking and analysis**, enhance emotional wellbeing and enable problem-solving, it is the ideal forum in which to have a supported discussion about professional development and is a core element in any learning organisation. A learning organisation is one which has a structure and culture which is open, creative and exploratory, including stakeholders (including employees and experts by experience) in decision-making and networking. It is effective in knowledge management and human resource practice promoting lifelong learning and skill acquisition (Blinston & Higham, 2009).

Main associated theory

Psychosocial Theory

Skill category

All

See also: critical incident analysis, emotional intelligence, ethical practice, evidence-informed practice, managing supervision, reflective practice, reflective writing, use of self and reflexivity

Further reading

Social Work England (2020) *Professional Standards*. Available at: www.socialworkengland. org.uk/media/1640/1227_socialworkengland_standards_prof_standards_final-aw.pdf (accessed 25 January 2021).

Professional judgement and decision-making

Sound professional judgements and good decision-making in social work are vital: lives and liberty depend on it. Put simply, a *judgement* is the process of evaluating and interpreting evidence to form an opinion, whereas *decision-making* is a conscious process leading to the selection of a course of action where there are two or more options. Taylor (2010) described a typology of social work decisions including:

- client decisions that might be facilitated by a social worker
- care planning decisions involving choice between two or more options for care
- choice between interventions or treatments
- protection or **safeguarding** decisions on behalf of society
- decisions about eligibility for services
- decisions to refer elsewhere or to take no action.

Arriving at a professional judgement and making a sound, defensible decision is a complex process as there are multiple, and often competing or contradictory, factors that need consideration. These include: legislation and your legal duty; statutory timescales; eligibility criteria and thresholds; risk as a dynamic variable; the availability of resources; ethical dilemmas; and many more. In addition, there are a number of pitfalls that can underpin poor, unreflective decision-making.

Danger zone

Professional judgements

Table P1   Professional judgements

Danger zones	
Anchoring	The tendency to rely too heavily, or 'anchor', on one piece of information when reaching a judgement (usually the first piece of information acquired).
Confirmation bias	The tendency to search for, interpret and stick to information that supports your existing hypothesis.
Continued influence effect	The tendency to believe wrong information even after it has been corrected and the misinformation continues to influence views and judgements.
Courtesy bias	The inclination to project an opinion that is more socially acceptable than your real opinion to avoid offending anyone.

Danger zones	
Empathy gap	The tendency to underestimate the strength or influence of emotions in oneself (or others).
Focusing effect	The tendency to incorrectly focus on, or overly emphasise, one aspect of an event.
Groupthink	The desire to avoid conflict by being compliant, or 'going with the flow', also known as the 'bandwagon effect'.
Hindsight bias	The proclivity to see past events as being predictable at the time those events happened, also known as the 'I knew it all along!' effect.
Information bias	The tendency to seek information even when it cannot affect your decision-making or actions.
Optimism bias	The tendency to be over-optimistic, overestimating favourable and positive outcomes.

Source: reproduced from Rogers et al., 2020: 131, Table 11.2. Reprinted by permission of SAGE Publications.

Professional judgements should be based on verifiable knowledge, sound reasoning and the use of robust methods. The rights, responsibilities, wishes and feelings of the individuals or families that you are working with are of vital importance. These should always be central to the decision-making process and/or when you are supporting an individual or family to make a decision. Moreover, it is broadly agreed that decision-making is most successful when the recipient of that decision is involved in its formation and implementation (Trevithick, 2012). It is this enabling and empowering approach that should underpin the process of judgement and decision-making where possible.

In the last decade, however, there have been many commentators who have drawn attention to the increased bureaucratisation and proceduralisation of social work **assessment** and case management (White et al., 2010; Featherstone et al., 2018). Whilst assessment models, procedures and tools can help to support good decision-making in this context, they also run the risk of serving 'to reduce rather than promote effective critical and analytical thinking' (Samsonsen & Turney, 2017: 131). A recent study by Symonds et al. (2018: 1923) found additional tensions in judgement and decision-making arguing that 'the biggest of those tensions still seemed to be the uneasy mix of professional judgement with the nurturing of autonomy and control in the client'. This was also framed against a background of working with diversity in that people were described as being located along a spectrum of self-determination and competence with some being highly competent decision-makers and others lacking capacity.

Skills in action

Lily

Lily was 54 years old when she moved into temporary supported accommodation; a house called Greenfields with 24-hour support for adults with learning disabilities. Greenfields was occupied by two other residents. Up until this point in time, Lily had lived in the family home with her elderly mother, Alice. Lily was moved into the accommodation after Alice had a fall which required hospitalisation as Lily lacked the life skills to look after herself. As a child Lily had been diagnosed as autistic and her family had been very protective of her. After her school years, Lily had remained in the family home: she had never held employment nor socialised outside of her family.

The move to shared accommodation represented a significant transition for Lily. Slowly she began to interact with her co-residents, joining in activities such as cooking and crafts. One day Lily's social worker, Barrington, raised the issue of returning home. Barrington and Lily discussed four future scenarios: returning home to live with Alice on her discharge from hospital; moving to live with her only other relative, Great Aunt Maureen; staying at Greenfields in the immediate future whilst exploring options further; and looking for permanent supported accommodation near to Alice and Great Aunt Maureen. Barrington helped Lily to understand that Alice may not be able to return home due to her age and health. He also enabled Lily to think about the benefits and disadvantages of the different options. Lily decided to return home once Alice was well enough to leave hospital, but with a plan in place to enable Lily to attend a day centre where Lily could meet the people that she had come to know at Greenfields and where she could attend classes to develop more life skills. The stay in hospital was longer than anticipated for Alice and over the weeks Barrington supported Lily to think about the other options. Lily indicated that her ultimate goal would be to move to permanent supported accommodation.

Main associated theory

Psychosocial Theory, Cognitive Behaviour Theory

Skill category

All

See also: active listening, critical thinking and analysis, empowerment and enabling, evidence-informed practice, observational skills, reflective practice, risk assessment, use of self and reflexivity

Further reading

Taylor, B.J. (2012) Models for professional judgement in social work. *European Journal of Social Work*, 15(4): 546–562.

Professional values and ethics Values and ethics are central to

social work practice. Combined, values and ethics provide you with a professional moral compass that can enable you to balance competing and conflicting demands, helping you to navigate complex, uncertain and risky situations. Values and ethics are closely linked to the concepts of *rights* and *responsibilities*, which apply to both you as a social worker and to those people that you are working to support.

There is a fundamental question, however, and this is what do we mean when we talk of 'values' and 'ethics'? The basic definition of a *value* is something (a quality or attitude) that we hold as important or useful, and the term *ethics* pertains to standards of conduct or moral judgement (Collins Dictionary, 2020a, 2020b). In this context, our values (those qualities or attitudes that we hold dear) can inform our ethics (our principles and moral code that inform our beliefs and behaviour).

There can be a difference between our *personal* values and ethics and our *professional* values and ethics. In social work practice, we are bound by duty and the requirement to comply with those professional values and ethics clearly articulated in our professional standards and codes of conduct. If there is conflict between our personal and professional ethics, then we must follow the professional standards as this forms part of the basic requirements for practice when you are a qualified and registered social worker.

As a starting point, in thinking about common or shared values, it is useful to reflect upon the global definition of social work provided by the International Federation of Social Work (IFSW):

> Social work is a practice-based profession and an academic discipline that pro-
> motes *social change* and development, *social cohesion*, and the *empowerment* and
> *liberation* of people. Principles of *social justice, human rights, collective responsibility*
> and *respect for diversities* are central to social work. Underpinned by theories of
> social work, social sciences, humanities and indigenous knowledge, social work
> engages people and structures to address life challenges and enhance wellbeing.
> The above definition may be amplified at national and/or regional levels. (IFSW,
> 2014, emphasis added)

The highlighted words all pertain to values that underpin practice. Now consider the six professional standards of Social Work England (2020), the regulatory body in England:

1   Promote the *rights, strengths* and *wellbeing* of people, families and communities.
2   Establish and maintain the *trust* and *confidence* of people.
3   Be *accountable* for the *quality* of my practice and the decisions I make.
4   Maintain my continuing professional development.
5   Act *safely, respectfully* and with *professional integrity*.
6   Promote *ethical practice* and report concerns.

In England, the framework underpinning social work practice includes a Code of Ethics offered by the British Association of Social Workers (BASW), which is the representative body for social workers. The Code of Ethics is built upon the three concepts of *social justice, human rights* and *professional integrity* (BASW, 2014). Despite some different terminology, you should be able to identify commonalities and overlaps between these three perspectives of an international agency, a country's regulatory body and representative agency.

Stop-reflect

Social Work England's Professional Standards

The first professional standard (Social Work England, 2020) is broken down into seven standards:

The standard: *Promote the rights, strengths and wellbeing of people, families and communities.*

1.1 Value each person as an individual, recognising their strengths and abilities.

1.2 Respect and promote the human rights, views, wishes and feelings of the people I work with, balancing rights and risks and enabling access to advice, advocacy, support and services.

1.3 Work in partnership with people to promote their wellbeing and achieve best outcomes, recognising them as experts in their own lives.

1.4 Value the importance of family and community systems and work in partnership with people to identify and harness the assets of those systems.

1.5 Recognise differences across diverse communities and challenge the impact of disadvantage and discrimination on people and their families and communities.

1.6 Promote social justice, helping to confront and resolve issues of inequality and inclusion.

1.7 Recognise and use responsibly, the power and authority I have when working with people, ensuring that my interventions are always necessary, the least intrusive, proportionate, and in people's best interests.

When you join the register held by Social Work England as a qualified social work practitioner, you commit to upholding each standard. Can you think of an example of how you might meet each one in your practice?

For example, you are working with an asylum seeking family. You find out that they are living in a run-down and overcrowded property, and the target of hostility within their local community. You work tirelessly to get the Housing Department to rehouse them. Which standards have you met?

We'd argue that this meets the following standards: 1.2 – promoting their human rights and advocating for them; 1.3 – you would not take action without discussing this with the family and should be working in partnership to agree a plan of action in an attempt to achieve a better outcome for them; 1.4 – you advocate that the Housing Officer accommodates them in a location near to other asylum seeking families from the same country and in this way you enable them to be connected to families from their own community (this also could meet 1.6); 1.5 – you would certainly meet this standard as you recognise discrimination in the family's account of everyday life that is taking place in the community which they leave behind once rehoused; and we would hope that you would use your position to advocate with the Housing Officer for a decision (to accommodate in a more appropriate residence and location) and, as such, use your power in the family's best interests (1.7).

Main associated theory

Psychosocial Theory, Cognitive Behaviour Theory

Skill category

All

See also: advocacy, anti-discriminatory practice, anti-oppressive practice, collaboration: working with experts by experience, critical thinking and analysis, cross-cultural practice, empowerment and enabling, ethical practice, questioning, use of self and reflexivity, valuing diversity, working with protected characteristics

Further reading

Banks, S. (2012) *Ethics and Values in Social Work* (4th edn). Basingstoke & New York: Palgrave Macmillan.

Banks, S. (2016) Everyday ethics in professional life: Social work as ethics work. *Ethics and Social Welfare*, 10(1): 35–52.

Questioning

Questioning The art of **interviewing** relies on skilled questioning techniques. This is the effective use of different types of questioning coupled with **active listening**. This chapter complements the chapter on **motivational interviewing** by describing types of questions that will enable effective data gathering, processing and analysis.

Open and closed questions: different types of questions are appropriate in different circumstances. For example, a closed question is suitable when checking information that you already have (that is, when you need a 'yes' or 'no' response) or when only a short answer is required (for example, when you need to get a person's name or address). As such, closed questions help to collect factual information. Closed questions have utility when working with children or adults with impaired cognition or limited mental capacity, or when working with someone who finds it difficult to speak up for themselves or articulate themselves. In contrast, an open-ended question enables the speaker to express their thoughts and feelings in their own words and helps to elicit a full, detailed response. Examples of an open-ended question are: what is your view of the concerns? How could we work together to find a solution? Open questioning is a tool for **active listening** and helps the speaker to feel that they are being listened to and that their thoughts, feelings and wishes are respected and taken into account.

Indirect questions: this is a type of question that is embedded within a statement, rather than being constructed as a direct question. Using indirect questions enables a person to have agency by making a choice about whether or not to respond, and in the type and length of response (Rogers, 2020). The Skills in Action box provides some examples of direct vs indirect questions.

Skills in action

Table Q1   Indirect questioning

Direct question	Indirect question
• Was that information difficult to hear?	• I'm thinking that information was difficult to hear.
• Would you like me to take my shoes off?	• I wonder if I should take my shoes off.

Probing questions: these are not intended to clarify information, but to develop and add more depth to responses. Probing questions help you to get below the surface and invite people to engage in critical thinking. Typically, probing questions are open-ended to elicit a fuller response. In addition, probes can be direct or indirect. The Skills in Action box provides examples.

Skills in action

Table Q2 Probing questioning

Indirect question	Probing question
• You seem upset, but I'm not sure what about.	• You appear to be very unhappy; can you tell me what has upset you?
• You seem disappointed, but I can't understand why.	• I'd really like to understand why you are disappointed so can you tell me why this is?

Hypothetical questions: the use of hypothetical questions is exemplified in strengths-based and solution-focused approaches. Both encourage a future-oriented position by reflecting on existing strengths and resources, and encourage a person to imagine using these to generate positive change. It is very easy to integrate hypothetical questions into every interview. Some examples include:

- What would you like to be doing in 12 months' time?
- What would you like to be the outcomes of our discussion?
- How do you think we could move forward to enable better care?

Funnelling: clever use of questioning can be used to funnel the respondent's answers. This technique gradually restricts a person's answer and is useful when there is very specific information that you need to glean. You might start off with some open questioning and become more specific by honing in on one part of a person's response. For example, 'Tell me about your recent period of abstinence', 'What was it about visiting the Rehab Centre that helped you not to drink?', 'Focusing on your relationship with that particular person, what about it motivated you to keep going'?

Circular questioning: this technique was developed in family therapy to be used when working holistically with a family (Trevithick, 2012). Circular questioning involves asking one family member to comment or reflect on the relationships or behaviour of two or more members. For example, 'Harrison, when Sally [sister] tells your mum she hates her, how does your mum respond?' Circular questioning allows for new connections and understandings of behaviour, interactions, meanings and impact.

Skills in action

Positive reframing

Whilst positive reframing is not a questioning technique *per se*, it is a communication technique that conveys active listening and uses questioning to help someone to move away from a negative position to imagine a positive outcome or future. Positive reframing involves being able to help a person to reflect on their situation or the presenting problem and identify what they would like to change *and* how they might effect that change. In this way, positive reframing can counter distorted thinking (the tendency to over-generalise, exaggerate, catastrophise), and polarised thinking (viewing everything in black or white). You can use the questioning techniques detailed in this chapter. Some examples include:

- I can understand why you feel like that, but I see it differently. For example, can you see how you have actually made a positive difference to the situation by being so focused on getting the right help, at the right time and calling our services?
- Imagine what life will be like in three months' time, when it will be very different and you've been working in partnership with me to get life back on track. What will life look like then?

There are some common pitfalls and barriers to effective questioning and you should bear these in mind when reflecting on your practice and the response of the people you've been working with. Some of these are: interruptions from people or the environment (a noisy road outside, for example); symbolic communication (the bag on the knee that represents a barrier or being late, which can communicate that your time is more important than the other person's); unconscious bias, assumptions and biased beliefs (these will lead to poor judgements and decision-making); confirmation bias (asking leading questions to confirm what you think you know); using the wrong question (closed or irrelevant questions); poor timing (asking sensitive or difficult questions before you have developed rapport); asking complicated or multiple questions in one go (overloading the respondent) (Rogers, 2020).

Main associated theory
Psychosocial Theory, Cognitive Behaviour Theory

Skill category
Assessment, communication

See also: challenging skills, counselling skills, critical thinking and analysis, giving and receiving feedback, non-verbal communication, use of self and reflexivity

Further reading

Kadushin, A. & Kadushin, G. (2013) *The Social Work Interview*. Columbia: Columbia University Press.

R

Radical social work The emergence of radical social work in the 1970s has had a significant influence on social work theory and practice (Kim, 2017). Radical social work is a value-driven model concerned with the values of equality and social justice. It is based on the idea that social work aims to improve people's lives not only by supporting individuals and families but also by striving for structural change. As such, it is easy to locate the roots of **anti-discriminatory** and **anti-oppressive practice** in the philosophies underpinning radical social work.

Understanding social justice

The notion of social justice is a core value of radical social work, but Kim (2017) raises questions about how it is understood and defined in contemporary social work. Reisch (2002) highlighted that the field of social work (including practice, policy and social work education) suffers from the absence of an agreed definition of social justice and that the absence of a conceptual and political framework for practice (whatever the area of practice) can be a detriment in different ways.

What is your understanding of social justice? We all have different interpretations, emphasis and ideas about social justice and it is likely that you may have a visceral and instinctive response that draws on personal experience, values and ethics. For example, if you have grown up as a Black and minority ethnic (BME) British person in a predominantly white neighbourhood your definition of social justice might tie notions of ethnic diversity to inclusion and equality goals. A person who has grown up with a physical disability might emphasise the barriers in the social and physical world which prevent or enable full social inclusion and participation in everyday life.

The absence of a shared understanding of social justice means that we may practice in contrasting ways as our ethical and political motivations and ideals are different. The emphasis we place on particular values or social conditions may differ but we should accept others' views as to what constitutes a social problem worthy of attention in the desire for social justice for all. We might tend towards our professional codes or standards for direction, but in a review of the descriptions of social justice in various social work organisations across the globe, Morgaine (2014) found no common and clear definition of social justice.

Radical social work challenges the status quo and dominant culture whilst aiming to tackle systems of oppression through community action, **advocacy** and social movements. This approach is not limited to local systems as radical social workers are concerned with the impacts of global capitalism, neoliberalism, austerity, inequality and oppression as well as understanding and responding to global social problems such as war, disasters and climate change. At the time of writing, radical social work collectives are mobilising against the impacts associated with the global pandemic caused by COVID-19 and the unequal ways this has affected BME communities as well as those people already affected by austerity and poverty.

Theory explained

Capitalism is an economic and political system which is dominant in the Western world. It is a system in which a country's trade and industry are controlled by private owners for profit, rather than by being owned by the state. Capitalism is characterised by free market competition which dictates production levels and pricing systems. Other characteristics include the growth of private property, capital accumulation, wage labour and competitive markets.

Neoliberalism is a political approach that is closely linked to capitalism. Neoliberal ideology emphasises the value of free trade and market competition, privatisation, price deregulation and flexible labour markets. In terms of the implications for individuals and communities, as neoliberalism sees competition as the defining characteristic of human relations, it redefines citizens as consumers. In a neoliberal framework, democracy is characterised by individual choice and autonomy.

Austerity refers to the state of being austere. In ideological terms, austerity is represented by a set of political and economic policies that aim to reduce government budget deficits through spending cuts, tax increases or a combination of both. Austerity measures are often used by governments in terms of economic challenge and when they are struggling to meet their financial commitments.

Main associated theory

Humanistic Theory, Empowerment Theory

Skill category

Anti-oppressive practice

See also: empowering and enabling, ethical practice

Further reading

Rogowski, S. (2010) *Social Work: The Rise and Fall of a Profession?* Bristol: Policy Press.

Turbett, C. (2013) Radical social work in the frontline: A survival toolkit for the UK. *Critical and Radical Social Work*, 1(2): 225–232.

Rapport building

Some of the people who you work to support may find your involvement threatening. As a social worker, you hold a great deal of power that can enable the provision of services or justify statutory intervention that some might see as controlling. Whilst you will be trained to develop a number of the skills described in this book, the opportunity for you to build a rapport with the people you are working to support may not be considered in equal depth. One reason for this is that rapport building is a difficult skill to teach or simulate. There may always be, for instance, intangible factors and perspectives that differ according to the individual circumstances of each interaction that you engage in.

The Skills in Action box below has been designed to show you that rapport is similar to trust. You can build trust and rapport simultaneously, but rapport focuses more on establishing a bond or connection, whereas trust relies more on establishing a reputation for reliability, consistency and keeping your promises.

Skills in action

Establishing a reputation for reliability

I First impressions count.

- When booking **home visits** and meetings it is essential that you are punctual. If you know that you are going to be late, telephone the person who you have arranged to meet and apologise. Respectfully request alternative arrangements.
- To avoid offence, you might do well to know in advance of a home visit whether cultural or religious mores should be observed.
- Observe the customs and traditions of social etiquette. This might mean, for instance, removing your shoes when entering a house, not putting your workbag on the furniture and not dressing too formally or too informally.
- Try to relax and smile, remember the names of the people who you are visiting. At all times, hold your head up and maintain a good posture.
- Some people will offer you a drink. If you are offered refreshments, consider carefully before you accept or decline. In our collective experience, we have found that some families expect you to share in the symbolic ritual of drinking tea and taking a small snack before any formal conversations can occur.

(Continued)

R

2   Find common interests.

- When appropriate, try to spend some time talking about a neutral subject before beginning a formal social work **assessment**. Perhaps try engaging the person in a conversation about the weather or a recent sporting event. Try to observe the surroundings and compliment the individual on their furniture, or choice of decoration. If they have a photograph or picture on the wall refer to that in the initial conversation. Even just expressing your shared frustration at the traffic that delayed your journey can help you to draw closer to someone.

3   Be empathic.

- Once you have permission and agreement from the individual, family or community to begin your formal assessment or meeting, and if you are meeting them for the first time, it is important that you explain why you are involved in their lives. Explain the procedure for recording and accessing case notes, the complaints procedure, and the right to **advocacy** and independent legal advice.
- Try to understand the lives of the people you are working to support by attempting to see the world from their perspective. Recognise and respect their emotions and the individual nature of their circumstance.
- At all times, try to demonstrate **active listening** skills that convey your genuine interest in the lives of the people you are working to support.

When seeking to build rapport it is important that you are genuine and sincere in your interactions. If you are overdoing things, you can appear disingenuous or too eager. Any perception that you are insincere or condescending can reduce your credibility.

Smiling and laughter can be a useful way to build rapport, but do use humour with care. Not everyone will have the same sense of humour. What might seem to you as acceptable sarcasm could easily cause offense to somebody else. For this reason, we strongly encourage you to avoid telling jokes or making light of complex situations.

Main associated theory

Psychosocial Theory

Skill category

Communication

See also: counselling skills, empathy, non-verbal communication, reflective practice, risk assessment, using humour

Further reading

Rogers, M., Whittaker, D., Edmondson, D. & Peach, D. (2020) *Developing Skills & Knowledge for Social Work Practice* (2nd edn). London: Sage.

Reflective practice is an essential element of social work. When exercised, it can lead to the improvement of services by enabling a continuous focus on individual and organisation learning. However, when opportunities for reflective practice are not exercised, or fully understood, there emerges an opportunity for social work practice to repeat the failings that have served to pepper our history. It has to be understood, therefore, that reflective practice is a skill. Like any other skill described in this book, it needs to be practised if you wish to become more proficient at it.

To start our summary of reflective practice it is perhaps worth thinking about why reflective practice is important. Put simply, reflective practice is a skill that encourages you to think about social work, before you do it, whilst you do it and after you do it. It is a skill that encourages you to think about what you are going to do, why you are doing what you are doing (and whether what you are doing is working), and how you might improve your practice if you were to be in a similar situation again.

There are a number of models that support reflective practice. It is our guess that you will probably be most familiar with the works of Schön (1983), Kolb (1984) and Gibbs (1988). Used widely in social work, the models provided by these authors support the template for reflective practice but they do not fully extend to account for or describe the skills needed to be a reflective social work practitioner.

Reflection is a personal activity but it is not a private one. It is something that you must do alone with some input and support from the people you are working to support and from the people who are working to support you. Throughout your career, you will be expected to talk about your reflections and analysis to substantiate and justify action. It is a reality of practice that you will make mistakes. Of course, you will not intend to, but you will be expected to be honest when mistakes happen and show that you are able to learn from experience. For this reason, the ability to learn from an experience is the primary skill for reflective practice.

As part of your work, you will expect the people you are working with to reflect on their own lives and situations and share their thoughts and feelings with you. In collecting evidence to inform your **assessment** of risk, you will also ask people to explain what they have learnt from the mistakes that they have made too. The main point is that reflective practice is an essential social work skill that applies to you and all of the people you work with. If you expect the people you are working to support to engage in a reflective process, the least you can do is engage in that process too. The main risks associated with reflective practice are listed in the Danger Zone box below.

Danger zone

Risk associated with reflection

Recognising that reflective practice is a skill is important because like any other example, some people are better at it than others. Without the ability to practise the skill of reflective practice capably, one of two things, which operate at the opposing ends of a spectrum, could happen.

At one end of the spectrum is arrogance. When thinking about social work practice, some people, new to the skill of reflection, may believe that what they did was fantastic, and that there is nothing they could do differently to improve.

At the other end of the spectrum is self-criticism. When thinking about social practice, other people, equally new to the skill of reflection, may believe that what they did was hopeless, and that they do not have the ability to be a social worker. Finding the middle ground is essential.

How might you ensure that you avoid arrogance and hopelessness in your own reflection?

When reflecting on social work practice, some people new to the skill tend to prefer the opportunity to reflect *on* action. This type of reflection occurs after an event and usually requires people to think about what they did well and what they might do to improve. As a starting point for reflection, we have no problem with reflection on action in principle. We recognise that the retrospective application of knowledge, values and skills is an opportunity to begin to articulate **evidence-informed practices** and enable the transition to reflect *in* and *before* action (Rogers and Allen, 2019). That said, we are concerned when reflection is tokenistic and limited to a broad description of practice that does not extend to an analysis of power. For this reason, the following Top Tips are presented to support the development of your critical reflection skills, regardless of the model that you use, and to help you find the middle ground that is so important to the principles of **anti-oppressive practice**.

Top tips

1 When considering an event for reflection, you will either focus on something that has happened (reflection *on* action), something that is happening (reflection *in* action) or something that is going to happen (reflection *before* action). You will begin to consider how you felt (or feel) and how your knowledge (formal or tacit), thoughts, feelings and behaviour might influence your practice. Honestly analysing the relationship between your knowledge, thoughts, feelings and behaviour is key to reflective practice.

2 As you begin to consider how your knowledge, thoughts, feelings and behaviour might influence your practice, it is equally important to consider the knowledge, thoughts, feelings and behaviour of the people you are working to support.

For example, if you imagine that a person might be concerned or suspicious about your involvement in their lives, what do you think you might need to do to facilitate an opportunity for trust or **collaboration** that is more effective?

3   Try to use reflection to evaluate the strengths and weakness of the skills described in this book. You should also be able to choose the most appropriate action according to your reflective observations of the situation at hand. For example, if you begin a meeting with an intention to use **mediation** skills, you should be able to use another skill if it appears that mediation is not working.

4   Always consider the power that you have as a key part of the reflective process. Moving to a position of reflexivity, consider how your identity as a social worker could enable or prevent effective action. Consider, for example how the person you are working to support might perceive you, the power that you have and your role in their lives.

Considering the impact of thoughts, feelings and behaviour, the application of theory, methods and social work skills, try to consider specific example of how you could promote the principles of **anti-oppressive practice**.

Main associated theory

Psychosocial Theory

Skill category

Critical thinking and analysis, reflection and reflexivity

See also: active listening, emotional intelligence, empathy, giving and receiving feedback, observational skills, questioning, reflective writing, use of self and reflexivity

Further reading

Rogers, M., and Allen, D. (2019) *Applying Critical Thinking and Analysis in Social Work*. London: Sage.

Reflective writing Consistent with **reflective practice**, reflective writing provides a purposeful activity in which you can analyse experiences, or your own practice, skills and responses to academic research, in order to learn and improve.

Reflective writing for an assignment should not involve merely describing a theory, method or something that happened. Nor does it mean writing down everything that you have learnt or read onto a page in an unstructured way. Reflective writing, like reflective practice, requires a clear line of thought, use of evidence or examples to illustrate your reflections, and an analytical approach.

Reflective writing is often presented in the first person. Consistent with reflective practice, it requires you to apply your knowledge (formal or tacit), thoughts and feelings to a topic to formulate a balanced argument and conclusion. An essential requirement of reflective writing is reading. Before you can apply your knowledge (formal or tacit), thoughts and feelings to a topic, you must first read around that topic as widely as you can within the time that you have.

Once you have read widely around the specific topic, we encourage you to structure you reflective writing around three core themes of recommendation, barrier and solution. See how these core themes are used to structure the hypothetical reflective writing example in the Skills in Action box below.

Skills in action

When you read the below example of reflective writing skills in action, consider how the writer develops a line of reasoning based on their own thoughts and experiences, and then links it to wider reading.

Please note that the references included in the example are fictitious and that different universities have different requirements and styles for writing and referencing. The approach shown below is just one example of an approach that you might take.

(Recommendation) After reading about crisis intervention (Rogers & Allen, 2020) I recognise that people who seek out support from social workers during an emergency are more likely to make the most progress. (Barrier) However, after considering the work of Allen (2020) I also understand that the decentralisation of social work agencies means that those people whose lives are characterised by oppression and marginalisation often feel that social work services are not accessible to them. The lack of accessible services suggests to me that when some people are in crisis, they might not know where to go for support. What is more significant, I also feel that their sense of isolation can be compounded with accompanying feelings of shame or embarrassment. (Solution) By way of solution, I support the conclusions of Allen and Rogers (2021) and believe that social work agencies need to engage in projects of community development so that services can be more accessible to those who need them. Being mindful of the nature of crisis, and the need for prompt and responsive support, I believe that sustainable support is arguably a key factor in the progress that comes from the experience of being in crisis. (Barrier) However, the task of ensuring accessibility, responsiveness, prompt support and community development in a time of international pandemic is a clear barrier to crisis intervention and the opportunity to provide services at those times and in those places where they are needed. (Solution) The response of social work to provide services at a time of national and international emergency … (and so on) …

In an assignment, reflective writing requires you to strike a balance between your personal perspective, and the requirements of good academic practice and rigorous thinking. Developing reflective writing skills in your social work training is essential. The skills that you develop now will be directly transferable to skills needed to produce analytical **assessments** and legal documents in practice.

Main associated theory

Psychosocial Theory

Skill category

Critical thinking and analysis, reflection and reflexivity

See also: case recording, evidence-informed practice

Further reading

Rogers, M., & Allen, D. (2019) *Applying Critical Thinking and Analysis in Social Work*. London: Sage.

Report writing Elsewhere in this book we have discussed other writing tasks (see chapters on **case recording** and **email communication**). Together, these three chapters illuminate the importance of writing skills in social work and, importantly, show that different approaches are needed for different writing tasks. The requirements when writing formal reports are different from case recording and emailing needs (albeit there will be some overlapping principles too). Formal reports might be required for: making referrals to other agencies; making requests for resources; court proceedings; child protection conferences; court applications to remove children into local authority care or in adoption cases; after a mental capacity **assessment** has been completed; or when using sections of the Mental Health Act 2007 to provide treatment.

To support evidence-based decision-making, be mindful that there could be several functions of a report including: to share information; to persuade and influence; to provide professional judgements, analysis and guidance to support decision-making. Reports should be produced with some core principles in mind:

1 The *purpose* of the report is clear.
2 All information provided is based on *evidence*.
3 The report has a strong *structure* and appropriate length with evidence and information that is broken down into accessible sections (use sub-headings and bullet points to make information easy to extract) to build a picture or argument.
4 All *sources of information* are clearly identified.

5   There is a clear delineation of *fact, opinion* and *analysis*.
6   *Language use* is appropriate for the report's *purpose* and *audience*.
7   The report is written *concisely* and all content is *relevant.*
8   Practical principles are attended to: page numbers are added; proofreading is undertaken (to identify errors); the report is signed and dated.
9   The report details all people who are copied into it (that is, to receive a copy).

Danger zone

Writing skills

*   *Spelling and word choice errors*: all professionally produced reports should be produced using word processing software and therefore there is no reason for any spelling errors. Word choices that are incorrect can change the whole meaning of the sentence or can make the meaning unclear.
*   *Ensure that your word choice is accessible*: for example, why use 'intangible' when 'unclear' will do? Or, why use 'skeptical' and not 'unsure'? Remember the advice of Jones (2016): KISS (**k**eep **i**t **s**imple, **s**tupid).
*   *Structure*: poor organisation and structure can result in repetition and a disconnected (rather than a developing) argument. This can significantly impact the response of the reader in terms of feeling sympathetic, ambivalent or frustrated with the content.
*   *Missing evidence*: if you make claims that are not supported by examples and evidence, the impact will be that the reader is not persuaded by your argument.

Any of these danger zones results in a report that undermines your professionalism and can ultimately result in lost credibility.

It is highly unlikely that you will be required to write a formal report that does *not* require you to integrate analysis alongside the necessary description and contextual information (Rogers & Allen, 2019). Analysis can include:

*   commentary on the significance and credibility of the information that you have gathered
*   analysis focused on impacts of decisions and actions
*   analysis focused on other influential factors whether at a micro or personal level (such an individual's employment status or ethnic background), at a meso-level (pertaining to the wider neighbourhood, e.g. the availability of community resources) or at a macro/structural level (such as the legal framework or dominant norms and social values)

- an exploration of emerging patterns in the life of the individual or family
- an evaluation of the information and/or situation (that is, the requirement for you to make professional judgements about the value of strengths and weaknesses of the individual/family/situation)
- analysis which includes contrast and comparison (assessing one piece of information in relation to another)
- some discussion of cause and effect.

Finally, it is perfectly acceptable to identify and name any information gaps that you have as you can articulate the additional information or action that is required. In doing so, you demonstrate skills in information gathering, assessment and evaluation, **critical thinking and analysis**. It shows that you have a comprehensive understanding of the individual, family or situation and can situate this in a broader context. If making recommendations, then do not merely describe what you think should happen next. You should provide evidence or a justification for each recommendation and, if necessary, underscore why this is the best option in this particular circumstance. If you can do all this in your report, then you demonstrate that you are a competent professional and critical thinker capable of providing a balanced and evidence-based report.

Main associated theory

Humanistic Theory

Skill category

Assessment, critical thinking and analysis

See also: chronologies, ecomapping, genograms

Further reading

Bogg, D. (2012) *Report Writing*. Maidenhead: Open University Press.

Rai, L. (2014) *Effective Writing for Social Work: Making a Difference*. Bristol: Policy Press.

Respecting confidentiality As you progress through your social work career, you will find yourself in situations where private and sensitive information is freely shared between professionals. This sharing of information is essential in matters related to **safeguarding** and public protection. Indeed, you may become so used to sharing private and sensitive information freely between professionals that there may be times when you are concerned that some organisations are not sharing information that you think is vital to your **assessment** and safety planning. However, you must remember that sharing private and sensitive information is subject to strict legislation and regulation. You could be breaking the law if you share information with people who have no right to access it.

Consider the example provided in the Stop–Reflect box below and see if you can answer the questions that are presented.

Stop-reflect

Talking about work outside of work

Tim and Julia are studying social work together and working at the same placement. On a Friday evening, after a particularly difficult week at work, they both agree to go out after work for an evening meal. In the restaurant, they sit down and look over the menu. After telling the waiter what they would like to eat, they start to talk about their work. They complain about a family that they have been working with and refer to individuals by name. They accuse the family of being hard to reach and refer to the father of the family in a very derogatory way. They do not notice the waiter standing close to the table. Engaged in their own debate, Tim and Julia agree on a course of action for the following week which involves using more statutory powers to work with the family. At the end of the meal, confident that the matter has been resolved, Tim and Julia both head home.

On Monday morning, the team manager of the placement phones Tim and Julia and asks them not to come into placement. The team manager explains that a concerns meeting is being convened because a formal complaint has been received from a member of the public who was at the restaurant that Tim and Julie went to on Friday evening. The complainant claimed that they were sitting opposite the pair and that the things that were being said in such a public place appalled them. The complainant said that he was a brother of the man that they were talking so rudely about and, as a result, knew which agency they worked for.

During the concerns meeting, it was decided that the placement offer would be withdrawn for both Tim and Julia.

1 Why do you think the placement made the decision to end the placement for Tim and Julia?
2 What have you learnt from this hypothetical example?

Confidentiality laws do not extend equally, and if there is a concern about the safety or welfare of a child, the conditions under which information can be shared may vary according to circumstances. For this reason, the skills associated with respecting confidentiality shown in the Top Tips box require you to respect the principles of individual privacy that apply to all of your relationships, both in and out of practice.

Things you must never do and things you must always do

As defined by the relevant data protection legislation, you must *never*:

- share information about the people who you work to support on social media
- take sensitive or confidential data home with you
- use your own electronic devices for work purposes
- talk to people outside of work about the people you are working to support.

As defined by the relevant data protection legislation, you must *always*:

- ensure that confidential information is only divulged with the consent of the person you are working to support or the person who has raised a concern to you
- share information with a relevant party based on a greater ethical requirement such as evidence of serious risk or the preservation of life.

Explain the nature of confidentiality to the people who you work to support, including those circumstances where confidentiality must be waived.

Main associated theory

Humanist Theory – but all actually apply

Skill category

All

See also: assessments, case recording, evidence-informed practice, reflective practice

BASW (2014) *The Code of Ethics for Social Work*. London: British Association of Social Workers. Available at: www.basw.co.uk/about-basw/code-ethics (accessed 25 January 2021).

Relevant Data Protection legislation according to the country within which you work.

Restorative practice is a model that binds theory, research and practice in diverse fields such as education, counselling, criminal justice and, finally, social work. It evolved from the concept and practices of restorative justice. Restorative justice is an approach to crime that moves away from the punishment model, rather it is concerned with resolving the injuries resulting from criminal behaviour by reconciling the needs

of victims, offenders, and the community. As such, there is a reparative function as restorative justice aims to repair the harm done (van Wormer, 2003).

Whilst restorative justice is a reactive approach which takes place after the event, restorative practice also includes the use of informal and formal processes that precede wrongdoing, those that proactively build relationships and a sense of community to prevent conflict and wrongdoing (Wachtel, 2016). Wachtel (2016) draws attention to the wider benefits as restorative practices helps to:

- reduce crime, violence and bullying
- improve human behaviour
- strengthen civil society
- provide effective leadership
- restore relationships.

In recent decades, restorative practice has grown exponentially in social work, which is unsurprising as a significant proportion of casework consists of working with persons or families who have been victimised or experienced some type of harm. In social work, family group conferences (FGCs), or family group decision-making (FGDM) as it is referred to across North America, has been the primary model growing in popularity across the globe since the 1980s.

FGCs originated in New Zealand as a response to concerns about the number of and outcomes for Maori children being taken into state care. The FGC model is based upon the concepts of democracy and empowerment as families are invited to make decisions in response to raised concerns. An FGC coordinator makes all arrangements and is a neutral guide through the process for the family. During the FGC, families and members of their support networks (including extended family and friends) meet privately, without professionals in the room, to make a plan to protect children in their own families from further abuse and neglect or to avoid the need for more punitive action (e.g. children being removed from their families to be accommodated by the state). Whilst designed for use within children and families social work, their use is wider as FGCs usage is growing across social care too in matters concerning elder abuse or mental health, for example.

Skills in action

The Fiddler Family

The Fiddler family included 25-year-old Yemesi, 28-year-old Ash and their son, 7-year-old Ben. Yemesi had a mild learning disability and poor mental health since experiencing post-natal depression (PND) following Ben's birth. Ben's social worker, Willow, was aware that Yemesi was struggling to cope and that she was feeling anxious and depressed. Ash was unemployed having struggled to find work as a plasterer since the firm he previously worked for went out of business. Ash also experienced poor mental health and had started to drink alcohol every day. The family were socially isolated with little money, no car and limited access to public transport. A police report was received following an incident of domestic abuse. Willow referred the family to the FGC service.

An FGC was held and attended by Yemesi, Ash and Ben as well as Yemesi's parents, older brother and Ash's sister. The extended family members had been unaware that Yemesi and Ash were both experiencing difficulties. Together the family was able to draw up a safety plan that included several supports:

1 Yemesi's mother agreed to look after Ben on two mornings each week to give Yemesi a break from her caring responsibilities.
2 On one of these mornings, Ash's sister agreed to collect Yemesi and drive her to a nearby community centre that ran a support group for women living with PND.
3 Ash's sister would also visit every Thursday morning to take Yemesi to the supermarket for the weekly shop and help her to plan for meals and budget.
4 To address the isolation of the family, on the last weekend in every month Yemesi, Ash and Ben would be collected by Yemesi's brother and driven to their parents for a family meal.
5 Ash agreed to make an appointment with his GP to discuss his mental health and alcohol use.
6 Yemesi found it difficult to manage her medication (frequently forgetting once she got up and became preoccupied with looking after Ben) which, obviously exacerbated her mental health condition. Yemesi's father offered to buy a medicine storage box (with daily compartments) and a pill reminder alarm.
7 Ash agreed to attend a free course offered by the employment agency to extend his skills and employability.

Three months after the FGC, a review was undertaken led by the FGC coordinator with the Fiddler family and Willow in attendance. There had been no further incidents of domestic abuse. Yemesi was taking her medication regularly, attending the support group and generally feeling less anxious and more in control. Ash had started a part-time job in the local newsagents. He wasn't using his skill in plastering but his self-esteem had improved and he wasn't drinking every day. A further review date was set, but Willow was happy that the safety plan arrangements were supporting the family to make positive steps.

Main associated theory

Humanistic Theory, Ecological Theory

Skill category

Interventions, relational practice

See also: advocacy, anti-discriminatory practice, anti-oppressive practice, conflict management and resolution, empowering and enabling, ethical practice, mediation

Further reading

Sen, R. & Webb, C. (2019) Exploring the declining rates of state social work intervention in an English local authority using family group conferences. *Child and Youth Services Review*. Available at: www.sciencedirect.com/science/article/pii/S0190740918311009 (accessed 25 January 2021).

Risk assessment and risk management are core issues in social work. The skills needed to recognise the risks posed by others enable you to develop opportunities for safer practice.

In child and family work, your role is to protect children from harm. In criminal justice, your role is to protect the community, and in community care, your role is to protect the vulnerable. However, in each example, you also have to protect yourself from the risks associated with your task.

Beck's (1992) influential text shows us that risk is a complex practice issue. As the social work profession consists of an amazingly diverse group of practitioners, there will always be different views and assumption on the nature of risk, including how to assess and manage it effectively (Kemshall, Wilkinson & Baker, 2013). As we will now consider in using the activity in the Stop–Reflect box below, creating a consistent approach to risk assessment is essential, but may not be achievable unless our assumptions are exposed to scrutiny.

Stop–reflect

The risk of smacking a child

Personal, professional and public attitudes towards risk are often developed and normalised by our socialisation. By way of example, consider the question 'Is it acceptable to smack a child?'

In response to this question, consider how much of your answer is informed by your own childhood, your knowledge of theories associated to human growth and development, your interpretation of law and safeguarding policy.

It is our prediction that there will be variable responses to the question 'Is it acceptable to smack a child?' Some readers may argue that it is not acceptable to smack a child in any circumstance. Other readers may argue that it is acceptable so long as the smack does not constitute abuse.

The point that we are making is that in relation to the act of smacking a child, there will be inconsistent views, opinions and reactions.

How might inconsistent views impact on a risk assessment of a foster carer who has told you that they have smacked their child?

The need to expose social work **assessments** and assumptions to scrutiny has been accentuated in the various inquiries and reviews that consider **safeguarding** issues and identify potential for improvement. Highlighting specific examples of variable risk tolerance (like that which might be associated with your opinion on smacking), the inquiries and reviews have created socio-political pressure that has resulted in risk averse social work practice (Warner, 2015). In other words, the pressure for social workers, and others involved in the task of public protection, to be disinclined or reluctant to tolerate risk.

The advantage of risk averse practice, if we could be so bold, is that there is an opportunity to develop more preventative services that offer flexible and accessible support at those times and places where they are needed. The reality of practice is, however, somewhat different. High caseloads and shrinking budgets mean that risk averse practice is also competing with heightened thresholds, the level used to determine whether or not social work intervention is needed. Not only does the competition between adverse practice and heightened thresholds destabilise any possible advantage that we advance in the spirit of fairness, it also results in structural inequality that becomes clearly visible when the organisation of social work makes oppressive assumptions about the people you are working to support.

It is also important to point out that the assumptions that inform a risk assessment can be based on an assessment of present factors, but that also extend to include potential future risk factors. Where a predictive assessment of potential future risks occurs, social work action is then tailored to prevent or reduce a risk that may or may not exist in the present. It is at this point that the care and control debate and Foucault's work on governmentality become particularly important (see for example Hardy, 2015) and it is why the following Top Tips are important.

Top tips

Risk assessment skills

1 When conducting a risk assessment, involve the people who you are working to support and the wider professional network if appropriate.
2 Use supervision as a method to scrutinise your assumptions. Try to replace your stereotypes with ethical decision-making through which the people you are working to support are engaged as an expert in managing their own life.
3 Extend the principle of 'least restrictive intervention' to your assessment. Recognise that any intervention should curtail people's basic rights and freedoms as little as possible.
4 Ensure that the assessments, interventions, monitoring and controls introduced to manage risk are proportionate to the scale of the risk being managed.

(Continued)

5   Recognise that behaviour is contextual, and that every environment will have formal or informal mechanisms for the assessment and management of risk. For this reason, the context of behaviour needs to be factored into the risk management process.
6   Discuss examples of risk in your team meetings. Try to develop an understanding that risk is nuanced and subtle rather than rule bound.

It is no simple task to risk assess effectively. Your primary aim as a social worker is to promote safety and welfare whilst supporting people to live as independently as possible and to facilitate opportunities for them to contribute to the wider society and fulfil their personal aspirations. At all times, you need to manage risk alongside your duty to respect rights, address need and meet other formal obligations. You cannot afford to be complacent as you seek to build a safer society. At times you will need to engage in risk taking as well as risk minimisation, risk management as well as risk assessment, so that the people you work to support can experience the most inclusive intervention as well as the least restrictive one.

In your own approach to the risk assessment, it is vital that you engage in **reflective practice** and take time to scrutinise your own assumptions. Each organisation that you work in will have a specific risk assessment framework. You would do well to take time to talk to your practice educator, supervisor or manager about this framework and about how the organisation's attitude towards risk derives from or drives local policies and practices.

Main associated theory

Crisis Intervention Theory – but all actually apply

Skill category

Assessment, interventions

See also: anti-oppressive practice, evidence-informed practice

Further reading

Beck, U. (1992) *Risk Society: Towards a New Modernity*. London: Sage.

Broadhurst, K., Hall, C., Wastell, D., White, S. & Pithouse, A. (2010) Risk, instrumentalism and the humane project in social work: Identifying the informal logics of risk management in children's statutory services. *British Journal of Social Work*, 40: 1046–1064.

Hardy, M. (2015) *Governing Risk: Care and Control in Contemporary Social Work*. London: Palgrave Macmillan.

Kemshall, H., Wilkinson, B. & Baker, K. (2013) *Working with Risk: Skills for Contemporary Social Work*. Cambridge: Polity.

Warner, J. (2015) *The Emotional Politics of Social Work and Child Protection*. Bristol: Policy Press.

Root cause analysis (RCA) is an umbrella term describing methods
and tools for the structured **assessment** process. In simple terms, RCA involves tracing a problem to its origin. In social work, the most effective examples of intervention are those that seek to address the cause of the problem rather than the effect. If we only respond to the effect of a problem, the packages of support that we implement might be required over and over again. However, if we can extend our assessments and try to identify the cause of the problem, we may be in a better position to support people to live as independently as possible.

RCA is a technique that helps people answer the question of why the problem occurred in the first place. Applied to adverse childhood experiences, social determinants of health, structural inequality and other areas, it seeks to identify the origin of a 'problem' using a specific set of steps, which can be supported by associated tools and methods, to find the primary cause of the problem.

Consistent with systems theory and narrative theories (Rogers et al., 2020) RCA assumes that events in a person's life are interrelated. An action or an event in one area of the system triggers an action or an event in another. As shown in the Skills in Action box below, by tracing back these actions or events in a formal assessment framework, you may begin to discover where the problem started and how it grew into the symptom you are now facing.

Skills in action

Root cause analysis in progress

Jess is living with anxiety. She tells her social worker, Eve, that her anxiety is making her panic when she is mixing with other people. Eve guides Jess through the following series of questions, being sensitive to Jess's emotions at all times.

1 *Explore and define the problem.* Eve starts by asking Jess to define anxiety. She asks Jess to explain what happens when she is anxious and what the symptoms are.
2 *Collect information about the problem.* Eve then asks Jess to explain how she knows that a problem with anxiety exists. Eve asks Jess to explain how she knows that her feelings are associated to anxiety and not nervousness or embarrassment. Eve then asks Jess to consider how long anxiety has existed and what impact anxiety has on her life.

(Continued)

3 *Identify possible causal factors.* Eve asks Jess to describe events that can make anxiety worse and what conditions allow the anxiety to occur. Once she has a full understanding of the casual factors, Eve asks Jess to consider what other problems are caused by anxiety.

4 *Identify the root cause(s).* Eve then asks Jess to consider when she realised that anxiety was influencing her life. She asks Jess about the occasions that can cause anxiety to occur and encourages her to give examples of when anxiety was not a problem.

5 *Recommend and implement solutions.* Eve asks Jess to consider what she can do to reduce the ability of anxiety to make her panic. She asks how that solution could be implemented and how Jess would know if the solution had worked. To conclude, Eve asks Jess to consider the risks of implementing the solution.

Adapted from Okes, 2009.

Main associated theory

Crisis Intervention Theory, Systems Theory

Skill category

Assessments, critical thinking and analysis

See also: active listening, empathy, observational skills, questioning, risk assessment

Further reading

Okes, D. (2009) *Root Cause Analysis: The Core of Problem Solving and Corrective Action.* Milwaukee, WI: ASQ Quality Press.

S

Safeguarding is a complex area of social work practice that is underpinned by a comprehensive historical, legal and policy context. Understanding this context is essential since you will only seek to support and safeguard people when these laws and policies enable you to do so. Once knowledge of the legal basis for intervention in the lives of others have been established, you will then need to consider the values, theories and methods that are used to safeguard people from harm.

The field of concern for safeguarding practitioners presents a constantly changing challenge that reflects developments in technology, social tolerances and the overarching challenges that relate to and are compounded by structural discrimination. As our contemporary knowledge and understating of risk evolves so does our understanding of safeguarding concern. In addition to broad definitions of physical, sexual and emotional abuse and neglect, safeguarding practitioners are also seeking to assess and prevent self-neglect, sexual exploitation, substance misuse, domestic violence, human trafficking, financial abuse, female genital mutilation, forced marriages, non-organic failure to thrive, controlling behaviour, child on parent abuse, online grooming and fraud.

Working to protect others from harm is a difficult and complex activity. For this reason, the Stop–Reflect box below encourages you to think about how supervision, case work discussions and counselling could help prevent or minimise the potential impact of vicarious trauma that you experience through others.

Stop–reflect

The emotional burden of safeguarding practice

We recognise that the behaviours and experiences associated with abuse and neglect might be upsetting for you. There has been a good deal written on the challenges associated with vicarious trauma, but there is an equal amount of information on the advantages of support that is offered to practitioners through supervision, counselling and peer mentoring. It is worth remembering that an interprofessional team that includes the police usually supports safeguarding practice. The whole team approach to safeguarding and the communities of practice within which you operate serve to safeguard people who are at risk of harm, but they also help to support your safety and wellbeing.

What type of support do you think you might need if you were to work in the field of safeguarding?

A number of skills needed for safeguarding practice are included in this book. At all times you should be alert to the signs and indicators of abuse, understand harm and risk, and be able to articulate your duties and responsibilities when responding to a disclosure. You will also need to develop the skills needed to keep yourself safe and to manage the stress and stains of safeguarding others. All of these skills and more should be supported throughout your social work training.

In our experience, assessing and responding to safeguarding concerns can be easier where there is clear evidence of harm. However, there will be some situations where your **assessment** involves the verification of harm. It is common for social work intervention to begin with a referral. This referral, sometimes provided by a concerned individual, indicates details of alleged abuse and neglect. Your responsibility in this situation would be to work with other professionals to verify the accuracy of this allegation. It is in the verification process that the skill for safeguarding practice emerges.

Throughout the history of public protection and safeguarding practice, tolerance of risk has changed. Most recently, safeguarding professionals have been accused of being slow to respond to risk (Featherstone, Morris and White, 2014). Delay, a preoccupation with structural inequality, humanistic practices and a genuine positive regard for all have been highlighted as some of the factors of professional practice that have resulted in professionals failing to protect those who are most vulnerable (Chisnell and Kelly, 2016).

The consequential reaction in safeguarding policy requires us to assume the presence of risk in our interventions (Smeeton, 2020). In other words, to assume that the allegation of abuse and neglect is an accurate representation of risk. With this assumption in mind, safeguarding practitioners then seek evidence to disprove this hypothesis. However, unless we reflect on this responsibility carefully, we might begin to see how any encouragement to assume risk, and the presence of harm, could stick a blade through the heart of human rights legislation and social work values and ethics.

For safeguarding practice, one of the most important skills, from which many of the others included in this book will follow, is the ability to recognise who is the focus of your intervention. If there is an allegation that a parent has assaulted a child, we assume risk and work with the police if necessary, to speak to the child and any other relevant person to identify evidence of safety. We do this to protect the child because we are primarily interested in the welfare of the child. In the same way, if there is an allegation that an adult carer is financially abusing somebody who they care for, we assume risk but gather evidence to verify this hypothesis. We do this to protect the person who is most vulnerable.

Remembering who is the primary focus of safeguarding practice helps to ensure that practice remains within the comprehensive legal and policy context. From this position follows another important skill. The skill of **anti-oppressive practice** and the location of an approach to intervention that sits between cultural relativism and pathologising reactions that are described in the Theory Explained box below.

Theory explained

Cultural relativism and pathologising reactions

Cultural relativism is a term used to describe the attribution of behaviour to a culture. For example, in our work with Gypsy and Traveller families, we have seen social work reports describing domestic violence as being normal within the 'Gypsy' culture. Attributing any behaviour to a culture is wrong because it assumes that all people who identify with that culture are complicit in that behaviour, belief, and tradition or custom. Cultural relativist reactions can lead to inaction in safeguarding practice.

Pathologising reactions can be seen in those occasions where risk is normalised or explained by attributing it to perceived personal, behavioural or cultural deficits. For example, in our work with victims of domestic abuse, we have seen social work reports describing women as being unable to leave the perpetrator because they are unable to recognise or prioritise the welfare of their children. Attributing any risk to the action of the victim not only adds to the absence of blame, but it also maintains a deficit view of women. Pathologising reactions can lead to overreaction in safeguarding practice.

Operating across a spectrum of possible reactions to risk, you will do well to use supervision to consider how and why your assumption and acceptance of risk reflects the evidence presented, rather than cultural relativism and pathologising reactions. We would also encourage a sustained approach to reflective and reflexive practice throughout the safeguarding process. In this way, your work to safeguard the welfare of others might also serve to safeguard the laws, policies, theories and methods that underpin your practice.

Main associated theory

Humanistic Theory – but all actually apply

Skill category

All

See also: ethical practice, person-centred communication, person-centred planning, reflective practice, risk assessments

Further reading

Chisnell, C. & Kelly, C. (2016). *Safeguarding in Social Work Practice: A Lifespan Approach.* Los Angeles: Learning Matters.

HM Government (2018) *Working Together to Safeguard Children: A Guide to Inter-agency Working to Safeguard and Promote the Welfare of Children.* London: HM Government.

Setting and maintaining professional boundaries

As social work is a relationship-based activity, it is important that you recognise how your attempts to transfer power, to build trust, to engage people and listen to their perspectives may lead to situations where the people who you are working to support may develop some level of emotional dependence on you.

As you develop close relationships with the people you are working to support, it is important that you are clear about what type of behaviour is appropriate. Throughout this book, we have highlighted the skills associated with social work practice, but we have not considered the importance of setting and maintaining professional boundaries in an equal way.

Appropriate relationships require you to recognise that you have considerable power. As you will be working with people who are vulnerable, a large proportion of your work will seek to facilitate opportunities to empower, enable, encourage and support them as much as possible. However, as shown in the Stop–Reflect box below, you must remember the importance of setting limits and agreements about what is acceptable and unacceptable behaviour. You must also recognise when your conduct, and the conduct of others, might cross the invisible line that separates professional and unprofessional practice.

Stop–reflect

When relationships cross the professional boundary

Blessing is working in a refuge designed to support women and children who are experiencing domestic violence. She has recently started to support a woman called Olivia.

After a few weeks, others living and working in the refuge begin to notice that Olivia is developing a strong attachment to Blessing. They have noticed that Olivia will often ask Blessing to stay on at the refuge, even after her shift has finished, so that they can talk. One afternoon, Olivia admits to having strong feelings for Blessing. Blessing also recognises that her relationship with Olivia is becoming too intimate.

In relation to setting and maintaining professional boundaries, what do you think Blessing and her manager can do to ensure professional practice?

Some suggestions might include:

- establishing a contract that sets out the expectations and limitations of the working relationship
- allocating a different key worker to Olivia
- increasing supervision for Blessing
- re-focusing on the codes of conduct for social work.

The key to setting and maintaining professional boundaries is understanding the difference between a professional and a personal relationship. In a professional social work relationship, you are responsible for the welfare of the person who you are working to support. For this reason, there are rules and boundaries that guide expectations about your conduct.

At all times, you are expected to place the needs of the people who you work to support at the centre of any decisions that you make about them and their lives, but information about yourself and your personal life should not be disclosed. You should also be aware of conflicts of interest. You should not hold more than one type of relationship with the people you are working to support. You cannot be their social worker and their friend. It is important, therefore, that you understand the limitations of your role and of your professional capabilities. If you feel ill equipped, unprepared or unable to set and maintain professional boundaries, you should seek support and advice from your manager.

Main associated theory

Humanistic Theory and Psychosocial Theory – but all actually apply

Skill category

Relational practice, anti-oppressive practice

See also: critical thinking and analysis, emotional intelligence, ethical practice

Further reading

Cooper, F. (2012) *Professional Boundaries in Social Work and Social Care: A Practical Guide to Understanding, Maintaining and Managing your Professional Boundaries.* London: Jessica Kingsley.

Solution-focused practice During the 1980s, Steve de Shazer and colleagues devised a therapeutic technique that provided an alternative to approaches that focused on deficits and problems (Shennan, 2019). Solution-focused practice values people as individuals who have strengths and resources. The approach is built upon the notion that individuals have the capacity to identify their own solutions to their problems. Specifically, when you employ the techniques of solution-focused practice you guide an individual to reflect on past experience and behaviours to identify incidences when positive outcomes have been achieved with the intention that such outcomes can be achieved once more.

Reflecting relationship-based principles, Shennan (2019: 2) describes solution-focused practice as a 'talking-based activity ... and one of the main activities of a solution-focused practitioner is to ask questions'. However, asking questions is not the limit of solution-focused practice, rather it is a specific approach that relies upon a set of solution-focused **questioning** techniques to enhance direct work with individuals. Solution-focused techniques are designed to help people move towards identifying solutions and away from self-criticism, self-blame and dwelling on past issues or problems. These goal-oriented techniques help individuals to move in a future-oriented direction. The core techniques of solution-focused practice are detailed here:

Problem-free talk: this represents an important first step in moving in a solution-focused and future-oriented direction. Try to encourage problem-free talk during your time with a person or their family. This helps them to move away from a position where they focus on the problem towards an imagined future where there is an achievable solution. In adopting problem-free talk at the start of any **home visit** or session, you are communicating an important message (that the person or family is not defined by the problem).

Scaling questions: scaling is a practical technique in which you ask the individual to reflect on their feelings, perspective or their situation in a rating exercise using a scale of 1 to 10: 1 is the worst case and 10 represents no problem at all. If a person gets 'stuck' and finds it difficult to mentally and emotionally move beyond the focus on the problem, then scaling can help to establish either a more pragmatic view of that problem or it can help to set a baseline. Once someone has scaled a feeling, perspective or situation, at the next visit or session you can revisit this to see what change has occurred. In this way, scaling questions are useful in the process of setting small goals and being able to measure these against previous thoughts, feelings or the situation.

Exception seeking: this is an important technique in solution-focused practice as by actively listening to a person, you will be able to identify a time when the problem was either absent, not as significant, or when the individual had managed the problem well (the exception to the problem). As O'Connell and Palmer (2005) point out, there are always exceptions waiting to be found. In this process, you will be able to highlight the skills, capability or strategy that the person has previously drawn on and encourage them to envisage doing so again. You can elicit this information by using other solution-focused techniques such as *competence seeking* or *coping questions* (where you ask the individual to describe a time when they have coped with the problem).

Competence seeking: this technique explicitly encourages a person to identify and acknowledge their own resources, strengths and qualities. You are asking the person to look in a mirror and identify positives. Some individuals can find this to be challenging, but it is of particular value if this is the case as it indicates that they have become so immersed in their problems that they may have lost sight and confidence in their ability to effect change.

Skills in action

Solution-focused question examples

Scaling questions:

* On a scale of 1 to 10, with 1 being not very much at all and 10 being as much as you can imagine, how confident are you about being able to do the tasks we have agreed?
* On a scale of 1 to 5, 1 being that it is very likely and 5 being it is not a priority, how likely is it that you will attend the first meeting of the Freedom Programme*? What would help to move you one number higher on that scale?

Exception seeking questions:

* When have you been able to manage your daughter's behaviour without expressing your anger or resorting to physical punishments? What happened?
* What happened that time when you overcame those feelings of anger/sadness/apathy/frustration?

Competence seeking questions:

* What discipline methods have worked with your son?
* What activities have you and your child enjoyed together in the past?
* What goals have you achieved so far in your life?
* How have you handled this problem successfully in the past?

*A programme for survivors of domestic abuse.

The miracle question: finally, the miracle question. This is one of the core techniques of solution-focused practice. Over the years, it has been reframed in various different ways, but essentially this questioning technique is at the very heart of solution-focused practice. Using this technique, you ask the person to imagine that a miracle occurs:

Now, I want to ask you a strange question. Suppose that while you are sleeping tonight and the entire house is quiet, a miracle happens. The miracle is that the problem which brought you here is solved. However, because you are sleeping, you don't know that the miracle has happened. So, when you wake up tomorrow morning, what will be different that will tell you that a miracle has happened and the problem which brought you here is solved? (DeJong & Berg, 1998: 77–78)

You can reword this in any way that feels more natural and comfortable for you, but the important thing is that the miracle question encourages the individual to engage in imagining a future where the problem has disappeared.

Solution-focused practice

Some people do not easily talk about their innermost thoughts and feelings. People with poor self-esteem, low confidence, or with poor mental health might find this particularly challenging and stressful. Can you think of ways you might encourage a person to do this?

Perhaps you could ask someone to draw a picture, or you could set a task from one meeting to the next and ask that person to write an account that portrays the strengths and resources that they feel they have or had in the past. Their picture or written account might depict a time when things were going well and you might ask them to describe what was different about that time. Alternatively, you might ask them to portray the 'miracle' in a drawing or written account.

If you are undertaking direct work with children or young people, there are solution-focused boardgames that have been devised to help to elicit and encourage conversations that focus on strengths, talents and positive aspects of a young person's character and situation. These can be most helpful in triggering conversations for children and young people who are not used to talking in a positive way about themselves or their lives.

Main associated theory

Humanistic Theory, Empowerment Theory, Psychological Theory

Skill category

Assessment, interventions

See also: active listening, building resilience, counselling skills, empowerment and enabling, motivational interviewing, task-centred work

Further reading

Shennan, G. (2019) *Solution-focused Practice: Effective Communication to Facilitate Change* (2nd edn). Basingstoke: Palgrave Macmillan.

Turnell, A. (2017) *The Signs of Safety: Comprehensive Briefing Paper*. Perth, Australia: Resolutions Consultancy.

Systemic practice techniques

The systemic approach originated in the field of family therapy. It is based on ecological systems theory which places importance upon relationships and acknowledges that individuals are embedded in their social context (Dallos & Draper, 2010). In this way, a person's capacity for growth and change is always influenced by their relationships and the wider processes and systems in which the individual and/or family exists. The growth of systemic practice in social work emerged from the 'Hackney Model', also known as the 'Reclaiming Social Work' model (Goodman & Trowler, 2011). The original model was designed to incorporate small pods of workers consisting of: a consultant social worker (the case holder for all work in the pod), a social worker, a childcare coordinator, a family therapist and a pod coordinator (an administrative role). The team benefitted from clinical supervision in a group format that was delivered by a clinical psychologist.

Early reviews of the model's implementation were mixed with some critiques outlining the different interpretations by local authorities as problematic (Pemberton, 2013). Contrasting reviews reported high quality practice and evidence of systemic ideas and change (Forrester et al., 2013) and in 2017 an evaluation of the Children's Social Care Innovation Programme recommended that policy-makers promote systemic social work (Sebba et al., 2017). This recommendation was based on the finding that outcomes improved following the inclusion of a systemic approach. Sebba et al. (2017: 70) argued that a systemic approach facilitated 'high quality case discussion, that is family-focused, and strengths-based, to build families/young people's capacity to address their own problems more effectively'.

Elsewhere in this book there are examples of techniques that can be used within a systemic approach such as the completion of a **genogram** or **ecomap**. There are additional techniques that you can employ to embed the principles of systemic practice:

> *Vision statement:* a vision statement is something that you create in partnership with an individual or family to help them to identify where they see themselves in the present and where they would like to be in the future. There are different ways to approach this activity. One approach could be to ask a parent or carer to state how they think their children would describe them as a parent or carer and then to imagine how they would like their children to describe them as a parent or carer in 20 years' time. This provides a benchmark and by comparing the two you enable the parent or carer to reflect on how they might move towards the vision and aspire to conform to that depiction of them in 20 years' time. To achieve this goal, you encourage the parent or carer to identify current challenges and the ways that these might be faced and overcome. It is much more empowering to ask somebody to identify challenges and solutions than for you to articulate your view as the authentic and overriding one and, at the same time, assert your position of power.

Stop–reflect

The art of visioning

Think about your life and identify one aspect of it that you would like to change. It may be that you need to improve your diet, study for the qualification that is blocking your

(Continued)

promotion at work, or address the guilt that you carry as a result of falling out with your brother last year over something rather trivial.

Consider the latter example, envisage that this relationship is fixed in five years' time and you have rekindled the supportive and close relationship that you previously enjoyed. How will you achieve this? Think about the first step to reaching this goal.

Circular questioning: another useful tool in systemic practice is circular questioning. This technique helps a person to look at something from a different perspective. It can enable a person to reflect on an existing situation, or it can be used to introduce an alternative idea, option or information. An example of circular questioning might involve asking a parent or carer to consider what their child, young person or cared-for adult might think about the current circumstances and the parent or carer's ideas/decisions/actions or the situation more broadly. In this way, you encourage that individual to be empathic and put themselves in someone else's shoes. Conversely, you might ask a child, young person or cared-for adult to reflect on the ideas/decision/ actions of their parent or carer to try to see things from their perspective. The point of circular questioning is to support a person to shift their thinking away from themselves, to consider the perspectives and motivations of another person who is important in their family system or support network. It can be used to diffuse tense situations. For example, a carer might say:

Joe flies off the handle whenever I suggest that we clean up his bedroom. He shouts at me to stay out of his room. I mean *shouts*. But it's a basic part of life skills training, and it smells. It's unhygienic. I tell him that he lives in shared accommodation and needs to follow rules.

Your response might be to encourage Joe to tell his carer why he 'flies off the handle'. Imagine that you lived in shared accommodation in which the only private space is your bedroom, or that there is a particular reason for the smell in the room that is embarrass-ing. There could be lots of reasons for Joe's reaction and you should try to help the carer to understand this situation from Joe's perspective.

Circular questioning can enable individuals or families to move forward if they reach an impasse (become 'stuck'). The technique can be used in conversations about future decisions or actions by asking the individual how another person might react.

Danger zone

Some barriers to implementing systemic practice techniques include:

- Individuals become so focused on the 'problem' and cannot see the other person's point of view.
- As a social worker, you rely too much on the techniques of systemic practice to the neglect of being reflective and understanding your impact on the relationship or situation.
- Using the techniques and a systemic approach in general can be hampered by the policies and priorities of your agency.
- Pressures of time and timely decision-making can result in a tokenistic approach to circularity and reflexivity resulting in hypotheses and judgements recreating pathologising discourses. (Bingle & Middleton, 2019)

Main associated theory

Systems Theory

Skill category

Assessment, interventions

See also: active listening, building resilience, counselling skills, critical thinking and analysis, empowerment and enabling, motivational interviewing, solution-focused practice, task-centred work

Further reading

Jude, J. & Rospierska, D. (2015) Embedding an integrative systemic style of working within a social care context. *Practice*, 27(3): 215–232.

T

Task-centred practice As you find when you read other chapters in this book, models for social work often have their roots in other disciplines or areas of practice (counselling and family therapy, for example). Task-centred practice is different as it was developed for social work and emerged out of research undertaken by Reid and Shyne (1969) in the USA. Task-centred practice provides a systematic model for working in partnership with people to identify and solve an identifiable problem. It does not have a distinct theory base (Marsh, 2008); it is a practical model to be used on a short-term basis. Task-centred practice involves working in partnership with an individual to identify specific goals that can be achieved by small steps or tasks. It is important that the individual identifies the goals, not you as their social worker. Task-centred practice is about working *with* people, not *for* people (Edmondson, 2020).

Enabling an individual to identify the goals and tasks helps you to assess their level of motivation to achieve the outcomes that they have identified. It also enables you to assess whether they have the skills, knowledge, resources and strengths to achieve the goals set (Trevithick, 2012). This is important as the agreed tasks need to be realistic and achievable; the last thing that you would wish to do is to set someone up to fail. If someone lacks or has limited skills, knowledge and resources at the time that you agree a goal and the tasks needed to achieve it, this then enables you to discern the amount and type of support that you will need to give that person to achieve their goals.

Stop-reflect

Opportunities for task-centred practice

Think about the broad areas of practice in social work (children and families services, mental health, adult social care) and the distinct areas and themes within each (care leavers, domestic abuse, older adults, family support, substance misuse). Can you think of aspects of social work in these areas where you might employ task-centred practice?

Here are some examples:

- *Improving relationships*: **mediation** between a parent and their adolescent child, enhancing community engagement, addressing social isolation.
- *Life skills*: budgeting, cooking, travelling on public transport.
- *Psychological distress*: supporting someone through loss, grief or bereavement.
- *Life transitions*: supporting care leavers to move out of their foster home, assisting one partner to come to terms with their partner's move to a care home.

- *Treatment and medical issues*: assisting someone to manage a medical programme of treatment, supporting someone to access mental health support.

This list is merely indicative and there are many, many more everyday examples that could be applied.

Depending on the goal, the support that people need may vary considerably. It might be that you coach someone to undertake a telephone call or approach someone for information. It may be that in deciding tasks, you both agree to undertake particular ones. In this part of the negotiation, it is important to remember that the core principles of task-centred work are focused on consolidating and building upon existing skills and resources of the individual in ways that are proportionate and relative to their existing lives.

Skills in action

Task-centred practice: Geoff

Geoff, a 62-year-old retired fire fighter, was referred to social care services by his community psychiatric nurse (CPN). Geoff had become very isolated since the death of his wife one year earlier. Isolation and loneliness were exacerbating his existing mental health condition. Geoff had been self-neglecting (not eating regularly nor attending to personal care and hygiene). The CPN referred Geoff with his consent. Margritte, a social worker located with the adult social care team in Newtown, was allocated the referral information as a new case. Margritte made contact with Geoff and scheduled a **home visit**.

On this visit Margritte spent some time building rapport with Geoff, which she found to be quite easy because Geoff obviously liked gardening as his front garden was full of beautiful plants (although clearly these had been a little bit neglected of late) and Margritte loved gardening too. Over the course of the visit Geoff admitted that he was lonely and had felt suicidal on occasion. With Margritte's support Geoff was able to admit that he did want to address his loneliness, get on top of looking after himself and his home and try to prevent his mental health from deteriorating further. Margritte asked about Geoff's family. Geoff described his daughter, Julie, and grandson as a 'lifeline' but admitted that he'd avoided Julie in the past few weeks as he did not want her to see him in a state as he knew that she'd worry. He did not want to be a burden or worry his family more than he had already done.

Margritte felt that Geoff had enough motivation to make some small changes to move towards reaching his goals: to feel back in control of his life, to be more connected to his family, and less socially isolated and lonely. Margritte and Geoff were able to identify two tasks that could be achieved in the two weeks until Margritte visited again. First, Geoff was to contact his daughter to suggest a day out to the local stately home which had an

(Continued)

179

animal farm, play park and beautiful garden. Second, Margritte said that she would make a telephone call to the Green Project, a local gardening project that needed volunteers to work with children and young people with learning disabilities. Geoff agreed that he would never have thought of doing anything like that but he'd give it a go.

Main associated theory

Task-Centred Theory

Skill category

Intervention

See also: active listening, advocacy, building resilience, counselling skills, empowerment and enabling, motivational interviewing, solution-focused practice

Further reading

Marsh, P. (2008) Task-centred work. In M. Davies (ed.) *The Blackwell Companion to Social Work* (3rd edn). Oxford: Blackwell Publishing.

Telephone skills Having a positive initial contact or introduction in any circumstances can be critical to an effective working relationship. First contact is often made via a telephone call in order to arrange a home visit or initial meeting; see the Stop–Reflect box for an example of how to do this effectively.

Stop–reflect

Introducing yourself

Imagine that you are the person who is due to receive a call from a social worker. What would you like them to consider before they call you? For example, do you have a preferred time, that is, avoiding meal times or the school run hour? Do you have a preference in how someone greets you, that is, would you prefer someone to use your first name or to take a more formal approach, using your title and surname, for example, addressing you as Mr/Mrs/Ms/Dr Ryan? What information would you like to get from that initial contact with a social worker: name, role, purpose of the visit?

Skills in action

Mustafa is a new social worker in a duty and assessment team. He needs to make an appointment to visit Carys Jones and her family as the school that she attends has made a referral due to concerns around neglect. Thirteen-year-old Carys mostly relies on a wheelchair as she has a congenital disease affecting her mobility and some loss of control of her limbs on her left side. The school have reported their concerns that for some weeks Carys has appeared gradually more unkempt (in a dirty and smelly school uniform). She is often hungry. The school are aware that her parents separated some months ago and they have been trying to call them in for a meeting, but have found it difficult to get either parent to turn up when meetings have been arranged. Mustafa makes a telephone call to Carys's mother to arrange a home visit:

Mustafa: Hello, is this Mrs Jones?
Mrs Jones: Yes, who's this?
Mustafa: My name is Mustafa Shakir. I am a social worker from Shoretown Services. Is now a good time to have a quick chat with you?
Mrs Jones: Yes. What is it?
Mustafa:| I have received a call from Carys's school as they are a little concerned about Carys. I think they have tried to hold a meeting with you about this. I'd really like to arrange a time to visit you to discuss this and see if there is any support that we can provide Carys. Are there any days or times that are not suitable for you?
Mrs Jones: Any day is fine. School finish time is no good though.
Mustafa: Of course, not a problem. I have some time on Wednesday afternoon after the school finish; would 4 p.m. be ok? Then I can chat with Carys too.
Mrs Jones: Yes, that is fine.
Mustafa: I have your address as 3 Lymn Road; is that correct? [Confirms address]. My telephone number is 01234 in case you need to contact me before Wednesday or need to rearrange. I look forward to meeting you then.

Mustafa is satisfied that he has conducted a telephone call to Mrs Jones in a respectful manner and prepares for the home visit.

There are obvious differences between face-to-face and telephone conversations such as not being able to see the other person. This limits the ability to 'read' the other person's **non-verbal communication** (body language, facial gestures) but someone's tone of voice can be highly informative. Remember to use your own tone of voice consciously to convey information (for example, you can convey respect, authority or empathy). The Top Tips box contains some other tips for managing telephone communications.

Top tips

Telephone skills

- When you make a telephone call, always check that the person who answers is the person that you need to speak to (don't assume it is just because they have answered).

(Continued)

- If you receive a telephone call, always make sure you take the name and telephone number of the caller (and write this down).
- Always give your name, explain who you are and why you are calling.
- It is respectful to check with the person that you have called that this is a convenient time to talk.
- Remember that silence does not operate in the same way that it does in face-to-face encounters and it can be quite difficult to manage in a telephone call. You need to be prepared to be active and vocal and to manage any silence well. If you are listening to another, use paralanguage ('ums' and 'ahs') to indicate that you are still actively listening and hearing the other person.
- If you are going to communicate with someone via text, rather than using the telephone to speak, then remember to maintain a professional tone: even if communicating with young people do not overuse text speak and emojis (these are not appropriate in professional communication). Keep your communication on a professional level by keeping it brief and to the point.
- Finally, if you find yourself having to leave a telephone message, you should talk slowly and be clear in your enunciation and, similar to texting, the information that you provide should be brief and to the point. Remember to leave your name and number.

Main associated theory

Humanistic Theory, Psychosocial Theory

Skill category

Communication

See also: emotional intelligence, home visits, observational skills, rapport building, setting and maintaining professional boundaries

Further reading

Koprowska, J. (2020) *Communication and Interpersonal Skills* (5th edn). London: Sage.

Time management is an important skill for a number of reasons. First, how you manage your time communicates important messages to the people that you work with and how you view the work that you undertake with them. Second, effective time management enables better service delivery. Third, good time management results in an appropriate work–life balance. Effectively managing time relies on a range of skills including:

- *Planning*: thinking ahead is fundamental and planning is a process that underpins effective time management.
- *Organisation*: at a basic level, staying organised can help you maintain a clear picture of what you need to do and when. This requires an up-to-date calendar, being diligent in recording, keeping and maintaining effective communication.
- *Prioritisation*: making an assessment of your tasks and responsibilities enables you to prioritise your work and in turn influences your management of time. You will need to consider levels of risk and need, statutory timeframes, the length of time to complete tasks, and you need to able to distinguish tasks that are urgent from ones that are important, but not urgent.
- *Goal-setting*: setting goals can help you to manage time. These could be task-related or specifically targeted at your professional training and development and career aspirations.
- *Delegation*: whilst it can be difficult to say no when someone asks you to undertake a task, similarly not everyone finds it easy to delegate work. This can be fundamental to good time management however.

The complexity and messiness of social work means that with the best will in the world, sometimes your excellent planning and organisation will go awry. It only takes a sudden crisis or **safeguarding** issue to throw your scheduling off course. One of the challenges in managing the working day is in how to allocate time for particular tasks or meetings. For example, whilst you always schedule a visit to Mr and Mrs Belfield for an hour, in reality you always stay for at least half an hour longer than that (despite good intentions). Therefore, it is critical that you are realistic and practical in scheduling and if you better understand how you use and manage time, you can make changes to be more efficient in time management.

Rymell (2015) suggests using a self-evaluation tool – a time diary – in order to understand this better. Whilst this might seem like another job on an already long 'to do' list, a little bit of investment in undertaking a time analysis will help you to reflect on and improve your time management skills. For example, it might show that you never allow enough travel time to see Mr and Mrs Belfield (let alone account for the lengthier visits). Therefore, your efforts at scheduling always go wrong on days when you visit this family resulting in you working into the evening or at the weekend to catch up on your admin tasks.

You should attempt to keep the diary for a week and segment each day into 30-minute periods (Rymell suggests 15-minute slots for a more detailed analysis). You should record 'planned' and 'actual' tasks and add comments in order to reflect the difference between the two. Your comments might include reflections about why you did not complete the planned task or why it took longer than anticipated; see the table below for a time diary example.

Table T1   Time diary example

Time	Planned Task	Actual Task	Reflection
09.00	Emails	Chatting with colleagues	A catch up is fine, but should keep it short and sweet
09.30	Travel to V Centre	Travel to V Centre	
10.00	Review meeting	Travelling still	Re-plan journey to account for commuter hour and roadworks ☺
10.30	Review meeting	Review meeting	Missed first 15 minutes
11.00	Travel to Smiths	Chatting with Practice Nurse	Chatted for 15 minutes to catch up what I'd missed, so running late
11.30	Smiths home visit	Travel to Smiths	Running late now
12.00	Smiths home visit	Smiths home visit	Arrived at 11.50 (not 11.30)
12.30	Travel to the office	Smiths home visit	Running later still
1.00	Lunch	Travelling back to the office	
1.30	Writing case records from the Smiths home visit and review meeting	Catching up on emails	Checking emails from yesterday, so playing catch up

Whilst keeping a time diary is a good idea, it is critical that you learn from the process. You might learn something about allocating time for routine activities, or how the time of day affects you in undertaking and completing certain tasks. Do you plan for the unexpected or crisis events? Good time management comes with experience and it is a skill that we have to develop for ourselves but there are some useful tips that can help in the Top Tips box below.

Top tips

- Keep details about appointments such as names, addresses and telephone numbers so that these are to hand. If you are delayed, a quick telephone call to someone is polite and professional.
- Allow adequate time for travel. If you think a journey will take 30 minutes in the middle of the day, add another 15 minutes in case of delays and particularly if you are travelling there for the first time (in case you get lost) and for breaks.

Comfort breaks for a drink and food are very important, but also factor in some time to write notes if you are going from one meeting or visit to another.
- Know yourself. Are you a morning or an afternoon person? If you are a morning person, then schedule your more challenging work for mornings.
- To manage deadlines, ensure that these are in your diary as soon as you have them. If you need to prepare a court report for a particular day, block out time to prepare the report in good time rather than try to find spare time in between visits and meetings. Build in contingency time (that is, extra time to complete the report in case you have to deal with emergencies during the time that you'd allocated to report-writing).
- Schedule meeting, conference and court dates as soon as you have them.
- Finally, make sure that you book your allocation of annual leave and take it. Do not use it to spend time catching up on admin. Everybody needs a break from work and you should view this as part of your strategy for self-care.

Main associated theory

All

Skill category

All

See also: chairing meetings, court skills, critical thinking and analysis, endings, home visits, presentation skills, report writing

Further reading

Murray, C. (2020) Time management skills. In M. Rogers, D. Whitaker, D. Edmondson & D. Peach (eds) *Developing Skills & Knowledge for Social Work Practice* (2nd edn). London: Sage.

Use of self and reflexivity

Earlier in this book, we discuss **emotional intelligence** and implicit to the very notion of emotional intelligence is knowledge of self (and knowledge of your emotional self in particular). Therefore, 'use of self' is intrinsic to social work and especially important in relationship-based practice (Ruch, Turney & Ward, 2010). Put another way, it is crucial that as a social worker you develop a sophisticated self-awareness of your own emotional states and responses to information, situations or people; as Howe (2008: 185) argued: 'the reference point for an understanding of others is one's self'.

Extending the notion of use of self, Dewane (2006) proposed that it involves combining aspects of one's personal self (including personality traits, belief systems, life experiences and cultural heritage) with the knowledge, values and skills gained through professional social work training. It enables genuineness and authenticity in relationship-based practice and enhances the micro skills involved in everyday interactions (e.g. **rapport building**, gathering and conveying difficult information).

Stop-reflect

Case study: Martin – unreflective practice

Martin's mother died in childbirth and as an only child without any extended family to take him in, he was officially looked after by the local authority throughout his whole childhood. Martin grew up with a loving and stable foster family and his experiences formed the basis of his motivation to pursue a social work career. Martin qualified when he was 24 years old. He transferred to a Looked After Children's team three years after qualifying having spent his first few years in a Duty and Assessment team.

In his first week Martin was asked to visit Mona, a 14-year-old young woman who was resident in secure accommodation. Mona had a history of running away from her previous foster carers (there had been several since the age of 9). She'd been groomed by local men in the city where she had been living and had experienced child sexual exploitation (CSE) from the age of 12. Martin felt that he didn't need to prepare much. He knew about CSE and he'd been a looked after child and so he knew how to get onto 'Mona's level'.

Is Martin right or wrong to assume there is no need to prepare? If wrong, what might he need to consider?

To start with, Mona has experienced an unsettled and unstable childhood and family life that was in total contrast to Martin's. She had experienced numerous changes of social worker and, she felt, none had really supported her as she'd have liked. Mona was a young woman and Martin was male. Mona didn't trust men. Some of the men who had abused her had been in their early twenties. They had mostly been white British (same as Martin); different from Mona's ethnic background as she had a mixed heritage.

Skills in action

Sami's reflexive foresight

Martin mentioned to one of his new colleagues, Sami, that he needed to organise a visit to Mona. Sami questioned this, highlighting the barriers that there might be as Mona lacked trust in social workers and may not have any degree of willingness to engage with Martin. In fact, Mona had made the request for a female social worker 'if [she] had to have one'. Sami felt that it was not appropriate for Martin as an unknown male social worker to visit Mona at this time. She was just beginning to make progress and had recently engaged with some therapeutic support. Sami thought Martin might trigger negative, and even traumatic, emotions for Mona. Martin went back to the Team Manager, Eli, who was also new and apologised, stating that he was not fully familiar with Mona's background, and they both agreed that someone else would be more appropriate.

Closely linked to use of self is the notion of reflexive practice, which relies upon a critical understanding of how your own knowledge, values, experiences, thoughts and feelings impact others, and vice versa, in everyday practice. Finlay (2002) proposes a typology that describes different reflexive processes including:

Introspection: this refers to those inner reflections that you might have when critically reflecting on your practice.

Intersubjective reflection: this is the process of exploring mutual understanding and agreements that emerge within relationships or partnerships whilst focusing on the context for that relationship (e.g. the nature of the social worker and child/adult/family/supervisor relationship).

Mutual collaboration: used in sociological, discursive and feminist approaches to co-production, collaboration, action research and wide-ranging methodologies.

Social critique: this refers to the process of engaging with notions of power imbalances. As such, whilst reflections might be on an individual level you should also acknowledge power and tensions arising from structural inequality and different social positions relating to gender, sexuality, age, religion, ethnicity, social class and physical ability.

Discursive deconstruction: this concept prompts you to think about the ambiguity of meaning in language and how this affects interpersonal communication and understandings.

Stop-reflect

Benefits and limitations of reflexive practice

Consider Finlay's (2002) description of different reflexive processes. Which one are you drawn to (i.e. which type of reflexive practice do you already engage in or do you feel reflects the way in which you think and act)? What are benefits and limitations of that particular process?

If you are drawn to social critique, one benefit might be that you consciously acknowledge the structural barriers that people face to social inclusion and equality (e.g. think about immigration policy and the way in which it dictates asylum seekers' experiences, life choices and opportunities). A limitation might be that you become so consumed with the macro-level (structural) factors impacting people's lives that you lose sight of the individual that you are working with.

Main associated theory

Humanistic Theory – but all actually apply

Skill category

Reflection and reflexivity

See also: counselling skills, critical thinking and analysis, cross-cultural practice, empathy, empowerment and enabling, ethical practice, reflective practice, valuing diversity, working with protected characteristics

Further reading

Trevithick, P. (2018) The 'self' and 'use of self' in social work: A contribution to the development of a coherent theoretical framework. *British Journal of Social Work*, 48(7): 1836–1854.

Using humour Whilst the judicious use of humour may not be one of the topics that you anticipate will be included in a book about social work, the sensitive and expert use of humour can be helpful in a range of circumstances that require skilled communication. These circumstances can range from those where embarrassment to anxiety to dismay preside. Humour is useful in these contexts as a means to help someone to manage their emotions and to be able to move beyond them.

The use of humour can be a great equaliser. By this we mean that humour can be shared across all groups and classes of humans as it places us on an equal footing. In this way, when interactions are experienced on a humane, mundane level, people are able to see one another as genuine and approachable. This is especially important and useful as many social work encounters are formal and, sometimes, serious. As such, the use of humour is key to relationship-based practice and helps to establish and facilitate relationships (Ruch, Turney & Ward, 2010).

Danger zone

Using humour

Using humour needs skilled communication as it is easy to get it wrong in terms of:

- *Timing:* this can be critical and if you get this wrong, you could be perceived as being offensive, oppressive and you could even cause distress.
- *Content:* is it appropriate? Is it politically correct? Are you belittling a problem or, conversely, exaggerating or even exacerbating it?
- *Place:* are you in a public or private setting? Are there other people within earshot which may affect the appropriateness of using humour within that setting?
- *Social and cultural differences:* are you knowledgeable enough about these to make a judgement about whether something will be received as humorous or otherwise?

Using humour in a self-deprecating way can be a great leveller as you are effectively positioning your humanity on a level with another. It is important if you do use humour in this way, that you are comfortable with the other person laughing at this aspect of yourself and, importantly, that you would be comfortable with them using humour targeting the very same. This raises a potential dilemma when working with others and that pertains to their use of humour, which can be prejudicial, biased and offensive: for example, in making racist, ageist or sexist 'jokes' or comments. As social work professionals it is important to think of ways to challenge such views and never endorse them. Finally, the use of humour can be very helpful in teams as it can enable you and colleagues to contexualise some of the thornier and more stressful aspects of everyday practice in ways that enable resilience and coping.

Main associated theory

Psychosocial Theory

Skill category

Communication

See also: active listening, building resilience, containing anxiety, critical thinking and analysis, emotional intelligence, use of self and reflexivity

Further reading

Jordan, S. (2017) Relationship based social work practice: the case for considering the centrality of humour in creating and maintaining relationships. *Journal of Social Work Practice*, 31(1): 95–110.

V

Valuing diversity The term 'diversity' refers to the wide range of human differences. This includes (but is not limited to) ethnicity, nationality, social class, sex, gender identity, sexual orientation, age, physical ability or attributes, cultural beliefs and religion. It can also include different characteristics or traits such as skin or hair colour, political beliefs, dietary habits (e.g. veganism) and the way in which we speak (our regional accent or dialect). Diversity is not a new phenomenon, but it remains a challenge in that not all people value diversity or respect the differences of other people or communities.

Valuing diversity is not limited to recognition of difference between people, it is the acknowledgement that these differences are a valued asset and enriching for individuals and communities. This is an important point and one that is often encapsulated in professional standards. For example, in England, the BASW (2014) Code of Ethics is built on the three value-based concepts of social justice, human rights and professional integrity, and as social work is a value-driven profession, acknowledging and valuing diversity and its relation to each of these concepts is fundamental. See the Skills in Action box for an example of how to value and promote diversity in everyday social work practice.

It is also the case that you might need to challenge someone's decisions or actions and this can be difficult if these are rooted to aspects of their difference. For example, Jehovah's Witnesses believe that the Bible prohibits the eating of blood and they do not accept blood transfusions as they believe that injecting blood into their veins is equivalent to eating it. Imagine you are supporting a family who are Jehovah's Witnesses and, unfortunately, a young member of the family has an accident and subsequently needs a blood transfusion, but the family refuse. As the child's social worker, you have a duty to safeguard that child.

Skills in action

Promoting diversity: Isaq

Isaq, who is 15 years old, arrived in England as an unaccompanied asylum seeker from Syria. Most of his family had been killed in the civil war. Isaq had a cousin and uncle living in the North of England. Isaq made his way to the UK in search of a better life. He undertook the journey alone. Isaq did not have any contact information for his uncle or cousin.

Isaq went to live with foster carers: the Whittle family. He seemed to settle very quickly. He got along well with Simon and Natalie, the Whittles' 10-year-old twins. Settling into

(Continued)

school took a little longer, but after a couple of months, Isaq had made friends with a small group of boys who lived locally. The Whittles were then worried when Isaq seemed unsettled and very low in mood some months later. On talking to Isaq's social worker, the Whittles were able to access mental health support which helped him to address some of the trauma resulting from his experiences.

The Whittles thought about their role in caring for Isaq and began to consider the ways in which they could help him come to term with his life experiences and remain connected to his roots. They decided to learn more about the community that Isaq was from. They made an effort to learn words in Arabic and found recipes for some Syrian dishes, cooking these for the whole family. The Whittles found a community group for Syrian young people and enabled Isaq to attend each week. It was quite a distance from their family home but Isaq really benefitted from being with people from his community, being able to speak his language, and there were other young people there who had similarly travelled to the UK on their own. Isaq benefitted from being with people with a shared culture, background and experiences.

Stop-reflect

Can you think of other ways that you might promote diversity?

Here are some more ideas:

- Seek to avoid the limited view of understanding diversity to mean ethnicity and culture.
- Seek to understand diversity from a global, not just a national, or even local, perspective.
- Involve diverse groups of people in problem-solving, decision-making and developing opportunities or services.
- Challenge your own and others' assumptions that limit opportunities, reflect stereotypes and are pathologising.
- Challenge others when they do not value or listen to the views or experiences of diverse groups of people; ensure everyone is heard equally.
- Remain sensitive to the fact that some people want their differences to be recognised whilst others do not.
- Be open and honest about the tensions and dilemmas of the practices, views and communication of diverse groups and the role and remit of social work.
- Use supervision to check your own conscious and unconscious views about diversity.
- Learn about different cultures (practices, customs, beliefs and communication).
- Look at issues and opportunities from others' viewpoints before making decisions.
- Finally, challenge organisational policies and practices that may be exclusionary. You can do this in lots of ways that can be seen as positive in terms of promoting diversity, rather than in a negative and critical manner.

Main associated theory

Humanistic Theory – but all actually apply

Skill category

All

See also: advocacy, anti-discriminatory practice, anti-oppressive practice, critical thinking and analysis, cross-cultural practice, empowering and enabling, ethical practice, use of self and reflexivity

Further reading

Gottlieb, M. (2020) The case for cultural humility framework in social work practice. *Journal of Ethnic & Cultural Diversity in Social Work.* DOI: 10.1080/15313204.2020.1753615.

W

Working with protected characteristics

Working with protected characteristics The notion of human rights has been central to moral, political and legal analysis for centuries albeit without consensus about the definition of human rights (Clucas, 2012; Ahmed & Rogers, 2016). In the UK, human rights are defined in law; primarily through the Human Rights Act (HRA) 1998 and the Equality Act 2010. Many of the rights established under the HRA 1998 were already protected under UK law (e.g. freedom) and the intention of the HRA was largely to integrate the European Convention on Human Rights into British law. The European Convention on Human Rights is an international human rights treaty between the 47 states who are members of the Council of Europe. In signing up to the Convention, those countries have made a legal commitment to abide by particular standards of behaviour and to protect the basic rights and freedoms of ordinary people.

This final chapter focuses on the case of human rights in England and another important law is the Equality Act (EA) 2010 which came into being on 1 October 2010. The EA 2010 replaced a number of different laws that provided protection from discrimination including: the Equal Pay Act 1970, Sex Discrimination Act 1975, the Race Relations Act 1976 and the Disability Discrimination Act 1995 as well as associated secondary legislation and numerous revisions. In this way, the EA 2010 streamlined, simplified and harmonised the hotchpotch of existing law and policy. Both the HRA 1998 and EA 2010 are governed and regulated by the Equality and Human Rights Commission (EHRC), a non-governmental organisation established in 2007 (see www.equalityhumanrights.com/en) which operates across England, Scotland and Wales. In addition to its governance role, the EHRC offers advice and guidance to individuals, organisations and public bodies.

We focus on the EA 2010 as this provides a framework that underpins social work and which is intended to address disadvantage and discrimination. The EA 2010 identifies nine protected characteristics making it unlawful to discriminate against someone on the grounds of:

- age
- disability
- gender reassignment
- marriage and civil partnership
- pregnancy and maternity
- race
- religion or belief
- sex
- sexual orientation.

In addition, the EA 2010 extended understanding of discrimination by embedding a typology to illustrate its multi-faceted nature (see Table W1). In relation to skill, this typology reminds us of what not to do, rather than giving us a template for what we should be doing. In actuality, the EA 2010 and the role of social work are intrinsically interwoven in a framework for practice which is centred on addressing disadvantage and discrimination, as well as seeking to achieve social justice, equality and fairness.

Table W1 Types of discrimination

Type	Description	Example
Direct discrimination	Where someone is treated less favourably than another person because of their protected characteristic.	John and Abdul, a same-sex couple, wanted to order their wedding cake from a local bakery but were refused service as the bakers do not believe in gay marriage.
Associative discrimination	Where someone experiences direct discrimination because they are associated with another person who possesses a protected characteristic.	Christine is looking for an afterschool club for her daughter who is five years old and mentions that she also wishes to transfer her son, who has ADHD and learning disabilities and is slightly older. She was initially told that there were places at the club, but after disclosing her wishes to transfer her son, she was then informed that there were none. Christine thinks that the club did not want to take her disabled son as well as her daughter.
Discrimination based on perception	Where someone experiences direct discrimination because others perceive that she/he/they possess a particular protected characteristic.	John was out with his friend, Marin. Marin has multiple sclerosis and uses a wheelchair when his mobility is affected. John and Marin went into a café. The waitress took John's order and asked him what his friend would like (making an assumption about Marin's lack of capacity and ability to speak for himself).
Indirect discrimination	Where you apply a rule or policy to everyone, but it disadvantages a person with a particular protected characteristic.	Judith is a Jewish woman who works in a local bank. Her manager decided to introduce a rota system when the bank decided that it would introduce Saturday opening hours. Judith was put on the rota and required to work every other Saturday. Judith explained that Saturday is a religious day. Her manager told Judith that she had to work the rota like every other employee or look for another job.

(Continued)

W

Table W1 (Continued)

Type	Description	Example
Harassment	Behaviour experienced as offensive by the recipient even if not directed at them.	An email is sent around members of a team that makes jokes about people with disabilities. One team member finds it offensive and forwards the email to the team manager.
Victimisation	Where someone is treated badly because they have either made or supported a grievance under the EA 2010.	Dee has previously made a claim of direct discrimination when she was gender transitioning and turned down for promotion at work. She continues to be allocated the most difficult and stressful work in her team and she believes that it is because she previously made a claim.

Stop-reflect

Working with protected characteristics

Pietr works in a large supermarket and told his colleagues that he had enjoyed a long weekend at Gay Pride and was feeling tired at the start of a week's shift (he is not gay but has gay friends who go each year). Subsequently Pietr noticed that he was being left out of social events, people appeared to be less friendly and when he ate in the work canteen people avoided sitting with him.

- What type of discrimination is this?

Carlos is 69 years old and approached the local college as he wished to undertake a beauty therapy course. The college website says there are lots of places left. When Carlos visits, the course leader tells Carlos that there are no places at all and they don't hold a waiting list.

- What type of discrimination is this?

A person who identifies as non-binary gender, Dasha, goes for a drink with their girl-friend, Sarah, in their local pub. Sarah goes to the bar but is refused service and asked to drink somewhere else.

- What type of discrimination is this?

As a social worker your manager tells you that there are limited resources for respite care and you can only recommend one family, but you have two: the Smiths and the Ahmeds. You feel that the Ahmeds' need is greater, but your colleague, Mike, suggests that you propose the Smiths as they're lovely, and the Ahmeds are notoriously difficult and even made a complaint against him that he was discriminating on race grounds just because he made a joke about Muslims (and he obviously meant no harm).

* What type of discrimination is this?

Main associated theory

Humanistic Theory – but all actually apply

Skill category

All

See also: anti-discriminatory practice, anti-oppressive practice, communicating with children and young people, communicating with people with lived experience of learning disabilities, cross-cultural practice, ethical practice, person-centred communication, valuing diversity

Further reading

Hudson-Sharp, N. (2018) *Transgender Awareness in Child and Family Social Work Education*. London: NIESR. Available at: www.niesr.ac.uk/sites/default/files/publications/Transgender_awareness_in_child_and_family_social_work_education.pdf (accessed 25 January 2021).

Speed, L. (2011) *Older People and Human Rights in Home Care: A Report of Two Surveys*. Research Report 80. Manchester: Equality and Human Rights Commission. www.equalityhumanrights.com/sites/default/files/research-report_80-older-people-and-human-rights-in-home-care-a-report-of-two-surveys.pdf (accessed 25 January 2021).

W

References

Ahmed, A. & Rogers, M. (2016) Diversity and exclusion in context. In A. Ahmed and M. Rogers (eds) *Working with Marginalised Groups: From Policy to Practice*. London: Palgrave.

Allen, D. (2017) Roma people: Are discriminatory attitudes natural? In K. Bhatti-Sinclair & C. Smethurst (eds) *Diversity, Difference and Dilemmas: Analysing Concepts and Developing Skills*. Maidenhead: McGraw Hill.

Allen, D. & Riding, S. (2018) *The Fragility of Professional Competence: A Preliminary Account of Child Protection Practice with Romani and Traveller Children in England*. Budapest: European Roma Rights Centre.

Allport, G. W. (1954) *The Nature of Prejudice*. Cambridge/Reading, MA: Addison-Wesley.

Antonopoulou, P., Killian, M. & Forrester, D. (2017) Levels of stress and anxiety in child and family social work: Workers' perceptions of organizational structure, professional support and workplace opportunities in children's services in the UK. *Children and Youth Services Review*, 76: 42–50.

Association of Palliative Care Social Workers (2016) *The Role of Social Workers in Palliative, End of Life and Bereavement Care*. Available at: www.apcsw.org.uk/wp-content/uploads/sp-client-document-manager/-1/the-role-of-social-workers-in-palliative-end-of-life-and-bereavement-care.pdf (accessed 25 January 2021).

Ataguba, O. A. & Ataguba, J. E. (2020) Social determinants of health: The role of effective communication in the COVID-19 pandemic in developing countries. *Global Health Action*, 13(1). DOI: 10.1080/16549716.2020.1788263.

Baginsky, M., Manthorpe, J. & Hickman, B. (2019) Social work teaching partnerships: A discussion paper. *Social Work Education*, 38(8): 968–982.

Baile, W., Buckman, R., Lenzi, R., Glober, G., Beale, E. & Kudelka, A. (2000) SPIKES – a six step approach for delivering bad news: Application to the patient with cancer. *The Oncologist*, 5: 302–311.

Baker, J., Lynch, K., Cantillon, S. & Walsh, J. (2004) *Equality: From Theory to Action*, Basingstoke: Palgrave.

Barker, R. L. (2003) *The Social Work Dictionary* (5th edn). Washington DC: The National Association of Social Work Press.

BASW (2014) *The Code of Ethics for Social Work*. London: British Association of Social Workers. Available at: www.basw.co.uk/about-basw/code-ethics (accessed 25 January 2021).

BASW (2020) *The Professional Capabilities Framework*. Available at: www.basw.co.uk/social-work-training/professional-capabilities-framework-pcf (accessed 25 January 2021).

Beck, U. (1992). *Risk Society: Towards a New Modernity*. London: Sage.

Bellinger, A. & Elliott, T. (2011) What are you looking at? The potential of appreciative inquiry as a research approach for social work. *British Journal of Social Work*, 41(4): 708–725.

Bingle, L. & Middleton, A. (2019) From doing to being: The tensions of systemic practice in social work – group reflective supervision in child protection. *Journal of Family Therapy*, 41(3): 384–406.

Birkenmaier, J., Berg-Weger, M. & Dewees, M.P. (eds) (2014) *The Practice of Generalist Social Work* (3rd edn). New York: Routledge.

Blinston, N. & Higham, P. (2009) Employment perspectives and learning organisations. In P. Higham (ed.) *Post-qualifying Social Work Practice*. London: Sage.

Bradt, L., & Bouverne-De Bie, M. (2009). Victim–offender mediation as a social work practice. *International Social Work*, 52(2): 181–193.

Broadhurst, K., Hall, C., Wastell, D., White, S. & Pithouse, A. (2010) Risk, instrumentalism and the humane project in social work: Identifying the informal logics of risk management in children's statutory services. *British Journal of Social Work*, 40: 1046–1064.

Butler, I. and Roberts, G. (2003) *Social work with children and families* (2nd ed), London: Jessica Kingsley.

Chisnell, C. & Kelly, C. (2016) *Safeguarding in Social Work Practice: A Lifespan Approach*. Los Angeles: Learning Matters.

Clucas, R. (2012) Religion, sexual orientation and the Equality Act 2010: Gay bishops in the Church of England negotiating rights against discrimination. *Sociology*, 46(5): 936–950.

Cocker, C. & Hafford-Letchfield, T. (2014) *Rethinking Anti-discriminatory and Anti-oppressive Theories for Social Work Practice*. Basingstoke: Palgrave Macmillan.

Collins Dictionary (2020a) *Value*. www.collinsdictionary.com/dictionary/english/value (accessed 25 January 2021).

Collins Dictionary (2020b) *Ethics*. www.collinsdictionary.com/dictionary/english/ethics (accessed 25 January 2021).

Cooper, J. (2020) Narrative social work. In M. Rogers, D. Whitaker, D. Edmondson & D. Peach (eds) *Developing Skills & Knowledge for Social Work Practice* (2nd edn). London: Sage.

Cooper, P. (2014) *Court and Legal Skills*. Basingstoke: Palgrave Macmillan.

Cooperrider, D.L. & Srivastva, S. (1987) Appreciative inquiry in organisational life. *Research in Organisational Change and Development*, 1: 129–169.

Cotterill, T. (2019). *Principles and Practices of Working with Pupils with Special Educational Needs and Disability: A Student Guide*. London: Routledge.

Crawford, K. (2012) *Interprofessional Collaboration in Social Work Practice*. Los Angeles: Sage.

Currer, C. (2010) *Loss and Social Work*. Exeter: Learning Matters.

Dallos, R. & Draper, R. (2010) *An Introduction to Family Therapy: Systemic Theory and Practice*. Maidenhead: McGraw-Hill Education.

De Dreu, C. (2007) The virtue and vice of workplace conflict: Food for (pessimistic) thought. *Journal of Organisational Behavior*, 29: 5–18.

DeJong, P. & Berg, I.K. (1998) *Interviewing for Solutions*. Pacific Grove, CA: Brooks/Cole.

Deutsch, M. & Coleman, P.T. (2000) *The Handbook of Conflict Resolution: Theory and Practice*. San Francisco, CA: Jossey-Bass.

Dewane, C.J. (2006) Use of self: A primer revisited. *Clinical Social Work Journal*, 34(4): 543–558.

Doel, M. (2016) *Rights and Wrongs in Social Work: Ethical and Practice Dilemmas*. London: Macmillan Education.

Edmondson, D. (2020) Task-centred practice. In M. Rogers, D. Whitaker, D. Edmondson & D. Peach (eds) (2020) *Developing Skills & Knowledge for Social Work Practice* (2nd edn). London: Sage.

Egan, G. (2013) *The Skilled Helper: A Problem-Management and Opportunity-Development Approach to Helping* (10th edn). Boston, MA: Cengage Learning.

Egan, G. (2018) *Student Workbook Exercises for Egan's the Skilled Helper* (11th edn). Melbourne: Brooks/Cole.

Featherstone, B., Morris, K. & White, S. (2014) *Re-imagining Child Protection: Towards Humane Social Work with Families*. Bristol: Policy Press.

Featherstone, B., Gupta, A., Morris, K. & White, S. (2018) *Protecting children: A social model*. Bristol: Policy Press.

Ferguson, H. (2011) *Child Protection Practice*. Basingstoke: Palgrave Macmillan.

Finlay, L. (2002) Negotiating the swamp: the opportunity and challenge of reflexivity in research practice. *Qualitative Research*, 2(2): 209–230.

Flanagan, J.C. (1954) The critical incident technique. *Psychology Bulletin*, 51: 327–358.

Fleming, J. & Ward, D. (2017) Self-directed groupwork – social justice through social action and empowerment. *Critical and Radical Social Work*, 5(1): 75–91.

Forrester, D., Westlake, D., McCann, M., Thurnham, A., Shefer, G., Glynn, G. & Killian, M. (2013) *Reclaiming Social Work? An Evaluation of Systemic Units as an Approach to Delivering Children's Services*. University of Bedfordshire: Tilda Goldberg Centre for Social Work and Social Care.

Gaskell-Mew, E. & Lindsay, L. (2016) Working with resistance. In K. Davies & R. Jones (eds) *Skills for Social Work Practice*. London: Macmillan Publishers Ltd.

Gibbs, G. (1988) *Learning by Doing: A Guide to Teaching and Learning Methods*. London: FEU.

Godsell, M. & Scarborough, K. (2006) Improving communication for people with learning disabilities. *Nursing Standard*, 20(30): 58–65.

Goldsworthy, K.K. (2005) Grief and loss theory in social work practice: All changes involve loss, just as all losses require change. *Australian Social Work*, 58(2): 167–178.

Goleman, D. (1995) *Emotional Intelligence: Why It Can Matter More than IQ*. Bloomsbury: London.

Goodman, S. & Trowler, I. (eds) (2011) *Social Work Reclaimed: Innovative Frameworks for Child and Family Social Work Practice*. London: Jessica Kingsley Publishers.

Government of India (2018) *Data on Language and Mother Tongue*. Available at: https://censusindia.gov.in/2011Census/Language_MTs.html (accessed 27 February 2021).

Gov.Scot (2020) Relaxation techniques. Available at: www.nhsinform.scot/healthy-living/preventing-falls/fear-and-anxiety-about-falling/relaxation-techniques (accessed 1 September 2020).

Grant, L. & Kinman, G. (2012) *Developing Emotional Resilience*. Community Care Inform (Practice Guidance). Available from: www.ccinform.co.uk/practice-guidance/guide-to-developing-social-workers-emotional-resilience/ (accessed 25 January 2021).

Green Lister, P. & Crisp, B.R. (2007) Critical incident analyses: A practice learning tool for students and practitioners. *Practice*, 19(1): 47–60.

Grotberg, E.H. (1995) *A Guide to Promoting Resilience in Children: Strengthening the Human Spirit*. The Hague: Bernard van Leer Foundation. Available at: https://bibalex.org/baifa/ attachment/documents/115519.pdf (accessed 25 January 2021).

Hammond, S.A. (1982) *The Thin Book of Appreciative Inquiry*. Bend, OR: Thin Book Publishing Company.

Hardy, M. (2015) *Governing Risk: Care and Control in Contemporary Social Work*. London: Palgrave Macmillan.

Harms, L. (2015) *Understanding Trauma and Resilience*. London: Palgrave.

Harrington, A. (2019) Chairing and managing formal workplace meetings: Skills for nurse leaders. *Nursing Management*, 26(5): 36–41.

Harrison, G. & Turner, R. (2011) Being a 'culturally competent' social worker: Making sense of a murky concept in practice. *British Journal of Social Work*, 41(2): 333–350.

Hartman, A. (1975) Diagrammatic assessment of family relationships. *Families in Society*, 76(2): 111–122.

Hatibo lu, B., Özate Gelmez, Ö.S. & Öngen, Ç. (2019) Value conflict resolution strategies of social work students in Turkey. *Journal of Social Work*, 19(1): 142–161.

Henderson, K. & Mathew-Byrne, J. (2016) Developing communication and interviewing skills. In K. Davies & R. Jones (eds) *Skills for Social Work Practice*. London: Macmillan Publishers Ltd.

Hester, M. (2011) The Three Planet Model: Towards an understanding of contradictions in approaches to women and children's safety in contexts of domestic violence. *British Journal of Social Work*, 41(5): 837–853.

HM Government (2018) *Working Together to Safeguard Children: A Guide to Inter-agency Working to Safeguard and Promote the Welfare of Children*. London: HM Government.

Howe, D. (2008) *The Emotionally Intelligent Social Work*. Basingstoke: Palgrave Macmillan.

IFSW (2014) Global definition of social work. Available at: www.ifsw.org/what-is-social-work/global-definition-of-social-work/ (accessed 25 January 2021).

Ion, G., Sánchez Martí, A. & Agud Morell, I. (2019) Giving or receiving feedback: Which is more beneficial to students' learning? *Assessment & Evaluation in Higher Education*, 44(1): 124–138.

Johnston, D.W. & Lordan, G. (2012) Discrimination makes me sick! An examination of the discrimination–health relationship. *Journal of Health Economics*, 31(1): 99–111.

Jones, R. (2016) Writing skills for social workers. In K. Davies & R. Jones (eds) *Skills for Social Work Practice*. London: Macmillan Publishers Ltd.

Kadushin, A. & Kadushin, G. (2013) *The Social Work Interview*. Columbia: Columbia University Press.

Karpetis, G. (2018) Social work skills: A narrative review of the literature. *British Journal of Social Work*, 48(3): 596–615.

Kellett, U., Moyle, W., McAllister, M., King, C. & Gallagher, F. (2010) Life stories and biography: A means of connecting family and staff to people with dementia. *Journal of Clinical Nursing*, 19: 1707–1715.

Kelly, P.L., Heyman, J.C., Tice-Brown, D. & White-Ryan, L. (2020) Interprofessional practice: Social work students' perspectives on collaboration. *Social Work in Health Care*, 59(2): 108–121.

Kemshall, H., Wilkinson, B. & Baker, K. (2013) *Working with Risk: Skills for Contemporary Social Work*. Cambridge: Polity.

Kim, H.C. (2017) A challenge to the social work profession? The rise of socially engaged art and a call to radical social work. *Social Work*, 62(4): 305–311.

Kolb, D. (1984) *Experiential Learning*. Englewood Cliffs, NJ: Prentice Hall.

Koprowska, J. (2020) *Communication and Interpersonal Skills* (5th edn). London: Sage.

Kriz, K. & Skivenes, M. (2010) Lost in translation: How child welfare workers in Norway and England experience language difficulties when working with minority ethnic families. *British Journal of Social Work*, 40(5): 1353–1367.

Laitila, M., Nummelin, J., Kortteisto, T. & Pitkänen, A. (2018) Service users' views regarding user involvement in mental health services: A qualitative study. *Archives of Psychiatric Nursing*, 32(5): 695–701.

Lazarus, R.S. & Folkman, S. (1984) *Stress, Appraisal, and Coping*. New York: Springer Publishers.

Lee, T., Kwong, W., Cheung, C., Ungar, M. & Cheung, M. (2010) Children's resilience-related beliefs as a predictor of positive child development in the face of adversities: Implications for interventions to enhance children's quality of life. *Social Indicators Research*, 95(3): 437–453.

Lefevre, M. (2013) Becoming effective communicators with children: Developing practitioner capability through social work education. *British Journal of Social Work*, 45(1): 204–224.

Lewis, J. & Erlen, N. (2012) *Resource Pack: Evidence Matters in Family Justice*. Totnes: Research in Practice.

Lishman, J. (2009) *Communication in Social Work* (2nd edn). Basingstoke: Macmillan/BASW.

Love, J.G. & Lynch, R. (2018) Enablement and positive ageing: A human rights-based approach to older people and changing demographics. *International Journal of Human Rights*, 22(1): 90–107.

Lyons, K. (2012) *The SAGE Handbook of International Social Work*. London: Sage.

Marsh, P. (2008) Task-centred work. In M. Davies (ed.) *The Blackwell Companion to Social Work* (3rd edn). Oxford: Blackwell Publishing.

McKeown, J., Ryan, A., Ingleton, C. & Clarke, A. (2015) 'You have to be mindful of whose story it is': The challenges of undertaking life story work with people with dementia and their family carers. *Dementia*, 14(2): 238–256.

McLaughlin, K. (2016) *Empowerment: A Critique*. Abingdon & New York: Routledge.

Merriam-Webster Dictionary (2020) *Skill*. www.merriam-webster.com/dictionary/skill (accessed 25 January 2020).

Miller, W.R. & Rollnick, S. (2013) *Motivational Interviewing: Helping People Change* (3rd edn). New York: Guilford Press.

Milner, J., Myers, J.S. & O'Byrne, P. (2015) *Assessment in Social Work* (4th edn). London: Macmillan Education.

Morgaine, K. (2014) Conceptualizing social justice in social work: Are social workers 'too bogged down in the trees'? *Journal of Social Justice*, 4: 1–18.

Morton, J. & Myers, S. (2016) Identity, difference and the meaning of 'culture' in health and social care practice. In A. Ahmed & M. Rogers. (eds) *Working with Marginalised Groups: From Policy to Practice*. London: Palgrave.

Moss, B. (2012) *Communication Skills in Health & Social Care* (2nd edn). London: Sage.

O'Connell, B. & Palmer, S. (eds) (2005) *Handbook of Solution-focused Therapy*. London: Sage.

Okes, D. (2009) *Root Cause Analysis: The Core of Problem Solving and Corrective Action*. Milwaukee, WI: ASQ Quality Press.

Okitikpi, T. & Aymer, C. (2010) *Key Concepts in Anti-discriminatory Social Work*. London: SAGE.

Pemberton, C. (2013) 'I am now anxious about how the Hackney model is being interpreted and rolled out'. *Community Care*, 24 October. Available at: www.communitycare. co.uk/2013/10/24/i-am-now-anxious-about-how-the-hackney-model-is-being-interpreted- and-rolled-out/ (accessed 25 January 2021).

Prayogo, E., Chater, A., Chapman, S., Barker, M., Rahmawati, N., Waterfall, T. & Grimble, G. (2018) Who uses foodbanks and why? exploring the impact of financial strain and adverse life events on food insecurity. *Journal of Public Health*, 40(4): 676–683.

Raghavan, R. (2015) Resilience of children and young people with intellectual disabilities. *Journal of Intellectual Disability Research*, 59(1): 82–83.

Randall, W.L. (2013) The importance of being ironic: Narrative openness and personal resilience in later life. *The Gerontologist*, 53(1): 9–16.

Reid, W.J. & Shyne, A.W. (1969) *Brief and Extended Casework*. New York: Columbia University Press.

Reisch, M. (2002) Defining social justice in a socially unjust world. *Families in Society*, 83: 343–346.

Riggall, S. (2016) The sustainability of Egan's skilled helper model in students' social work practice. *Journal of Social Work Practice*, 30(1): 81–93.

Roberts, M. (2014) *Mediation in Family Disputes: Principles of Practice* (4th edn). Farnham: Ashgate Publishing Ltd.

Rogers, C.R. (1951) *Client-centered Therapy: Its Current Practice, Implications and Therapy*. London: Constable.

Rogers, C.R. (1980) *A Way of Being*. Boston: Houghton Mifflin.

Rogers, M. (2020) Interviewing. In M. Rogers, D. Whitaker, D. Edmondson & D. Peach (eds) (2020) *Developing Skills & Knowledge for Social Work Practice* (2nd edn). London: Sage.

Rogers, M. & Allen, D. (2019) *Applying Critical Thinking and Analysis in Social Work*. London: Sage.

Rogers, M., Whitaker, D., Edmondson, D. & Peach, D. (eds) (2020) *Developing Skills & Knowledge for Social Work Practice* (2nd edn). London: Sage.

Rosengren, D.B. (2018) *Building Motivational Interviewing Skills: A Practitioner Workbook* (2nd edn). New York: The Guilford Press.

Ruch, G. (2010) The contemporary context of relationship-based practice. In G. Ruch, D. Turney & A. Ward (eds) *Relationship-based Social Work*. London: Jessica Kingsley Publications.

Ruch, G., Turney, D. & Ward, A. (eds) (2010) *Relationship-based Social Work*. London: Jessica Kingsley Publications.

Rymell, S. (2015) *Time Management: How to Feel More in Control of your Work Load*. Community Care Inform (Practice Guidance), July. Available at: www.ccinform.co.uk/practice-guidance/guide-to-time-management/ (accessed 25 January 2021).

Samsonsen, V. & Turney, D. (2017) The role of professional judgement in social work assessment: A comparison between Norway and England, *European Journal of Social Work*, 20(1): 112–124.

Schön, D. (1983) *The Reflective Practitioner*. London: Temple Smith.

Sebba, J., Luke, N., McNeish, D. & Rees, A. (2017) *Children's Social Care Innovation Programme: Final Evaluation Report*. London: Stationery Office.

Shennan, G. (2019) *Solution-focused Practice: Effective Communication to Facilitate Change* (2nd edn). Basingstoke: Palgrave Macmillan.

Shulman, L. (2008) *The Skills of Helping Individuals, Families, Groups, and Communities*. Boston, MA: Cengage Learning.

Skolnik, S. (2019) Coming together: Factors that connect social workers to group work practice. *Social Work with Groups*, 42(1): 2–17.

Smale, G.G., Tuson, G. & Biehal, T. (1993) *Empowerment, Assessment, Care Management and the Skilled Worker*. London: HMSO.

Smeeton, J. (2020) 'A murky business': A phenomenological ontology of risk in child protection social work. *Qualitative Social Work: Research and Practice*, 19(2): 284–300.

Smith, M., Gallagher, M., Wosu, H., Stewart, J., Cree, V., Hunter, S., Evans, S., Montgomery, C., Holiday, S. & Wilkinson, H. (2011) Engaging with involuntary service users in social work: Findings from a knowledge exchange project. *British Journal of Social Work*, 162: 1–18.

Smith, R. (2013). Castells, power and social work. *British Journal of Social Work*, 43(8): 1545–1561.

Social Work England (2020) *Professional Standards*. Available at: www.socialworkengland.org.uk/media/1640/1227_socialworkengland_standards_prof_standards_final-aw.pdf (accessed 25 January 2021).

Spong, S.J. (2012) The challenge of prejudice: Counsellors' talk about challenging clients' prejudices. *British Journal of Guidance & Counselling*, 40(2): 113–125.

Stevens, R.A. (2008) Social models of disability and social work in the twenty-first century. *Ethics and Social Welfare*, 2(2): 197–202.

Strier, R. & Binyamin, S. (2014) Introducing anti-oppressive social work practices in public services: Rhetoric to practice. *British Journal of Social Work*, 44(8): 2095–2112.

Sue, D.W. (2006) *Multicultural Social Work Practice*. Hoboken, NJ: John Wiley and Sons Inc.

Symonds, J., Williams, V., Miles, C., Steel, M. & Porter, S. (2018) The social care practitioner as assessor: 'People, relationships and professional judgement'. *British Journal of Social Work*, 48(7): 1910–1928.

Taylor, B.J. (2010) *Professional Decision Making in Social Work*. Exeter: Learning Matters.

Taylor, B.J. (ed.) (2011) *Working with Aggression and Resistance in Social Work*. Exeter: Learning Matters.

Think Local Act Personal (2016) 'Ladder of co-production' model. Available at: www.thinklocalactpersonal.org.uk/latest/National-Children-and-Adult-Services-Conference-2016-/ (accessed 10 December 2019).

Thomas, J. (2004) Using 'critical incident analysis' to promote critical reflection and holistic assessment. In N. Gould & M. Baldwin (eds) *Social Work, Critical Reflection and the Learning Organisation*. Aldershot: Ashgate.

Thompson, N. (2018) *Promoting Equality: Working with Diversity and Difference* (4th edn). London: Palgrave.

Toner, L. & Black, R. (2020) *The Power of Small Gestures: Emotions and relationships in social worker practice*. Sheffield: The University of Sheffield.

Trevithick, P. (2012) *Social Work Skills and Knowledge: A Practice Handbook* (3rd edn). Maidenhead: Open University Press.

Trevithick, P., Richards, S., Ruch, G. and Moss, B (2004) *Knowledge review: Teaching and learning communication skills in social work education*. Bristol: Policy Press.

Tripp, D. (1993) *Critical Incidents in Teaching: Developing Professional Judgement*. London: Routledge.

Tuckman, B.W. (1965) Developmental sequence in small groups. *Psychological Bulletin*, 63: 384–399.

Turbett, C. (2014) *Doing Radical Social Work*. Basingstoke: Palgrave Macmillan.

van Wormer, K. (2003) Restorative justice: A model for social work practice with families. *Families in Society*, 84(3): 441–448.

Wachtel, T. (2016) *Defining Restorative*. Available at: www.iirp.edu/images/pdf/Defining-Restorative_Nov-2016.pdf (accessed 25 January 2021).

Walsh, T. & White, S. (2019) *Reassessing Attachment Theory in Child Welfare: A Critical Appraisal*. Bristol: Policy Press.

Warner, J. (2015) *The Emotional Politics of Social Work and Child Protection*. Bristol: Policy Press.

Westlake, D. & Jones, R.K. (2018) Breaking down language barriers: A practice-near study of social work using interpreters. *British Journal of Social Work*, 48(5): 1388–1408.

Whitaker, D. (2020) Court skills. In M. Rogers, D. Whitaker, D. Edmondson & D. Peach (eds) *Developing Skills & Knowledge for Social Work Practice* (2nd edn). London: Sage.

White, S., Wastell, D., Broadhurst, K. & Hall, C. (2010) When policy o'erleaps itself: The 'tragic tale' of the integrated children's system. *Critical Social Policy*, 30(3): 405–429.

Whittington, C. (2007) *Assessment in Social Work: A Guide for Learning and Teaching*. SCIE Guide 18. London: SCIE.

Winter, K., Cree, V., Hallett, S., Hadfield, M., Ruch, G., Morrison, F. & Holland, S. (2017) Exploring communication between social workers, children and young people. *British Journal of Social Work*, 47(5): 1427–1444.

Wolfensberger, W. (1983) Social role valorization: A proposed new term for the principle of normalization. *Mental Retardation*, 21(6): 234–239.

Yan, B., Chen, X. & Gill, T.M. (2020) Health inequality among Chinese older adults: The role of childhood circumstances. *The Journal of the Economics of Ageing*, 17. DOI: 10.1016/j. jeoa.2020.100237.

Yee, J.Y. & Dumbrill, G. (2003) Whiteout: Looking for race in Canadian social work practice. In A. Al-Krenawi & J.R. Graham (eds) *Multicultural Social Work in Canada*. Don Mills, ON: Oxford University Press.

Index

www.ingramcontent.com/pod-product-compliance
Ingram Content Group UK Ltd.
Pitfield, Milton Keynes, MK11 3LW, UK
UKHW031553170425
457560UK00006B/237